DECONSTRUCTING A DISCIPLE'S DOUBT

DECONSTRUCTING
A DISCIPLE'S DOUBT

Dr. Jason Lee McKinney

WordCrafts

This book dedicated to:
my fellow doubting Thomases and denying Peters.

This book is dedicated to:
all the doubting disciples like me—the unsettled, the unsteady,
the beat down, and beat up, for those who don't feel secure in
their faith and yet still feel compelled to seek for truth wherever
and to whomever that leads.

This book dedicated to:
those who have cried like our brother Rich Mullins,
"Hold me Jesus 'cause I'm shaking like a leaf."

You are not alone.
I'm with you.
I understand.

Contents

Introduction

The book before you is one half philosophy of religion textbook; one half autobiography, and one half pop culture fish wrap for easy digestion. Perhaps the only comfort you can take from the previous statement is that this book for sure is not an advanced arithmetic (or even basic arithmetic) textbook. If that is what you are looking for go ask your local librarian to find it using the Dewey decimal system or type in "Books by guys who know something can't have 3 halves" into the Amazon search bar, this book is not for you. In fact, this book is NOT a lot of things. It is not a book for philosophers to continue in their circular self-congratulating co-misery of championing how much smarter they are than everyone else. Nor is it a book for those who treat reasonable questions of faith, existence, and the meaning of life like witchcraft. It is not for those who counter those who struggle with their beliefs with the platitude of "you just gotta believe brother!" This book is not for the settled and the steady, the safe and the secure. It's not for the atheist who thinks people of faith are militant backwoods uneducated idiots who are fooled by fairytales nor is it for people of faith who just cannot fathom why and how someone might not believe in God. This book is for doubting Thomases and denying Peters; it's for atheists whose fondest memories are of their devout grandmothers reading them the old stories of the faith. This book is for the believer who does not understand for the life of them why certain things appear to be the way they are. This book is for the atheists who understand

1

why their friend has faith and it is for the friend who understands how someone could be an atheist. This book is for the wonderers and wanderers. Those who not only doubt but are brave enough or plagued enough to doubt everything. This book is absolutely for those who doubt their doubt. This book is for those who ask the questions: why does existence exist at all? Is there a point and a purpose to the universe being the way it is? What is the true nature of truth? Why is there so much evil? Is there such a thing as evil if there is not purpose? Is there a difference truly between the world's religions that connects to ultimate reality?

For non-philosophers the language in this book may at times get a bit technical. Some of the concepts are really big and to speak to them with any sort of intellectual currency, precision of language is vital. I will do my best to define each of the technical words in as plain of language as I can as well as providing context, analogy, analysis and metaphor to ease the understanding. I will use dialogue from movie scenes that illustrate the concepts as well as my own song lyrics and QR codes to the songs (I promise this is not an ego play just hopefully an aid in helping you understand). Conversely for those trained in philosophy or theology this book will surely be viewed as pop philosophy with many simple anecdotes from my life along with movie quotes and song lyrics that will come across as reductionist and pedantic given the broad and deep nature of the subjects at hand. I freely admit the latter will be a fair criticism, but the aim of this book is not for philosophers. The aim of this book is for the average person who still asks and is kept up late at night by the big questions. This book is for the parents at St. Jude's tonight who like the father of a sick boy in Mark 9:24 can barely get the words out "I believe, help my unbelief." That often uttered but rarely admitted prayer; said in sincere weakness and crushing exhaustion but with purity of heart.

In fact, Flannery O'Connor in *The Habit of Being* states, "Lord, I believe; help my unbelief'... is the most natural and most human and most agonizing prayer in the Gospels, and I think it is the foundation prayer of faith."[1] Doubt is seen far too often as a weakness. I think this is because humans are so uncomfortable with uncertainty. My good friend, author and sound engineer Justin Patton says, "Certainty is a helluva drug!" The one thing humans can't escape is that certainty is most certainly uncertain. John Calvin states in his work *Institutes of the Christian Religion, 3.2.1*, "Surely … we cannot imagine any certainty that is not tinged with doubt, or any assurance that is not assailed by some anxiety."[2]

Paraphrasing David Hume conceptually here who put forth just because the sun has always risen does not mean we can be certain it rises tomorrow. There will be a day when the sun has risen for the last time. We cannot know it will rise tomorrow. Now based upon past evidence it is reasonable to assume it will rise tomorrow but we cannot be certain of it. When we are dealing with the really big issues like those listed earlier, we are all (Atheists, Christians, Agnostics, Muslims, Jews, etc.) dealing in plausibility and probability. None of us can ever be certain in the true sense of the word. Alfred, Lord Tennyson in his poem *The Ancient Sage* artfully articulates this point,

> *For nothing worthy proving can be proven,*
> *Nor yet disproven; wherefore thou be wise,*
> *Cleave ever to the sunnier side of doubt.*[3]

From a Christian perspective Charles Spurgeon in his sermon *The Desire of the Soul in Spiritual Darkness* delivered on June 24, 1855, asserts, "I do not believe there ever existed a Christian yet, who did not now and then doubt his interest in Jesus. I think, when a man says, "I never doubt," it is quite time for us to doubt him."[4] Richard Dawkins who many consider to be the world's most famous atheist in a 100-minute debate with Archbishop of Canterbury Rowan Williams on Feb. 23, 2012, himself said that he cannot know that God does not exists and that "we are playing with estimates of probability."[5] For those who profess faith in anything, a religion, science, a spouse, etc. certainty is never within grasp. I would posit that doubt is not the opposite of faith, certainty is. Doubt is necessary, it is not juxtaposed to faith but rather runs alongside, each informing the other. Show me a person who has never once doubted their beliefs—be they deist or theist of any sort or atheist and I will show you either a person who is shallow or a liar!

If certainty is not within any of our grasps, then all of us are wrestling with what is plausible and trying to work our way abductively to what is probable to form and maintain our worldview. If this is the case, then wrestling with doubt no matter what your worldview is seems to me to be quite normal and predictable. Perhaps Flannery is right that the foundation of a prayer of faith is asking for help in one's lack of faith. I know for me it has been.

In Christianity there are numerous accounts of those who walked closely with Jesus having doubts. Even Jesus' own cousin who announced him as the one to the public had a time of doubting his own words. Matthew 11:2–6 speaks to when John (the Baptist), who was in prison, heard about the deeds of the Messiah, he sent his disciples to ask him, "Are you the one who is to come, or should we expect someone else?" Jesus replied, "Go back and report to John what you hear and see: The blind receive sight, the lame walk, those who have leprosy are cleansed, the deaf hear, the dead are raised, and the good news is proclaimed to the poor. Blessed is anyone who does not stumble on account of me." Finally, if you are one of the blessed ones whose doubts are few and far between and you are Christian, the book of Jude1:22 calls you to, "have mercy on those who doubt."

Religious belief does not come easy for me. Philosophy did not give me my religious faith, but it has talked me back into my religious faith many times (you will see this phrase again and again in this book). My religious faith did not give me my philosophy, but my religious faith has inspired me to dig deeper into philosophy many times. For me they have gone hand in hand, and each has strengthened the other. Both have kept me from despair when I would have otherwise been trapped in it. I am a natural doubter. Since I was a child, I have had a hard time taking anything at face value. I wanted to not only know why, but how and what was the reason for how and what was behind the motivation for why. Yet I consider myself (and have for many years) also a person of faith. I believe in the metaphysical. I believe in the transcendent. I believe truth is complex and multi-faceted. I am not only a person of faith but a specific faith. I am a disciple of Jesus Christ. My faith has changed over the years. It has evolved. There are some beliefs which I held early on in my religious faith that I no longer hold. There are also parts of my faith that I am exponentially more assured of today than I have ever been. In that regard I have deconstructed parts of my faith. The fact that belief does not come easy to me I used to see as a weakness, a flaw. I no longer see it that way. I see doubt as neither strength nor weakness but rather just a part of who I am. I venture to say all humans doubt their worldview, doubt their faith or doubt their lack of faith. That is the truth of the matter when we are honest and brave enough to admit.

John E. McKinney Sr., 63, of Evansville, Indiana, passed away Monday, July 31, 2006, at Deaconess Hospital. He is survived by two sons, John E. McKinney Jr. of Boonville, Indiana, and Jason Lee McKinney of Nashville, Tennessee. The previous words were all that was left of the biggest, strongest, funniest man I had ever known after the cancer had its way with his nearly 6'5" 250lb frame. My Dad was a rugby player and worked for Norfolk Southern railroad (see my song *Norfolk Southern Trains* if you are curious about more). As a kid he was my hero. I adored him. I was the kid who would still have his dad carry him everywhere when he was six years old. I was a shy kid, so I literally and figuratively clung to him. So much so that his nickname for me was Roo, based off of the young Joey character in the Winnie the Pooh children's book series. The character was always jumping into his mother Kanga's pouch. My Dad compared this to me jumping into his arms and ignoring the world outside of that protective space. I was for sure a Daddy's boy when I was younger. Later, when my dad remarried when I was 10 years old there was a shift and things got complicated. His new wife was jealous of the amount of attention he gave me when I was around, and she made him choose between us. There was a period of about six years that I only saw my dad on Christmas day. This created an ongoing tension with my dad and an on and off again nature to our relationship for the rest of his life.

In my entire life I can honestly say I have never seen my dad be afraid of anything. In that regard he was steady. Even when he contracted cancer, he carried on like everything was fine, not like in a denial sort of way but in a brave and pragmatic way. In fact, he did not even tell me he had cancer for a long time because he didn't want to worry or burden me. When it got to the end though, when he was on a feeding tube and was severely disfigured from the radiation, I saw fear in his eyes. He never uttered a word, but I could see it. He was afraid to die.

My dad was raised by devout Christians. My grandparents were amazing people. They had a profound impact on me spiritually (see Sing a Prayer). Although he was raised as a Christian, I would describe my dad's spiritual beliefs as agnostic. The few conversations I could get him to have about ultimate reality and metaphysical things he indicated that there had to be something out there he just didn't know what. He didn't particularly connect with any religion and so he just left it at acknowledging there had to be something to him that was good enough. He also seemed secure in that until at the end, I could see he wondered; it wasn't in the words. Like I said before he never actually questioned anything out loud. That wouldn't have been his way. It was in the silences. It was in the long pauses when we would talk about the end. It was about how he would listen more to me ramble about my belief.

I made sure my dad knew what I thought about God, and Jesus and salvation but I never told him I forgave him for what I perceived to be abandoning me. I never uttered the words of how much it hurt that he chose to cut me out of his life so he could keep the peace with my step-mother. In a two-year time frame where both of my grandparents had died and my parents got divorced, a time that I really needed him, he chose not to be there. I should have said all of that, let him know how bad I was hurt but also offered him complete and total forgiveness because as he approached death the roles were reversed. He really needed me. I failed him just as much as he failed me. I never brought myself to say those words and it is the single biggest regret of my life. He died doubting where he would go or if there was anywhere to go. He died doubting whether he had my forgiveness. Truth is he died with me doubting where he would go. He died with me doubting whether he had my forgiveness. My Christianity demanded I forgive him as an act of faith. Mark 6:14 says, "For if you forgive other people when they sin against you, your heavenly Father will also forgive you." I had to wrestle with whether I really believed in Christianity when I could not bring myself to forgive my dad when he most needed it. I deconstructed from knowing whether I really believed in Christianity or not. I deconstructed from knowing I was forgiven when I could not extend forgiveness myself.

Truth Is

V.1
He used to be the strongest man I knew
Now he's just wasted through
I brush his teeth cause he's too weak to
His breath reeks of death, gums black and blue
The doctor's cure is worse than the damned old disease
His life comes down to memories and facing mortality

Ch.1
Truth is we're all scared to die
Truth is we all question why
But most of us can't stand to face the proof
Truth is we all have our doubts
Truth is we don't have it all figured out
But we wear our masks of belief, too scared to lose
Truth is we all do

V2.
He sneaks Jack into his feeding tube
Says he's got nothing else to lose
Spend nights by the glow of Law and Order reruns
While the world has forgotten big John
We'll talk music and our all time favorite lines
That's one love we share, that he passed down right

Ch.2
Truth is we don't have a choice
Truth is that's most of the point
We take our last breath and surrender to the grave
Truth is down deep inside
When you strip away the noise and the pride
We all hope there's something beyond this damned place
The truth is we're all searching for some grace

Ch.3
Truth is he wore my crown
Truth is he mostly let me down
Truth is I didn't forgive and now he's gone
Truth is we never made things right
And I'll have to live with that the rest of my live
I could have set him free instead of holding on

Ch.4
Truth is we all live alone
Trapped in our little comfort zones
Scared to let ourselves be really known
The truth is we're all put to the test
We all end up in our Sunday best
With no time left for a second chance
What are we gonna do with the time we get?
What are we gonna do with what's left?[6]

Sing A Prayer

V. 1
Grandma used to sing a prayer over me (x2)
Begging please Lord keep you hand on this child
Grandpa used to put me up on his knee (x2)
Read to me about calvary the Lord's sacrifice

Ch.
My brothers and my sisters
I'm so grateful for it
When I'm lost in the darkness
It's the fire that lights it
When I don't know the answers
I remember her melody
When I'm crushed by my failures
The words of life redeem me

V.2
Grandma used to sing a prayer over me (x2)
For the blood to keep me from pharaoh's hand
Grandpa used to put me up on his knee (x2)
Read to me the stories of the promised land[7]

This book is titled *Deconstructing a Disciples Doubt*. I want to now dissect what each of these words and concepts mean.

DECONSTRUCTING

THE WIZARD

Can I believe my eyes? Why have you come back?

DOROTHY

Please sir, we've done what you told us. We brought you the broomstick of the Wicked Witch of the West. We melted her.

THE WIZARD

Oh, you liquidated her, eh? Very resourceful.

DOROTHY

Yes, sir. So we'd like you to keep your promises, if you please, sir.

THE WIZARD

Not so fast, NOT SO FAST! I'll have to give the matter a little thought. Go away and come back tomorrow.

DOROTHY

Tomorrow? Oh, but I want to go home now!

TIN MAN

You've had plenty of time to think already!

COWARDLY LION

Yeah!

THE WIZARD

DO NOT AROUSE THE WRATH OF THE GREAT AND POWERFUL OZ! I SAID COME BACK TOMORROW!

DOROTHY

If you were really Great and Powerful, you'd keep your promises!

THE WIZARD

[As Toto reveals him behind a curtain] You presume to criticize the Great Oz?! You ungrateful creatures! You're lucky

11

that I'm only holding this till tomorrow, instead of the next TWENTY YEARS from now! [They notice him] Er ... the Great Oz has spoken. [Redraws the curtain hastily] PAY NO ATTENTION TO THAT MAN BEHIND THE CURTAIN! THE GREAT, er ... OZ ... HAS SPOKEN!!

DOROTHY

[Pulling aside the curtain] Who are you?

THE WIZARD

Oh, er, [Into a microphone, which increases his voice dramatically] I AM THE GREAT AND POWERFUL [In normal voice] ... Wizard ... of Oz.

DOROTHY

You are?! I don't believe you.

THE WIZARD

I'm afraid it's true. There's no other Wizard except me.

SCARECROW

You humbug!

TIN MAN

Yeah!

THE WIZARD

Yes. That's exactly so. I'm a humbug.

DOROTHY

Oh, you're a very bad man!

THE WIZARD

Oh, no, my dear, I ... I'm a very good man—I'm just a very bad Wizard.[8]

According to Merriam-Webster deconstructing is, "a philosophical or critical method which asserts that meanings, metaphysical constructs, and hierarchical oppositions (as between key terms in a philosophical or literary work) are always rendered unstable by their dependence on ultimately arbitrary signifiers." According to the Cambridge Encyclopedia of Philosophy deconstruction is, "a demonstration of the incompleteness or incoherence of a philosophical position using concepts and principles of argument whose meaning, and use is legitimated only by that philosophical position.[9] Philosophically the term deconstruction gained prominence in the work of postmodern French philosopher Jacques Derrida. Derrida's basic premise is that meaning cannot be fully shared because meaning is not repeatable and further language is inadequate to fully comprehend and communicate meanings (in this regard his thoughts align with Thomas Aquinas). Philosophically deconstruction is about ridding oneself of presuppositions (something akin to Phenomenology's philosophical attitude, more on that later). Deconstruction is about taking that which is orthodox (or commonly assumed to be true or assumed to be the meaning of the thing- concept, text, etc.). Deconstruction is to question that which is accepted and to look at the context culturally for why that came to be accepted. Philosophical deconstruction is challenging you to look at the man behind the curtain and ask why is he behind the curtain? Why does he have the power and for what purpose does he use that power? Why are you assuming he is everything he says he is and most importantly why are you taking him at his word? What is his intended purpose? Is there any meaning being communicated that the man behind the curtain does not intend?

Philosophically deconstruction however is not destruction. It is a breaking down of a thought or concept not the breaking apart. This is where the term deconstruction philosophically departs from the term deconstruction theologically. Theological deconstruction is the rejection of the assumed orthodox tenets of your faith. The fundamental difference often is that philosophy by nature allows for varying points of view, so the rejection of philosophical orthodoxy does not necessarily lead to a destruction of the concept or text itself. For example, I can reject Descartes notion of an evil genius while still maintaining many other Cartesian beliefs. I can even still call myself a rationalist. It would be exceedingly rare to find any one philosophical assertion that would lead me to denounce all together a whole line of philosophical thinking. Theological deconstructing in this regard has higher stakes. When an old belief can't explain new data philosophically a dialectic movement occurs, and a higher understanding is reached (see Hegel). But when this occurs theologically it can (not always) shake the very foundation of someone's thoughts on the meaning of life. If I question everything about a particular philosophical movement it does not follow that I would even conceivably end up rejecting philosophy, but it is conceivable that I could end up rejecting theology as a whole if I reject certain tenets of theology.

Theology is the study of God and God's relation to the universe. Philosophy deals with nature of knowledge (epistemology- how we know what we know and what are the limits to what we can know) and existence (metaphysics- why is there anything, what is real, why does real exist, what is beyond the objective world). Theology begins with the assumption of a metaphysical reality and a divine revelation. There is a particular nature to theology and thus a theological deconstruction is more likely to be a complete and total destruction of a belief system than that of a philosophical deconstruction.

- Deconstructing- According to *Merriam Webster,* "a philosophical or critical method which asserts that meanings, metaphysical constructs, and hierarchical oppositions (as between key terms in a philosophical or literary work) are always rendered unstable by their dependence on ultimately arbitrary signifiers."
- Theology- the study of God and God's relation to the universe.
- Philosophy- the study of the nature of existence and knowledge.

DISCIPLE

In the closing scene of the movie *The Dead Poet's Society*, Robin Williams' character Mr. Keating has just been fired and the school headmaster has taken over teaching his class.

INT. KEATING'S CLASSROOM—DAY

[The students are all seated at their desks in silence. Everyone looks as the door opens. They quickly stand as Mr. Nolan enters the room.]

MR. NOLAN

I'll be teaching this class through exams. We'll find a permanent English teacher during the break. Who will tell me where you are in the Pritchard textbook? Mr. Anderson?

TODD

Uh, in the, in the Pr-

MR. NOLAN

I can't hear you, Mr. Anderson.

TODD

In the, in the, in the Pritchard?

MR. NOLAN

Kindly inform me, Mr. Cameron.

CAMERON

We skipped around a lot, sir. We covered the Romantics and some of the chapters on Post Civil War literature.

MR. NOLAN

What about the Realists?

CAMERON

I believe we skipped most of that, sir.

MR. NOLAN

All right, then, we'll start over. What is poetry?

[There is a knock at the classroom door.]

MR. NOLAN

Come. The students look back as the door opens.

[They quickly turn away when they see it is Keating.]

KEATING

Excuse me. I came for my personals. Should I come back after class?

MR. NOLAN

Get them now, Mr. Keating. Gentlemen, turn to page 21 of the introduction. Mr. Cameron, read aloud the excellent essay by Dr. Pritchard on "Understanding Poetry."

[Todd slowly closes his book. Keating opens the door to the tiny room off the classroom.]

CAMERON

That page has been ripped out, sir.

MR. NOLAN

Well, borrow somebody else's book.

CAMERON

They're all ripped out, sir.

MR. NOLAN

What do you mean, they're all ripped out?Never mind. [Mr. Nolan takes his own book over to Cameron's desk and then slaps the open page.] Read!

[As Cameron begins to read, Keating looks out at Todd as he puts his scarf on. Todd looks at him for a moment and then glances away.]

CAMERON

"Understanding Poetry" by Dr. J Evans Pritchard, Ph.D. To fully understand poetry, we must first be fluent with its meter, rhyme and figures of speech, then ask two questions: 1) How artfully has the objective of the poem been rendered and 2)

[The door squeaks as Keating shuts it behind him. Cameron pauses.]

CAMERON

How important is that objective? Question 1 rates the poem's perfection; Question 2 rates its importance. And once these questions have been answered, determining the poem's

greatness becomes a relatively simple matter. If the poem's
score for perfection is plotted on the horizontal of a graph—"
[Keating passes by Todd and the others and gets to the back of
the classroom before Todd leaps up from his seat and turns to
face him.]

TODD

Mr. Keating! They made everybody sign it.

MR. NOLAN

[Mr. Nolan gets up from his desk and approaches Todd.]
Quiet, Mr. Anderson.

TODD

You gotta believe me. It's true.

KEATING

I do believe you, Todd.

MR. NOLAN

Leave, Mr. Keating.

TODD

But it wasn't his fault!

MR. NOLAN

Sit down, Mr. Anderson!
[Todd reluctantly returns to his seat.]
One more outburst from you or anyone else, and you're
out of this school! Leave, Mr. Keating.
[Keating hesitates at the back of the classroom.]
I said leave, Mr. Keating.
[Keating slowly turns and heads to the door. As he opens it, Todd,
stands upon his desk and turns to Keating.]

TODD

O Captain! My Captain!

MR. NOLAN

Sit down, Mr. Anderson!
[Keating pauses at the door and looks back at Todd on his desk.]
Do you hear me? Sit down! Sit down! This is your final
warning, Anderson. How dare you? Do you hear me?

[After a moment of indecision, Knox climbs up onto his desk.]

KNOX

O Captain! My Captain!

MR. NOLAN

Mr. Overstreet, I warn you! Sit down! [Pitts climbs up onto his desk, followed by several others, including Meeks.] Sit down! Sit down. All of you. I want you seated. Sit down. Leave, Mr. Keating. [More students stand on their desks until half the class is standing.] All of you, down. I want you seated. Do you hear me? Sit down!

[Keating stands in the doorway, staring up at the boys in wonder. A smile comes to his face.]

KEATING

Thank you, boys. Thank you.[10]

Merriam Websters defines a disciple as "a convinced adherent of a school or individual who assists in the spreading the doctrines."[11]

A disciple is a follower of a leader who believes in the doctrine of a leader and imitates the example of a leader. A disciple is more than a student. Students may or may not believe or adhere to a leader's teachings, a disciple is one who not only believes in the teachings of the leader but also imitates those teachings and spreads the message. In other words, a disciple is indoctrinated by the teachings or philosophies of the leader. They are willing to follow wherever the leader may lead them regardless of personal loss or risk. They are willing to stand on a desk and repeat the teacher's favorite poem even at the risk of being kicked out of school. To borrow a term from marketing they are not just users of the brand they are brand champions. Brand champions are external storytellers who spread the vision, values and cultivate the brand to anyone who will hear. Every leader needs committed and passionate brand champions/disciples in order for the message to spread. Disciples being equivalent to brand champions are not casual consumers of a leader, they are super fans.

There are three communities of followers. There are ambient followers who are the casual consumers of the leader's doctrine or message or teachings. Ambient followers may pick through the leader's teachings ala carte. They may adhere to some and others not. They may consume some of the leader's material (be they books, sermons, lectures, etc.) and remain intentionally or unintentionally unaware of others. Then there are the engaged followers. Engaged followers are those who are students of the leader, even to the point of giving the leader's doctrine preferential place over and above other teachers but not to the point of championing the leader's teachings to other people and not to the point of great personal sacrifice, risking their own personal career, reputation and well-being. For engaged followers the leader may be their favorite leader. The leader's message may be their favorite, but their commitment does not go to the point of being indoctrinated. Finally, there are disciples. Disciples are fully indoctrinated and committed to the point significant personal sacrifice and risk. Disciples are all in.

- Disciple- a convinced adherent of a school or individual who assists in the spreading the doctrines.

To sum up, the three communities of followers for a leader are
1. Ambient Followers
2. Engaged Followers
3. Disciples

All humans have instances in their lives where they fit into each of the communities. For instance, I am a huge basketball fan. I will watch any basketball if there isn't anything else on. I will watch middle school basketball and enjoy it if there isn't any better option on TV. I am not however going to drive to and pay for a ticket to a middle school game (unless my kid is playing). For college basketball I am an engaged Butler Bulldog fan. I will buy and do own T-shirts and tickets to the games. I will work my schedule around when the games are on TV if I can (or certainly make time to watch the replay). I will not however sacrifice time at work or with family nor put my family in financial risk to support the team. For my own son's team, I am a disciple. I never miss a game (and if I do I call in for the play by play) I root for them at any time. I spend far more money supporting that team than I care to mention. I think that team and him as a player are the absolute best and I spread the message on all social media platforms to preach the message of him as a player. I am biased? Yes! Part of being a disciple of anything requires you being biased towards the leader, or in this case team/player.

Every human is a disciple of something and often a number of things. Everyone is indoctrinated in and biased to something or someone. While we often filter the word indoctrination as negative, this isn't necessarily so. According to Merriam Webster indoctrination is, "to imbue with a usually partisan or sectarian opinion, point of view, or principle."[12] In other words, indoctrination is to fully accept a set of beliefs or doctrine/philosophy. This is something all humans do. You are indoctrinated. We are indoctrinated by our parents, culture, friends, churches, the media, art, entertainment, etc. Have you ever argued with a spouse or roommate about what the proper way to squeeze toothpaste from the tube or which way the toilet paper should go? You are imbuing a partisan point of view on the matter, you are indoctrinated. Another example is if I handed you a small green piece of 75% cotton and 25% linen paper measuring 2.61 inches wide and 6.14 inches long with a picture of Alexander Hamilton on it what value would you assign that paper? It would be fair to assume you would value it at $10. It would be assumed by both myself and you that I am handing you $10 because we have been indoctrinated that bill is worth that much. Indoctrination is everywhere and unavoidable. We cannot choose whether we will be indoctrinated only what we will be indoctrinated by. There are beliefs you have that you no longer question, that you no longer think critically about on a regular basis. In these areas you are indoctrinated. To have a worldview you must be indoctrinated, and all worldviews hold certain bias of what is and what is not true (even relativism, but more on that later.) In his work *Loving Wisdom*, Paul Copan affirms, "every philosophy of life will have limits as to what is true or acceptable and what is not."[13] To have a conception of the world and to live and function within that view, indoctrination is necessary. Indoctrination is necessary to communicate effectively. Words have meaning based upon a foundation of assumptions and biases. While the postmodernists view this is a negative it is actually a base level necessity for culture to exist.

In this regard the first two words in the title of this book have an oxymoronic relationship to one another. This is not lost on me, I kind of think it is humorous. You are a disciple of something, a person, an ideology, a worldview. We all have presuppositions. We need these presuppositions to function in the world. We function in the world by making assumptions based upon a worldview. There are things you would climb up on a chair and risk it all to spread the message about without thinking through it critically. Whatever those things are you are an indoctrinated disciple of those things be they message or manifesto; object or oration; ethic or epistle; ideal or idea; person, place, or thing. This is also why deconstructing can be a very good thing from time to time. Deconstructing our assumed beliefs and narratives helps insure we don't move from indoctrination to brainwashing. We also can't stay in a cycle of questioning all our beliefs all the time. If we did, we would either end up clinically insane or in a total state of existential nihilism. However, taking inventory about our assumed beliefs and allowing our doubting to move us into deconstructing them from time to time can be a very scary but very healthy thing.

It is important here that I make a distinction between indoctrination and brainwashing. All disciples are indoctrinated but not all disciples are brainwashed. There are important distinctions between the two. Indoctrination gives partisan, bias, and loyalty towards a particular leader or set of philosophies, teachings, or principles. With indoctrination this is done out of the individuals volition. As the indoctrinated person becomes aware of alternative philosophies, teachings, principles they are free to continue to accept the current paradigm, expand their acceptance of the new information along with the current paradigm, or to abandon the current paradigm and be indoctrinated into the new paradigm of philosophies, teachings, or principles. With indoctrination the only limiting factor is ignorance. Nothing is forced. Indoctrination occurs through influence. My 3rd grade teacher Ms. Olsen heavily influenced my love for Americana authors who wrote of the struggles and life of the American south. She did this by exposing me to authors and books within this genre and championing its merits in class. She read me *Where the Red Fern Grows* and multiple works by Mark Twain. She indoctrinated me into a love for it, but she did not brainwash me. I could choose to continue to read books about southern life outside of what Ms. Olsen assigned or not. Brainwashing requires blind allegiance and a relinquishing of personal autonomy and volition. Brainwashing is about control. The Oxford English Dictionary defines brainwashing as "pressuring someone to adopt radically different beliefs by using systematic and forcible means."[14] It often implies mind control, and other unethically manipulative methods of persuasion. Ms. Olsen for sure indoctrinated me in that she biased me towards a certain style of literature that I then chose to adopt as a part of my literary worldview. She did not force me to adopt it. She may have forced the exposure to it by way of her being the teacher and me the student, but she in no way forced me to continue in it or to think it was the only literature worth reading. Brainwashing is manipulative where indoctrination is influencing. In brainwashing you cannot question authority, in indoctrination you absolutely can. I could hand you that $10 bill and you could say it holds no value for you. My mom may have had the rule that I had to squeeze the toothpaste tube from the bottom growing up, but I can freely choose to abandon that as an adult, even if my mom had to move in with me for her elderly years, I do not have to continue in it and I have the capacity to consider the merits of that method of using the toothpaste. Brainwashing removes one's sense of self, where indoctrination can give a sense of self. Humans all want to belong; we are herd animals scientifically and spiritually speaking religions are built upon communities and gatherings. Being a part of communities should add to our sense of self. When you ask someone who they are they often speak about roles within communities. I am a father, husband, professor, musician, etc. I have been indoctrinated into all those roles. I have a bias of perspective, yet all of these add to my sense of self. I am in the community of fathers. There are certain societal norms and mores that shape how I think about what a father should be. Some of these I accept and assume to be true and others I reject. I am indoctrinated yes, but free to operate and apply the indoctrinated role as I see fit. Brainwashing requires groupthink and often a total loss of self.

Having a worldview requires us to live within a certain framework that assumes certain principles. One of the great benefits of a disciple deconstructing is that we avoid committing the logical fallacies of appeal to ignorance, fallacy of origins, and appeal to common belief fallacy.

- Worldview- A particular conception of the world.
- Indoctrination- to imbue with a usually partisan or sectarian opinion, point of view, or principle.
- Brainwashing- Pressuring someone to adopt radically different beliefs by using systematic and forcible means.
- Appeal to Ignorance Fallacy- A type of false dichotomy that assumes a proposition is true or false only based upon the lack of contrary evidence.
- Fallacy of Origins- Assumes a proposition is true or false

based upon the origin of the proposition (who said it) and not the merit of the assertion.

- Appeal to Common Belief Fallacy- Assumes the truth of a proposition based solely on the number of people who hold that proposition to be true or false.

Conversely one of the dangers of being a disciple who is deconstructing is committing the same fallacies. Just because most academics do not believe in God is not a good reason to deconstructing into atheism. Just because your church said something is true does not automatically mean it is true, it also does not automatically mean it is false or even that it is a binary proposition. Just because someone who follows a philosophy or teaching hurt you (emotionally, physically, or spiritually) does not negate the merits of the philosophy or teaching. Let me give an extreme example for a moment. What if someone found archival footage of Hitler giving a math lesson to some school children. In the footage Hitler tells the children 6 x 3 is 18. Would you believe what Hitler was saying or dismiss it because it was Hitler who said it? Is the math equation somehow false because of the origins of who is saying it?

The real trick is to judge our own motivation soberly. Are we deconstructing our discipleship in order to reach a new level of synthesis? Is it to reach a higher level of ultimate truth? Is the deconstruction for the purpose of gaining a better understanding of true orthodoxy of our belief system? Is it even for the aim of abandoning our current belief system because we have begun to suspect it may be false? All these in my estimation are positive reasons to deconstruct. Or is it to excuse some behavior that goes against our current belief system? Is it to try and avoid wrestling with the hard questions? Is it to try and avoid living in the tension of a paradox? Are you running towards the truth or running away from it?

DOUBT

A few snippets of dialogue form the movie *The Matrix*.

[COMPUTER SCREEN TYPING]

Wake up Neo…

NEO:

What?

[COMPUTER SCREEN TYPING]

The Matrix has you.

NEO:

What the hell?

[COMPUTER SCREEN TYPING]

Follow the White Rabbit?

NEO:

Follow the White Rabbit?

UNKNOWN VOICE

Knock Knock Neo!

MORPHEUS:

I imagine that right now; you're feeling a bit like Alice. Hmm? Tumbling down the rabbit hole?

NEO:

You could say that.

MORPHEUS:

I see it in your eyes. You have the look of a man who accepts what he sees because he is expecting to wake up. Ironically, that's not far from the truth. Do you believe in fate, Neo?

NEO:

No.

MORPHEUS:

Why not?

NEO:

Because I don't like the idea that I'm not in control of my life.

MORPHEUS:

I know *exactly* what you mean. Let me tell you why you're here. You're here because you know something. What you know you can't explain, but you feel it. You've felt it your entire life, that there's something wrong with the world. You don't know what it is, but it's there, like a splinter in your mind, driving you mad. It is this feeling that has brought you to me. Do you know what I'm talking about?

NEO:

The Matrix.

MORPHEUS:

Have you ever had a dream, Neo, that you seemed so sure it was real? But if were unable to wake up from that dream, how would you tell the difference between the dream world and the real world?

NEO:

This can't be.

MORPHEUS:

Be what? Be real?[15]

Often called the father of modern philosophy French Philosopher Rene Descartes focused his attention on epistemology (how do we know what we think we know). Descartes was a rationalist and definitely the O.G. of deconstruction and doubt. Descartes became concerned with the assumed truths he had once believed. He wanted to find better grounds for knowledge than that which he had previously assumed. He set out on a thought experiment to assume nothing (though he did assume words still held their basic meanings). He used doubt as a way to move towards removing false beliefs but also as a way to conquer doubt about those things that can be known and trusted. "His goal was to use doubts in order to defeat skepticism and to find firm grounds for knowledge that would be secure from all doubt."[16]

His doubt and deconstruction had the aim and purpose of

finding solid ground. Descartes aimed to "rid myself of all opinions which I had formerly accepted and commence to build anew from the foundation."[17]

He had every intention of rebuilding his belief, of reconstructing it. He attempted to take what phenomenology would call a philosophical attitude (more on that in Part 3 of the book). He is getting at the fact that our perception of reality seems like a true reality but only to our perceptions. There is no way for us to ever know how closely the reality we perceive is to true reality by the senses. It must be assessed by the mind. Descartes makes the analogy that dreams and sleep form out of resemblance to something with formal reality (occurring in space and time) An example is a unicorn. A unicorn has objective reality in that it is an idea, but that idea is constituted by something with formal reality, a horse. Descartes begins his reconstruction with the famous statement, cogito ergo sum or loosely translated "I think therefore I am." Doubt comes in two primary categories global doubt and local doubt. Global doubt is to doubt everything while local doubt is to doubt a particular experience or a particular set of information.

- Doubt- The attitude of equally questioning all paradigms, information, rules, presuppositions, and all other points that govern one's understanding of the world.
- Local doubts- Those are doubts about a particular sense experience or some other occurrence at a particular point in time.
- Global Doubt- Doubting existence itself.
- Philosophical Attitude- The disengagement and distancing from the immediacy of your life to the reflecting upon it.

Descartes famous statement is very basically asserting that because he can have local doubts answers the question of global doubt. Because I can ponder whether or not I exist is a really good argument that I do in fact exist. Descartes concludes the inference to the most reasonable conclusion is that he does in fact exist. Does he prove this fact? Could we all be in the matrix right now? Maybe. But Descartes decides abductively the most reasonable conclusion is that he does exist and no longer continues to doubt that fact. Descartes then chooses to place his faith in the fact that he does exist. This movement is much like Hegel's dialectic where you go from thesis (a belief) to antithesis (some new information or teaching or philosophy that makes you question or rubs against your current paradigm), to synthesis (reaching a higher understanding of your current belief, reasonably ruling out the new information as false/unhelpful or assimilating the new information into your worldview). This movement is healthy and helps us all reach a little closer to ultimate reality. What is not healthy is continuing to question all your worldview all of the time. "Merely having an open mind is nothing. English writer and philosopher G.K. Chesterton said, "The object of opening the mind, as of opening the mouth, is to shut it again on something solid."[18]

Just as every worldview has indoctrination as a building block within it, every assumed belief is an act of faith. Everyone lives by faith. Atheist and theist alike. Remember if we are dealing in plausibility and probability whatever we choose to believe is an act of faith. Doubt and belief should be influenced by the weighing of evidence and not popularity. Alvin Plantinga in his book *God, Freedom, and Evil* states, "The mere fact that a belief is unpopular at present (or at some other time) is interesting from a sociological point of view but evidentially irrelevant." There are valid and sound logical arguments for the existence of God. There are valid and sound arguments for there not being a God. There are substantial evidential arguments for God and substantial evidential arguments for there not being a God. Neither side is in the business of provability, no one is certain. Everyone is putting their faith in their belief system (see more on that in Part 3).

CONCLUSION

All humans will have doubts about their belief system and worldview. All humans live putting their faith in their belief system and worldview. This does not mean that all humans doubt their beliefs to the same degree or have the same faith in their beliefs. We humans are individuals first and foremost, so my doubts will not be the same doubts or to the same degree as any of you reading this. Some of you will doubt very few of your beliefs and not doubt them very much while others are plagued by doubt about almost everything. What the rest of this book will do is walk you through how I have wrestled through my own journey with doubt and faith. The rest of this book lets you be a fly on the wall to how I have wrestled with and found answers I find to be sufficient. It gives you a peak into philosophers who have helped me to reshelve the issues back into the faith category. You may find these answers sufficient or not. You may find some of the things I wrestled with are not the same things you wrestle with and that is okay. What I do think is for the majority of people the things I have wrestled with (and continue to on some days) are at least in the vicinity of what they wrestle with. Things such are why does existence exist, why is existence the way it is, what is true and how can I know it is true, why is there so much evil and suffering, how do I know which religion to follow and does it matter, is there such a thing as a soul and if so what is a soul, what about my own personal experience how much weight should I give that? Truth is my dad died with me doubting where he would go. Was his agnostic belief in something good enough? I doubt it. How far did grace reach? Did it reach far enough to compel him to make a death bed confession? All that was beyond my kin to answer and beyond my control. What was in my control and what I failed to make sure of was that he died not doubting whether he had his son's (who claimed to be Christian) forgiveness. If I really believed in Christianity, why did I not forgive him? I had to reconstruct my belief of the assurance that I really believed in Christianity. Mark 6:14 says, "For if you forgive other people when they sin against you, your heavenly Father will also forgive you." I had to wrestle with whether I really believed in Christianity when I could not bring myself to forgive my dad when he most needed it. Ultimately I had to forgive myself for not forgiving my dad while he was still here. I had to cry out to Jesus, "I believe, help my unbelief."

If I had to sum up in one sentence where I find myself today it would be found in the Bible John 6:66–69, "From this time many of his disciples turned back and no longer followed him. 'You do not want to leave too, do you?' Jesus asked the Twelve. Simon Peter answered him, 'Lord, to whom shall we go? You have the words of eternal life. We have come to believe and to know that you are the Holy One of God.'"

Doubters Prayer

V1.
I cry out, to you for help
Do you hear me when it hurts to speak?
I stretch out, my weary hands
Will I be left uncomforted?
I daydream about long ago
When it was easier to hold on to hope
Will I never know your favor again?
Did you forget about all your promises?
I meditate on all your words
The less I know the more I learn
Time and time again I fail
You carried the cross but I drove the nails
In you oh in you

Ch.
I believe help my unbelief (x2)
When I don't understand
Can't comprehend
All of these doubts keep filling my head
All the pain that I see
Don't make sense to me
I still believe help my unbelief

V2.
In the dark when I'm lonely
It don't help at all that your thoughts are beyond me
But who am I to question you
Cause you know all and I'm just getting through
No matter how long a night can get
Your thunder is heard in the whirlwind
Not a shooting star is unaccounted for
Or a grain of sand on the ocean floor

Bridge
Though the circumstance hasn't change I believe
I need your love to light the way I believe
You're not shaken by all my questions
I'm not forsaken so let my faith awaken[19]

DISCUSSION QUESTIONS

1. Why do you think Flannery O'Connor called the doubter's prayer the foundation of faith?
2. What is meant by certainty is a helluva drug? Do you agree or disagree and why?
3. What is the difference between plausibility and probability?
4. Do you agree that certainty is the opposite of faith? If so, what is your reason?
5. In the lyrics of *Truth Is* what do you think is meant by the lines "But we wear our masks of belief, too scared to lose; Truth is we all do?" Do you agree we all wear masks to hide our doubts at times?
6. In the lyrics for *Sing A Prayer* the lines, "When I don't know the answers; I remember her melody" refers to the spiritual base the author's grandparents instilled in him. Considering the concept of indoctrination, do you think this instilling of a particular religious view is beneficial or damaging? If damaging what is a more positive option?
7. How did new information allow/push Dorothy to deconstruct her limited worldview when it comes to the Wizard?
8. Do you believe there is a difference between a deconstruction of a belief and a destruction from it? Should the doubting disciples first aim be to completely disregard a held belief or to try integrating new information to maintain it?
9. Compare Todd's devotion to Mr. Keating to that of Peter's declaration in Matthew 26:35?
10. Why would a disciple's doubt be more surprising or concerning than the doubt of an engaged follower or an ambient follower?
11. Has your understanding of indoctrination been changed or expanded by reading what the author has to say on the subject?
12. Articulate in your own words the primary differences between indoctrination and brainwashing?

13. Compare the concepts of doubting and deconstruction to Morpheus' "splinter in your mind" and "how would you tell the difference between the dream world and the real world?"

14. Look up Rene Descartes concept of the evil genius, how does this compare to some people's perception of God? What role could this play in causing someone to doubt?

15. What is the difference between Descartes use of doubt in his deconstruction with what you have seen in those around you in your life who have deconstructed from faith?

16. Do you struggle more with local doubts or global doubts? Why do you think that is?

17. John 6:66–69 speaks about some disciples who no longer followed (destruction of faith) and Peter who says there is no were else to go. What do you think the difference is between those who doubted but were able to maintain their faith and those who lost their faith?

18. Think back to times in your life when it was "easier to hold on to hope." What made it easier? Think to times when hope was harder to hold on to. What made it harder? Was it intellectual challenges? Was it emotional grief? Was it broken dreams? Was it circumstantial? Was it theological?

19. If it is true that in the big questions of life, we are not dealing with what can be proved, is it possible for "all of the pain that I see" to make sense? Is it required for us to maintain belief? Can our doubt be satisfied with reasonable evidence that the pain we see plausibly or probably has a good purpose?

20. Do we need the circumstances of our belief to change in order to maintain it?

21. How does the quote from Lord Tennyson about not be able to prove the big questions rub against our craving for certainty? How do we honor our doubts without being trapped by them?

DISCLAIMER

I do want to take a few sentences to make a disclaimer. I have not been through a singular deconstruction; I have been through several over different issues and at different times in my life. While everyone of the personal stories I will use in this book are true, they are not necessarily written about in chronological order. I chose rather to write about the issues of deconstruction starting at the largest and most general and working down to the more specific. My own deconstructions and doubts did not happen in this order. Additionally, while the thought processes and philosophies that helped me deconstruct and reconstruct are accurately represented in principle, I make no claims that all the books I reference were a part of my deconstructions and reconstructions at the time of my going through them. Some of the books were not even written when I went through the issues they address, however the works I reference are the types and their assertions and philosophies do represent accurately the way I cognitively ascended to a cogent return to faith. That is not to say that none of the books referenced played a role at the time I was going through the specific deconstructions and reconstructions but not all of them did. Some of the books I did not encounter until much later.

BIBLIOGRAPHY

Audi, Robert. *The Cambridge Dictionary of Philosophy*. Cambridge, MA: Cambridge Univ. Press, 1999.

"Brainwashing." brainwashing noun - Definition, pictures, pronunciation and usage notes | Oxford Advanced Learner's Dictionary at OxfordLearnersDictionaries.com. Accessed January 13, 2022. https://www.oxfordlearnersdictionaries.com/us/definition/english/brainwashing?q=brainwashing.

Calvin, Jean, and Henry Beveridge. *The Institutes of the Christian Religion*. Lexington, KY: pacps, Pacific Publishing Studio, 2011.

Dead Poets Society (Motion Picture). United States: Buena Vista Pictures Distribution, 1989.

"Disciple." In *Merriam-Webster.com*. Accessed January 13, 2022. webster.com/dictionary/disciple.

Illustrated London News, October 10, 1908.

"Indoctrination Definition & Meaning." Merriam-Webster. Merriam-Webster. Accessed January 13, 2022. https://www.merriam-webster.com/dictionary/indoctrination?utm_campaign=sd&utm_medium=serp&utm_source=jsonld.

Langley, Noel, Florence Ryerson, Edgar Alan Woolf, Mervyn LeRoy, Herbert Stothart, E. Y. Harburg, Harold Arlen, et al. *The Wizard of Oz*, n.d.

Martinich, A. P., Fritz Allhoff, and Anand Jayprakash Vaidya. *Early Modern Philosophy: Essential Readings with Commentary*. Malden, MO: Blackwell Publishing, 2007.

O'Connor, Flannery. *Habit of Being*. New York, NY: Farrar, Straus & Giroux, 1999.

"Richard Dawkins versus Rowan Williams: Humanity's Ultimate Origins." YouTube, November 7, 2012. https://youtu.be/zruhc7XqSxo.

Spurgeon, C. H. *Spurgeon's Sermons*. Peabody, MA: Hendrickson Pub., 2011.

Tennyson, Alfred Tennyson. *The Works of Alfred Lord Tennyson.* Ware, UK: Wordsworth, 2008.

Wachowski, Lilly, Lilly Wachowski, Lana Wachowski, Lana Wachowski, Joel Silver, Don Davis, Bill Pope, Owen Paterson, Zach Staenberg, and Yuen Wo Ping. *The Matrix*, n.d.

Endnotes

1. Flannery O'Connor, *Habit of Being* (New York, NY: Farrar, Straus & Giroux, 1999).

2. Jean Calvin and Henry Beveridge, *The Institutes of the Christian Religion* (Lexington, KY: pacps, Pacific Publishing Studio, 2011).

3. Alfred Tennyson Tennyson, *The Works of Alfred Lord Tennyson* (Ware, UK: Wordsworth, 2008).

4. C. H. Spurgeon, *Spurgeon's Sermons* (Peabody, MA: Hendrickson Pub., 2011).

5. "Richard Dawkins versus Rowan Williams: Humanity's Ultimate Origins," YouTube, November 7, 2012, https://youtu.be/zruhc7XqSxo.

6. Written by Jason Lee McKinney (Zekers and ZiZi Music (BMI)

7. Written by Jason Lee McKinney (Zekers and ZiZi Music (BMI)

8. *The Wizard of Oz*, n.d.

9. Robert Audi, *The Cambridge Dictionary of Philosophy* (Cambridge, MA: Cambridge Univ. Press, 1999).

10. *Dead Poets Society* (Motion Picture) (Buena Vista Pictures Distribution, 1989).

11. "Disciple," in Merriam-Webster.com, accessed January 13, 2022, webster.com/dictionary/disciple.

12. "Indoctrination Definition & Meaning," Merriam-Webster (Merriam-Webster), accessed January 13, 2022, https://www.merriam-webster.com/dictionary/indoctrination?utm_campaign=sd&utm_medium=serp&utm_source=jsonld.

13. Paul Copan, *Loving Wisdom: Christian Philosophy of Religion* (Grand Rapids, MI: Chalice Press, 2012), 19.

14. "Brainwashing," brainwashing noun - Definition, pictures, pronunciation and usage notes | Oxford Advanced Learner's Dictionary at OxfordLearnersDictionaries.com, accessed

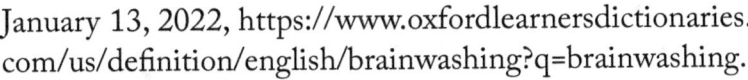

January 13, 2022, https://www.oxfordlearnersdictionaries.com/us/definition/english/brainwashing?q=brainwashing.

15. *The Matrix*, n.d.

16. A. P. Martinich, Fritz Allhoff, and Anand Jayprakash Vaidya, *Early Modern Philosophy: Essential Readings with Commentary* (Malden, MO: Blackwell Publishing, 2007), 76.

17. A. P. Martinich, Fritz Allhoff, and Anand Jayprakash Vaidya, *Early Modern Philosophy: Essential Readings with Commentary* (Malden, MO: Blackwell Publishing, 2007), 88.

18. *Illustrated London News*, October 10, 1908.

19. Written by Jason Lee McKinney (Zekers and ZiZi Music (BMI)

Part 1

Why Does Existence Exist?
(A Cosmological Argument from Contingency)

In the movie *Rudy* starring Sean Astin, the character Rudy Ruettiger's dream is to play football for Notre Dame (as any normal human would #GOIRISH!). Rudy however has very little athletic ability as well as not being a great student. His intent was to try and walk-on the team since his lack of athleticism prevented him from being offered a scholarship. In order to walk-on though you have to be a student at the university which left the issue of his grades. Two years earlier Father John Cavanaugh pulled some strings to get Rudy into the local junior college, Holy Cross. Rudy has just finished his final semester at Holy Cross and is waiting to see if he will finally get into Notre Dame as a student. This is his final chance.

[Father Cavanaugh walks into the church to find Rudy praying]
FATHER CAVANAUGH
Taking your appeal to a higher authority?
RUDY
I'm desperate. If I don't get in next semester, it's over. Notre Dame doesn't accept senior transfers.
FATHER CAVANAUGH
Well, you've done a hell of a job kid, chasing down your dream.
RUDY
Who cares what kind of job I did if it doesn't produce results? It doesn't mean anything.

FATHER CAVANAUGH
I think you'll find that it will.
RUDY
Maybe I haven't prayed enough.
FATHER CAVANAUGH
I don't think that's the problem. Praying is something we do in our time, the answers come in God's time.
RUDY
If I've done everything I possibly can, can you help me?
FATHER CAVANAUGH
Son, in thirty-five years of religious study, I've come up with only two hard, incontrovertible facts; there is a God, and, I'm not Him.[20]

Tilda Swinton's character the Ancient One in the *Doctor Strange* movie states as Strange is traveling in between dimensions:

THE ANCIENT ONE
You think you know how the world works? You think that this material universe is all there is? What is real? What mysteries lie beyond the reach of your senses? At the root of existence, mind and matter meet. Thoughts shape reality. This universe is only one of an infinite number. Worlds without end. Some benevolent and life giving. Others filled with malice and hunger. Dark places where powers older than time lie ravenous ... and waiting.[21]

Gottfried Wilhelm Leibniz asked in his work *Monadology*, "Why is there something rather than nothing?"[22] This is the biggest metaphysical question of all. Why does existence exist? The particular area of metaphysics that deals with this question is cosmology and answering the question requires a cosmological argument. This has nothing to do with make up or making someone look attractive.

- Cosmology- the branch of philosophy dealing with the origin and general structure of the universe, with its parts, elements, and laws, and especially with such of its characteristics as space, time, causality, and freedom.[1]
- Cosmological Argument- According to Bruce Reichenbach from the Stanford Encyclopedia of Philosophy, "a general pattern of argumentation (logos) that makes an inference from particular alleged facts about the universe (cosmos) to the existence of a unique being, generally identified with or referred to as God. Among these initial facts are that particular beings or events in the universe are causally dependent or contingent, that the universe (as the totality of contingent things) is contingent in that it could have been other than it is or not existed at all."

Humans have long asked why are we here and what does it mean? Even this question has a question behind it, why is there anything? How did anything get here? For my life to have meaning the universe must have meaning. For there to be a reason why I am here, there first has to be a reason why anything is here. Ponderance of meaning is a feature that is exclusive to humans here on earth. Phenomenological and existential German philosopher Martin Heidegger in his work *Being and Time* argues that humans are qualitatively different from the rest of creation by the fact that we search for meaning. Heidegger asserts humans are different by our, "capacity to put [our] existence into question. [We] are creatures for whom existence as such, not just particular features of it, is problematic."[23]

Beyond the reason for existence of humanity what was before nothing and what caused nothing to become something? One theory is that there once was nothing then Chuck Norris round-house kicked nothing and told it to get a job and the universe sprang forth. Chuck Norris jokes aside, didn't something have to preexist what we describe as nothing for there to ever be something?

In my own life I have wrestled with this from an early age. It seemed to me even as a child I received one of two pat and trite answers to the origin of the universe:

1. The big bang
2. God

Now I don't deny the legitimacy of either of those answers in and of themselves, but it always seemed like a cop out on both sides. It appeared to me just saying either was committing a sort of hypothesis of the gaps. People don't know so they would say either big bang which didn't really answer the question of the origins of the universe but rather just stops at the first effect of a cause humans can know. The big bang answer just side steps causality all together. The God answer is like the kid in Sunday school who always answers "Jesus!" to every question. It may be technically true (and I ultimately personally accepted and continue to accept that it is), but I was searching for a little more thorough answer. It also always bothered me that these two answers were almost universally pitted against one another. This always came across to me as a false dichotomy. I was never able to buy that the big bang or God were the only and competing options. People who gave the big bang option seemed to be digging their own ditch into an epistemic regress and those who asserted God without doing the homework commit a God of the gap's fallacy. Now as stated before in all of these big ideas, humans are dealing with plausibility and probability not provability. In my own deconstruction process, I set out to see if I could move the needle in from doubt to plausibility and even to probability that reconciles both the causal necessity for agency in regard to the beginning of the universe while also showing how the big bang could in fact not be evidence against a causal agent but actually evidence for it. If that evidence was on purpose so to speak then there must be a purpose for my existence and yours. If without a cause the origins of the universe are an infinite regress, then there must be a cause (literally everything else in the universe has a cause so why not the universe). If there is a cause then there must be a reason for that cause, if there is a reason for the universe to exist there is a reason for humans to exist. Perhaps the reason humans exist is to reflect the creator.

- False dichotomy or dilemma fallacy- Limits two elements of a premise into binary options. The fallacy committed is not one of form but in premise. Not all binary premises are committing this fallacy. The fallacy is committed when there is at least one other option and perhaps many others beyond the two elements in the premise.

Freedom

A.
Freedom (Freedom)
Whoah oh Freedom (Freedom)
Freedom it isn't free
Freedom (Freedom)
Whoah oh Freedom (Freedom)
Feedom, it was bought and paid for upon the tree

V.1
When the universe came to exist
There must have been a cause for the effect
I wasn't there but reason persists
Love broke through nothing we exist

Pr.
What is proof without evidence
What is truth without consequence

V.2
Oh, What makes a man a man
It's the choice he has to make a stand
Oh, Love's more than utility
Divine spark in you and me[24]

Plato, speaking from the character Timaeus of Locri, "Now everything that comes to be must of necessity come to be by the agency of some cause, for it is impossible for anything to come to be without cause."[25]

It seems paradoxical to speak of what condition must exist before the first moment of the universe. What are the conditions needed for the first moment? If a song is the result, and the mechanisms are a guitar, pen, paper, and a recording device, is anything else required? Or, if given the right amount of time and the precise shifts, will the mechanisms eventually form a song? Does there need to be a songwriter involved? Does there need to be a causal agent for the song to exist? Does the knowledge of what mechanisms were used to create the song dismiss the need for a songwriter?

In Appendix C of John C. Lennox's book *Seven Days That Divide the World*, Lennox quotes Leon Kass from his book *The Beginning of Wisdom*, who provides a critical insight about how modern naturalistic cosmology is ill-equipped to answer questions of first cause when he states, "About this too, modern cosmology cannot help but agree: 'What was there before the big bang?' God only knows. Despite all our sophistication, the utter mysteriousness of the ultimate beginning and its source cause cannot be eradicated."[26]

Lennox again in chapter four of *God's Undertaker* begins with a critical takeaway quote from professor and Christian philosopher Keith Ward stating:

"To the majority of those who have reflected deeply and written about the origin and nature of the universe, it has seemed that it points beyond itself to a source which is non-physical and of great intelligence and power. Almost all of the great classical philosophers—certainly Plato, Aristotle, Descartes, Leibniz, Spinoza, Kant, Hegel, Locke, Berkeley— saw the origin of the universe as lying in a transcendent reality. They had different specific ideas of this reality and different ways of approaching it, but that the universe is not self-explanatory, and that it requires some explanation beyond itself, was something they accepted as fairly obvious."[27]

The mechanisms for writing a song do not explain the song; they are not self-explanatory. The lack of being self-explanatory does not diminish the mechanisms nor make them incongruent with the process of writing the song. It merely means they are the tools with which a causal agent used to create the song. The example of a song correlates with the universe, as is the big bang to the mechanisms and the songwriter to a necessary causal agent. The song and the mechanisms are contingent upon the songwriter. The principle of sufficient reason affirms the songwriter is necessary for the song to exist. The song is not necessary, and neither are the mechanisms; they are both subject to the songwriter's will. The songwriter could have written a different song or used a piano instead of a guitar, but for a song to exist, the songwriter is a necessary first cause.

- Sufficient Reason- everything that exists has a reason to exist; everything that exists was caused.
- First Cause- An ultimate cause which does not have a cause. A necessarily existing first mover.

The cosmological argument from contingency asserts there is something rather than nothing because of a necessarily existing first causal agent. The necessity of first cause is congruent with big bang cosmological theory. Five points of congruence between the contingency cosmological argument and big bang cosmological theory are pinpointed and posited within this part. This part of the book gives explanation of the cosmological argument from contingency and shows how the principles of sufficient reason and first cause substantiate the contingency cosmological argument. The very assertions of big bang theory prove the need for sufficient reason because there is something instead of nothing. An argument explaining how the big bang theory has no theological or logical conflict with the contingency cosmological argument is made.

EXPLANATION OF THE COSMOLOGICAL ARGUMENT FROM CONTINGENCY

Though numerous voices contribute to the contingency cosmological argument, I will focus on two: a primary and a secondary. The primary philosopher, whose cosmological argument I will reference is Gottfried Leibniz. The secondary is Thomas Aquinas. Aquinas is drawn upon solely for the way his cosmological informed and influenced Leibniz.

In answer to the question, "Is there a God?" Thomas Aquinas stated in Article 3 of the Summa Theologiae, "It is certain, and obvious to the senses, that in the world some things are moved. But everything that is moved is moved by another."[28] Aquinas cosmological argument centered on the necessity of a first cause; Aquinas asserted a necessary first cause for every second cause. He gives the example of a piece of wood and fire. A piece of wood has the potential to be hot, but that potential does not make the wood hot; there must be a first mover. Only a first mover can convert potential into actual. Leibniz builds upon Aquinas and states, "Thus God alone (or necessary causal agent) has this privilege, that he must exist if he is possible. And since nothing can prevent the possibility of what is without limits, without negation, and consequently without contradiction, this by itself is sufficient for us to know the existence of God a priori."[29]

Leibniz made a distinction between things that exist necessarily and things that exist contingently. Necessarily existing propositions exist by necessity of their nature.[30]

It is impossible for necessarily existing things not to exist; for example, numbers and mathematics are necessary in existence. They are not caused. They exist simply by their nature. Contingently existing things are caused to exist by something else; they are moved, as Aquinas posits. The overwhelming majority of things do not have to exist. Contingently existing propositions only exist because something caused them to exist. Necessarily existing propositions are necessary in any possible world, while contingently existing things could exist or not exist depending on which world was actual. Humans innately know by the laws of motion and the observed cause and effect, what is contingent and what is necessity. What moves is moved by a first cause. Leibniz argued a necessarily existing first cause from an *a posteriori* position; he did believe in innate ideas. Therefore, contingent in a cosmological sense is anything that does not exist in and from it self. A contingent is "a being that is causally dependent for its existence on some other being."[31]

In other words, contingently existing things are not self-existent. Conversely necessarily existing things exist out of their own nature and are sustained from and by that nature.

- a posteriori- things you know before you observe them. Things that are known as matter of fact or from past experiences. Things assumed to be true, like the sun rising in the east tomorrow.

Leibniz cosmological argument for a necessary causal agent comes from the following reasoning: if X is a necessary causal agent and is possible, then X must exist; otherwise, it is not necessary.[32] Leibniz states, "If a necessary [causal agent] is possible, it follows that it exists is the pinnacle of modal theory, and makes the first transition from possibility to being, that is from essences of things to existences ... such a transition is necessary, otherwise nothing would exist."[33]

Everything that exists has an explanation of its existence, either in the necessity of its nature or an external cause. The fact that a universe exists and all in that universe is contingent, a metaphysical necessary causal agent must exist in order to avoid an infinite regression. The contingent cosmological argument is as follows:

1. If the universe has an explanation of its existence, that explanation is grounded in a necessarily existing causal agent.
2. The universe exists.
3. The universe has an explanation of its existence.
4. The explanation is grounded in a necessarily existing causal agent.
5. The necessary causal agent explaining the existence of the universe must possess will and intellect in order to be causal.
6. Therefore, the universe exists and the existence is explained in a necessarily existing causal agent possessing will and conscious intellect.

Some examples of contingently existing propositions are the big bang causing galaxies, parents getting down to cause a child, or bees making honey. Without anything necessarily existing and only contingent things existing, all matter and knowledge is an infinite regression. This regression is analogous to a kid asking in infinitude, "But what was before that? What caused that?" Leibniz argued that the whole universe is contingent; it did not necessarily have to exist.

Nothing present at the big bang necessarily existed. Thus, time, matter, space, or energy did not have to exist. In fact, there is nothing necessary about the universe. The big bang, if assumed to be the singularity (which birthed time, space, matter, and energy) is contingent and not necessary, the singularity could not have created itself. Contingent things are never self-creating.

If the universe is contingent and did not create itself, metaphysically how could it have come to be? The big bang is a reasonable perhaps even probable theory of operationally how naturally the universe came to exist, but it does not address why or how metaphysically the universe exists. The universe must have a cause beyond the natural since it is contingent. The cause must be a necessarily existing proposition, which include: abstract objects, mathematical equations, or a necessary causal agent. Necessarily existing propositions like abstract objects and mathematical truths are not causal agents as they lack will and conscious intellect. They are self-existing and self-evident but have no extension beyond themselves. Additionally, this necessarily existing proposition must have the intellect (knowledge) and will (power) to birth the contingent universe. The necessary causal agent "has power, which is the source of everything, knowledge, which contains the diversity of ideas, and finally will, which brings about changes or products in accordance with the principle of the best."[34]

An example is the necessity of mathematical truths; the truths do not have an intellect or will in and of them. Leibniz states:

"Therefore, since the ultimate ground must be in something which is of metaphysical necessity, and since the reason for an existing thing must come from something that actually exists, it follows that there must exist some one entity of metaphysical necessity, that is, there must be an entity whose essence is existence, and therefore something must exist which differs from the plurality of things, which differs from the world, which we have granted and shown is not of metaphysical necessity."[35]

The inference to the most logical conclusion is that the universe comes from a causal agent that necessarily exists. Everything about the big bang is contingent and a second cause. There is still the need for a first causal agent, which must be necessary and self-existing.

In summary, what did create the universe must be necessary, beyond space and time, immaterial, uncreated, and self-existing causal agent.[36]

This causal agent must be non-temporal; otherwise, it is not necessary since time itself is contingent. Leibniz substantiates the source of existence being a necessary causal agent. "The ultimate reason for the reality of both essences and existences lies in one thing, which must of necessity be greater than the world, higher than the world, and must have existed before the world did, since through it not only existing things, which make up the world, but also possibles have their reality. Moreover, it can be sought in but one source, because of the interconnection among all of these things."[37]

Outlining the Principles of First Cause and Sufficient Reason

In chapter 3 of *God's Undertaker*, Lennox references Thomas Aquinas' cosmological argument stating, "He regarded God as the First Cause—the ultimate cause of all things; God directly caused the universe to exist, and it was thus dependent on him."[38] Aquinas highlights a difference between direct causation and secondary causation.[39] Though Aquinas lived in the thirteenth century, his argument for God, which was reframed and extended by Gottfried Leibniz, is still a significant obstacle for atheism's science cosmology. The syllogism of the cosmological argument for God delineates between things existing contingently and thus only capable of secondary causation, and those that exist as necessary and are capable of first causation. The "therefore" pivot in the deductive argument contends that the big bang, matter, time, and existence are contingent and therefore not self-existing. Contingents must rely on a necessary in order to avoid infinite regression. Atheistic science cosmology is left to "re-deify the universe by endowing matter and energy with creative powers that they cannot be convincingly shown to possess."[40] Not only is a second causation contingently existing thing incapable of being a first causation, even a necessarily existing thing such as a mathematical certainty is incapable of first causation. The first causation must result from agency, an agency with intellect and volition. Lennox asserts the question of first causation can never be ultimately answered by science, since science deals with processes of reducing questions of how to their measurable parts.[41]

Sufficient Reason and Inference to the Best Explanation

Leibniz was a rationalist and believed in the principle of sufficient reason.

The Leibnizian definition of sufficient reason argues from cause to effect in a pre-Kantian way.[42] Leibniz uses the term to mean both a rationale for existence as well as its efficient cause.[43] Leibniz states, "No fact can be real or existing and no statement true without a sufficient reason for its being so and not otherwise."[44] Leibniz rejected the notion that for something to be known, it must be experienced; instead, he believed that reason could sufficiently reveal what experience lacks. Richard Taylor in his book *Metaphysics* gives an analogous illustration on the principle of sufficient reason. Imagine walking in a forest and seeing a strange object, "a large ball, about your own height, perfectly smooth and translucent."[45] The sight of this object so out of place is "puzzling and mysterious." The logical inference to the best explanation for this object is that some agent has caused it to be there. The idea that it might have come from nothing at all, that it might exist without there being an explanation for its existence, is one that few people would consider worthy of entertaining.[46] Analogous to the contingency argument's assertions on the origin of the universe, the concept of the origin of life is discussed in chapter eleven of *God's Undertaker Has Science Buried God*. Lennox principally affirms, "What we are clearly towards considering is the idea that information and intelligence are fundamental to the existence of the universe and life and, far from being the end products of an unguided natural process starting with energy and matter, they were involved from the very beginning."[47] The inference to the best explanation and the principle of sufficient reason both suggest it is unnecessary to experience or observe what proceeded the big bang to know that something necessarily did proceed with the big bang in order for the singularity of the big bang to have existed. Leibniz states:

Beyond the world, that is, beyond the collection of finite things, there is some One Being who rules, not only as the soul is the ruler in me, or, better, as the self is the ruler in my body, but also in a much higher sense. For the one Being who rules the universe not only rules the world, but also fashions and creates it; he is above the world, and, so to speak, extramundane, and therefore he is the ultimate reason for things.[48]

- Rationalism- the position that reason has precedence over other ways of acquiring knowledge. Knowledge comes from the mind, from thought. Reduces consciousness is everything. Intellectualism ends in absolute subjectivity where everything is thought. Usually thought of in opposition to empiricism. Phenomenology takes the middle ground between the two (more on phenomenology in Part 3 of the book).
- Empiricism- knowledge comes through the senses. Knowledge comes to us through the world and as it really is. The objective world is given. Humans are born as blank slates (tabula rasa) and the world is given to us as it really is through the senses. Reduces consciousness is nothing it is just material. Empiricism ends in absolute objectivity.

OUTLINING THE PRIMARY ASSERTIONS OF AND PIECES OF EVIDENCE FOR THE BIG BANG THEORY

The big bang is a term that is commonly and colloquially interwoven into the modern linguistic lexicon while simultaneously remaining a mysterious concept. According to the Merriam-Webster dictionary, the big bang is "the cosmic explosion that marked the beginning of the universe." The big bang theory explicitly asserts that in the beginning the universe suddenly expanded and has continued to expand since. The consensus view of the universe being infinite, constant, and static was upended by the big bang theory's assertion of an expanding universe from a single point in the finite past. The primary assertions of the big bang theorists are

1. The universe had a first moment birthed out of a cosmic singularity; evidenced by the Hubble relation of galaxies; galaxies are moving away from each other.[49]
2. The universe is expanding; the net result of this is "every point in space is alike at a given moment of time, and so is every direction."[50]
3. The existence of a cosmological horizon evidenced by Olbers' Paradox. According to the Encyclopedia Britannica, Olbers' Paradox is a "cosmological paradox relating to the problem of why the sky is dark at night." If the universe is uniform and constant, the night sky would appear to terminate at the surface of a star; thus, the night sky would be equally bright throughout.[51]
4. The appearance of nucleosynthesis, leading to the abundance of elements needed to form stars, is a primary piece of evidence for the big bang theory. According to the Encyclopedia Britannica, nucleosynthesis is the "production on a cosmic scale of all the species of chemical elements from perhaps one or two simple types of atomic nuclei, a process that entails large-scale nuclear reactions including those in progress in the Sun and other stars.[52]

The proceeding description of the assertions and evidence of the singularity's conditions to produce the first moment or big bang does not adequately address how the conditions moved from the stasis of potentiality into an actual universe.

POTENTIAL VERSE ACTUAL

For the universe in potentiality to have sprung forth from a dense pellet or gas shifts (big bang) to cause the actual universe's existence, there logically needs to be an actuality of a causal agent in existence already.[53] Without the causal agent existing non-temporally prior to the big bang event, the pellet or gas shift would remain in a stasis of potentiality. The self-existence of a causal agent is necessary to move the potential universe to an actual universe. Thomas Aquinas states:

"But a thing cannot be led from potentiality into actuality except through some being that is in actuality in a relevant respect; for example, something that is hot in actuality—say a fire—makes a piece of wood, which is hot in potentiality, to be hot in actuality, and it thereby moves and alters the piece of wood…. For what is hot in actuality cannot simultaneously be hot in potentiality; rather it is cold in potentiality. Therefore, it is impossible that something should be both mover and moved in the same way and with respect to the same thing, or, in other words, that something should move itself. Therefore everything that is moved must be moved by another."[54]

The possibility of an infinite can only exist in potentiality; there is no actual infinite. "This conception of the infinite prevailed all the way up to the nineteenth century. The medieval scholastics adhered to Aristotle's analysis of the impossibility of an actual infinite, and the post-Renaissance thinkers, even Newton and Leibniz with their infinitesimal calculus, believed that only a potential infinite could exist."[55]

The importance of this in reference to the big bang is that for the universe to have sprung forth from a dense pellet or gas shifts to cause the universe would not ever happen in actuality without a causal agent in actuality already existing. The self-existence of a causal agent is necessary to move the potential universe to an actual universe. The need for an agency to move potential to actuality does not mean to Leibniz that all things possible in potentiality are possible in actuality. If a possibility in potentiality is incompatible with the actuality of a necessary causal agent, then that possible in potentiality is impossible in actuality.[56]

- Potentiality- state of affairs which do not actualize in form.

- Actuality- state of affairs which are in fact reality.
- Olbers Paradox- First put forth in 1823 by the German astronomer Heinrich Wilhelm Olbers. According to the Encyclopedia Britannica, Olbers Paradox is a "cosmological paradox relating to the problem of why the sky is dark at night."

The Very Assertions of Big Bang Theory Prove the Need for Sufficient Reason Because There is Something Instead of Nothing.

DEFINING NOTHING

For there to be a possibility, there must be an actuality. Is nothing (used in noun form like "the nothing" from the movie "Never Ending Story") merely a state of non-being or is nothing truly nothing at all?[57] William Lane Craig ties together the connection between reality and possibility by stating, "For if there is reality in essences or possibles, or indeed, in transcendent truths, this reality must be grounded in something existent and actual, and consequently, it must be grounded in the existence of the necessary [causal agent], in whom essence involves existence, that is, in whom possible being is sufficient for actual being."[58]

Dennis Fried states of Leibniz treatment of possibles, "So, for instance, we might judge that the complete concept of Superman (if we could know this concept) "does not imply contradiction"; God could have created Superman if he had wished. However, even though Superman does not exist, we cannot deny the predicates of being caped, being the strongest man in the world, to this individual conceived as possible. Speaking of possibles, Leibniz is satisfied if true propositions are formed concerning them. Leibniz aims at true propositions about beings and worlds that a necessary causal agent could have created. So, Leibniz wants the propositions expressed by "Superman is caped" and "Superman is the strongest man in the world" to be true. The containment conception of truth, which is intentional rather than extensional, allows Leibniz this result.[59] For a possibility of nothing to exist, there must be something in actuality upon which the possibility of nothing is grounded.

In a letter to Arnault in *Philosophical Texts*, Leibniz posits, "If we tried to reject pure possibles absolutely, we would destroy contingency and freedom; for if there were nothing possible other than what God actually creates, then what God creates would be necessary, and if God wanted to create something else he would not be able to create anything else, and would have no freedom of choice."[60] For Leibniz, a proposition of a possible must have the roots of a real proposition in actuality. Therefore, nothing is a proposition that has no root in an actual term. For example, Jason McKinney exists in reality (Descartes said so), and therefore Jason McKinney not existing is not nothing as it could have been if God chose to make the world actually in which Jason McKinney did not exist. The person Jason McKinney does not exist necessarily. Nothing can exist if there is not a correlating real term, but not empirically so. Nothing as an actuality cannot be observed or sensed or measured; therefore, even the concept of nothing without a necessary causal agent is logically absurd.[61]

THERE IS SOMETHING RATHER THAN NOTHING

The most certain statement that can be made and agreed upon within this part of the book is that there is something. There is a universe that does, in actuality, exist. Therefore the burden of proof is on the concept of nothing, not the fact that there is something. Something can be experienced. Additionally, it cannot be reasoned by the human mind a true concept of nothing as no individual has experienced anything analogous that can be extrapolated to conceive of nothing. What can be proven to exist is Cartesian in nature. Even Descartes himself could not conceive of nothing, as he was a thinking thing; he was an immovable observer in his experiment to clear away all to the end of nothing. Leibniz, as did Augustine, conceded to the fact of existence as man is in the middle of existing and does not have access to the conception of nothing either be induction or deduction. To explain the existence of something when man has not the capacity to conceive of nothing leaves the explanation of existence to a comparison to something else which actually exists. Man does not have the ability to conceive of nothing and thus cannot compare something to nothing.[62] For Leibniz, the question of the fact that it is was not as important as why it is and even more intriguing how it is metaphysically speaking.

DEMONSTRATING THE BIG BANG THEORY HAS NO LOGICAL OR THEOLOGICAL CONFLICT WITH THE CONTINGENCY COSMOLOGICAL ARGUMENT.

From an abductive[63] and deductive[64] view there is logical validity and consistency to affirming both a cosmological argument based upon contingency and the big bang theory. What are the implications of a non-temporal cosmology that requires a necessary agent in order for there to be a temporal big bang? William Lane Craig states, "the prospect of this empty, beginningless duration prior to the inception of the universe has seemed scandalous to many, since in the absence of anything which endures it seems bizarre to maintain that duration itself exists."[65] One of the primary questions is whether the big bang is temporal. If the big bang birthed time, space, and matter does, then can the big bang be considered a part of the temporality the singular event created? If the big bang happened non-temporally, can it be considered an "event" as humans understand events?

An argument against this assertion is that the big bang is not an "event" since it begins non-temporally. In his book *A Brief History of Time*, Stephen Hawking states that the finite universe has no space-time boundaries and lacks a singularity and a beginning.[66]

Time might not be linear or exist at all, thus making beginning singularity nonsense. A universe without beginning, which is constant as Plato posited, does not require a cause. In this view, the universe is finite in relation to the past but does not need a beginning event. William Lane Craig, in his book *The Kalam Cosmological Argument*, differs from Hawking's assertion and claims, "If the big bang occurred in a super dense pellet existing from eternity, then why did the big bang occur only 15 billion years ago?"[67] Craig goes on to state, "If it be alternatively suggested that prior to the big bang there was a contraction of gas which collapsed and then exploded, one may ask how the gas came to be scattered in the first place."[68] Craig finally concludes, "A literal application of the big bang model in which the universe originates in an explosion from a state of infinite density, that is, from nothing, provides a simple, consistent, and empirically sound construction of how the universe began."[69]

- Deductive reasoning- The process of drawing a conclusion based on premises that are generally assumed to be true. Reasons from general to specific instances.
- Inductive reasoning- The process of taking multiple premises that are believed to be true and combining them to draw a conclusion. It is a process that works in the opposite direction to deductive reasoning. A method of reasoning in which a body of individual observations is synthesized to come up with a general principle.
- Abductive reasoning- The process of starting with an observation or set of observations and then seeks the simplest and most likely conclusion from the observations. This process, unlike deductive reasoning, yields a plausible conclusion but does not positively verify it. Abductive conclusions are thus qualified as having a remnant of uncertainty or doubt, which is expressed in retreat terms such as "best available" or "most likely."

One can understand abductive reasoning as inference to the best explanation.

If the big bang is conceded to be the first moment for the universe, then a deductive argument can be used to show its consistency with a contingent cosmological argument would go as follows:

1. There exists a series of events starting with the big bang.
2. The series of events of the universe and its expansion (time, space, matter, history) exist as caused and not as uncaused (necessary).
3. Because the events begin temporally as contingent, the necessary agent is the non-temporal cause of all contingents associated with the big bang.
4. Thus, there is no incongruence between the contingent cosmological argument and the big bang theory.

A fair criticism of the asserted thesis statement of this argument is that it is using abductive reasoning. Based upon observed natural laws of contingency and reasoning infinite regression, the inference to the best explanation is that the regress must cease at a certain point. Neither the big bang nor what non-temporally occurred prior to the big bang event can be observed and thus are both the inference of abductive reasoning. One cannot be treated as any more inductive than the other. Analogously both are observing the symptoms of the universe and attempting to diagnose the condition. Additionally, both the contingency cosmological argument and the big bang theory can co-exist in the same diagnosis. As stated earlier, the inference to the best explanation being that of a necessary causal agent is logically valid and well reasoned.

THEOLOGY

In his book, *Creation and the World of Science*, biochemist Arthur Peacock posits, "Theology is agnostic about the how of creation...

Whether the big bang wins out or not is irrelevant theologically."[70] Ultimately the contingency cosmological answer to the question, why is there something rather than nothing is a necessarily self-existing metaphysical beyond being conscious intelligent causal agent (beyond being because this causal agent cannot be contained within being). To Leibniz and Aquinas, this equated to God.[71] Leibniz could not conceive of existence without a necessary causal agent. He deemed existence without a necessary causal agent as impossibility and states:

"All which we see and experience, are contingent and have nothing in them to render their existence necessary, it being plain that time, space, and matter, united and uniform in themselves and indifferent to everything, might have received entirely other motions and shapes, and in another order. Therefore one must seek the reason for the existence of the world, which is the whole assemblage of contingent things, and seek it in the substance which carries with it the reason for its existence, and which in consequence is necessary and eternal."[72]

From a theological framework, the contingency cosmological argument is analogous to the theological necessitarian argument for God. In this case, the big bang is simply the natural methodological process by which a necessary actual God created the actual contingent universe from an infinite number of potential universes.[73] Michael V. Griffin, in his book *Leibniz, God, and necessity*, states, "The existence and perfection of God are necessary. It's necessary that a perfect [causal agent] choose to actualize the best of all possible worlds. So the actuality of the best of all possible worlds is entailed by God's existence and perfection."[74]

The move from potential to actual needs an actualized mover. Nothing moves from potential to actual without God.[75] Genesis 1:1 says, "In the beginning God created the heavens and the earth." There is no tension between the move from a non-temporal pellet or gas condition to a temporal singular first moment, and God created the heavens and the earth. In the book Wisdom of Solomon included in the Septuagint, chapter 9:1 states, "God of the fathers and Lord of mercy, who made all things by your word and by your wisdom formed human beings."[76] Finally, Leibniz states:

Now, as there is an infinity of possible universes in the Ideas of God, and as only one of them can exist, there must be a sufficient reason for God's choice, which determines him toward one rather than another. Moreover, this reason can be found only in the fitness, or the degrees of perfection, that these words contain since each possible thing has the right to claim existence in proportion to the perfection it involves.[77]

In summary from a theological perspective a universe without God only leaves nihilism. God is both the cause and the meaning giver for the universe. The big bang if given to be the natural method by which God operationally brought the universe into existence only speaks to God's wisdom not his necessity.

- Nihilism- the belief that all values are subjective and that nothing objective can be known and there is no meaning to life. Nothing can be known and thus nothing believed. Meaning is only created by the individual for the individual and even that has no meaning beyond the meaning the individual assigns it.

CONCLUSION

The cosmological argument from contingency asserts there is something rather than nothing because of a necessarily existing first causal agent.[78] The causal agent is congruent with big bang cosmological theory.[79] This part of the book intersected five points of congruence between the contingency cosmological argument and big bang cosmological theory showing that neither precludes the other and they plausibly perhaps probably complement one another. At the end of my deconstructing what I had been taught, I was at least left with the same conclusion that Father Cavanaugh gave Rudy, "there is a God, and I am not him." I was satisfied that there must be a first mover, a first cause, a causal agent that exists necessarily and whom plausibly and very probably used the big bang as the mechanism to write his cosmic Bohemian Rhapsody. I am contingent. I did not have to exist for the universe to exist. In fact, the universe itself did not have to exist but for the universe to exist it must have had a necessary causal agent behind it. That fact alone implies intent. Intent plausibly implies that love is not just the synapses of my brain implying meaning to myself biologically where there is not. If it is observable that love exists because the universe exists. Maybe the fools who believe in God got it right which means it is plausible that there is a purpose beyond utility. Like the cadence and chords of harmony to melody, big bang cosmology must have a necessarily existing causal agent to stack on top of; there is no harmony without first a melody. This does not answer the question of whether the intent or the execution of existence (i.e. the universe, time, space, matter) was wise or the way it was actualized was the wisest way it could have been actualized. I will tackle this in Part 2 where we will again spend some time with our Leibniz (some of you can't let any time lapse and will just turn the page and keep reading while others of you will never freely choose to actualize reading the next part at all...sorry that was a super nerdy philosophy joke but also to show that I am not unaware of Plantinga's criticism of Leibniz).

Fools and Fairytales

Looking at the vast I'm too small
Put the math to test it don't add at all
Feeble and weak, fallen down
Cling to belief in the face of doubt
I'm no martyr man no rebel cause
I don't pretend to know it all

CHORUS
I'll take my chances
When its hard to find
Maybe Fools and Fairytales got it right this time

V.2
When you pick and choose and fight to win
We all lose that game in the end
I just can't believe we're on the throne
Top of the heap in the cosmos[80]

DISCUSSION QUESTIONS

1. On the surface Father Cavanaugh's statement to Rudy seems like an oversimplification and not much help. However, a deeper look shows Father Cavanaugh is making not only a profound statement about certainty, but also cosmology as well a commentary of the status of humans against the backdrop of postmodernity. In your own words, explain how you think Father Cavanaugh is commenting on certainty, cosmology and postmodernity?

2. The movie quote from The Ancient One, "At the root of existence, mind and matter meet" speaks to the heart of the Leibnizian cosmological argument from contingency. Explain how this quote correlates with the six points of the cosmological argument?

3. Human Exceptionalism is the idea that humans have a unique nature and a unique place in the universe. Only humans have moral agency and wrestle with the concept of their meaning within the universe. The question asked by Leibniz is an example of this. Do you agree with human exceptionalism as a concept? Do you agree with Heidegger that humans questioning of the nature of existence sets humans apart from the rest of the universe?

4. Do you think the hypothesis of the big bang is evidence for or against a necessary causal agent? Does the process of a thing (how) explain the cause of the thing (why)? Does it explain the sufficient reason?

5. In the song *Freedom*, dissect line by line the cosmological stance the first verse is taking?

6. Was it surprising to you how many of the classical philosophers believed in a transcendent reality? Why or why not?

7. Can you explain the difference between potentiality and actuality?

8. Can you explain the difference between a contingently

existing thing and a necessarily existing thing?

9. Can a metaphysically necessarily existing thing not exist? Why or why not?

10. Does the logical necessity of a first moving causal agent for the existence of the universe make an impact on your global doubts? Why or why not?

11. How does the concept of the inference to the best explanation of the universe beginning with a cosmically singular event from a necessarily existing first causal agent impact your doubt?

12. How did the author's discussion of the concept of "nothing" impact your understanding? How is our understanding of the term nothing impacted by the concept of time?

13. Discuss the differences between the three types of logical reasoning. In terms of discussions surrounding the origins of the universe which type(s) are most often used? Are there any that are impossible to use?

14. Give your reasoning for why Arthur Peacock is right or wrong about theology being agnostic about the big bang?

15. What is your understanding of the analogy of melody and harmony to the big bang and the contingency cosmological argument?

16. In *Fools and Fairytales*, the first two lines discuss humanity's tenuous epistemic situation regarding knowledge of the beginning of the universe. Juxtapose this with the line in Freedom, "what is proof without evidence, what is truth without consequence?" Take into consideration the following quotes

    i. Renowned atheist and evolutionary biologist Richard Dawkins states biology is "the study of complicated things which give the impression of having been designed for a purpose" (Lennox, *God's Undertaker*, 79).

    ii. Logic would again infer that a design has a designer and did not arise by chance.

iii. Meyer states the theory of intelligent design holds that there are telltale features of living systems in the universe—for example, digital code in DNA, the miniature circuits and machines in cells, and the fine-tuning of the laws and constraints of physics—that are best explained by an intelligent cause rather than an undirected material process" (Meyer, *Four Views*, 180).

iv. The fine-tuning of the physical laws of the universe are a strong argument for the intelligent design view.

   a. John Lennox in God's Undertaker states, "recent research has shown that many of the fundamental constants of nature, from the energy levels in the carbon atom to the rate at which the universe is expanding, have just the right values for life to exist. Change any of them just a little, and the universe would become hostile to life and incapable of supporting it" (Lennox, *God's Undertaker*, 70).

   b. Hugh Ross states, "cover America with coins in a column reaching to the moon (380,000 km or 236,000 miles away), then do the same for a billion other continents of the same size. Paint one coin red and put it somewhere in one of the billion piles. Blindfold a friend and ask her to pick it out. The odds are about 1 in 10 (to the 40th power) that she will" (Lennox, *God's Undertaker*, 71).

   c. It is a mathematical absurdity that the universe should contain stars, let alone earth and life on earth by chance alone.

v. The complexity of the origin of life is a strong argument in favor of the intelligent design view.

   a. Geophysicist and college professor Stephen C.

Meyer points out that the informational properties of DNA seem to point to an intelligent cause. Meyer draws the authors of the book *The Mystery of Life's Origin.* He states, "chemistry and physics alone could not produce information any more than ink and paper could produce the information in a book" (Meyer, *Four Views*, 198).

b. Life's origin has particular complexity, which dictates "identifying causes known to have the power to produce the kind of effect, feature, or event in question" (Meyer, Four Views, 200).

c. John C. Lennox states, "It is a perversion of language to assign any law, as the efficient, operative cause of anything. A law presupposes an agent; for it is only the mode, according to which the agent proceeds: it implies a power; for it is the order, according to which that power acts. Without this agent, without this power, which are both distinct from itself, the law does nothing; is nothing" (Lennox, *God's Undertaker*, 65).

17. In the process of deconstructing our beliefs is it possible to "cling to beliefs" while also deconstructing?

18. In *Fools and Fairytales,* the last line in the first verse, speaks to epistemic humility. Unpack what is epistemic humility and why it is so important both for those who are solid in their belief about the origins of the universe as well as those who doubt.

19. Revisit the Ancient Ones line; she states, "You think that this material universe is all there is? What is real? What mysteries lie beyond the reach of your senses?" Juxtapose this with the line in *Fools in Fairytales*, "I just can't believe we're on the throne." What are these lines trying to assert of the nature of existence?

20. How has this part of the book impacted your thoughts on the origins of the universe?

SOURCES DOCUMENTED/CITED

Aquinas, Thomas. *Summa Theologiae* found in Chapter 28 of Bruce V. Foltz ed, *Medieval Philosophy: A Multicultural Reader.* (London, UK: Bloomsbury Academic, 2019).

Crawford, Dan D. "The Cosmological Argument, Sufficient Reason, and Why-Questions." *International Journal for Philosophy of Religion* 11, no. 2 (1980): 111–22. https://doi.org/10.1007/bf00136760.

Craig, William Lane. *The Kalam Cosmological Argument.* Portland , OR: Wipf and Stock, 2007.

———. "God and the Beginning of Time: Reasonable Faith." Reasonable Faith, 2017. https://www.reasonablefaith.org/writings/scholarly-writings/divine-eternity/god-and-the-beginning-of-time/.

Douven, Igor. "Abduction." Stanford Encyclopedia of Philosophy. Stanford University, April 28, 2017. https://plato.stanford.edu/entries/abduction/.

Encyclopaedia Britannica, ed. "Nucleosynthesis." Encyclopædia Britannica. Encyclopædia Britannica, inc., November 7, 2011. https://www.britannica.com/science/nucleosynthesis.

———. "Olbers' Paradox." Encyclopædia Britannica. Encyclopædia Britannica inc., January 17, 2018. https://www.britannica.com/science/Olbers-paradox.

Foltz, Bruce V., ed. *Medieval Philosophy: a Multicultural Reader.* London, UK: Bloomsbury Academic, 2019.

Fried, Dennis. "Necessity and Contingency in Leibniz." *The Philosophical Review* 87, no. 4 (1978): 575. https://doi.org/10.2307/2184461.

Griffin, Michael V. *Leibniz, God and Necessity.* Cambridge, UK: Cambridge University Press, 2015.

Hawking, Steven. *A Brief History of Time.* New York, NY: Bantam Books, 1988.

Knopp, Richard. "Cosmology and Creation." PH605 Fall 2020.

Leftow, Brian. "A Leibnizian Cosmological Argument." *Philosophical Studies* 57, no. 2 (1989): 135–55. https://doi.org/10.1007/bf00354595.

Leibniz, Gottfried Wilhelm, Roger Ariew, and Daniel Garber. *Discourse on Metaphysics and Other Essays: Discourse on Metaphysics, On the Ultimate Origination of Things, Preface to the New Essays, The Monadology*. Indianapolis, IN: Hackett, 1991.

———. "Copyright© Lloyd Strickland 2003-2020." Scholarworks at University of Massachusetts Amherst. University of Massachusetts Amherst, February 2014. http://www.leibniz-translations.com/ultimateorigination.htm.

———. *Philosophical Texts*. Oxford, UK: Oxford University Press, 2011.

———. *The Monadology: and Other Philosophical Writings*. Oxford, UK: Clarendon Press, 1898.

———. *Theodicy: Essays on the Goodness of God, the Freedom of Man, and the Origin of Evil*. Withorn: Anodos Books, 2017.

Lennox, John C. *God's Undertaker: Has Science Buried God?* Oxford, UK: Lion, 2009.

———. *Seven Days That Divide the World: the Beginning According to Genesis and Science*. Grand Rapids, MI: Zondervan, 2011.

McKinney, Jason. Final unpublished paper for Modern Philosophy PH701. Summer 2020.

Melamed, Yitzhak Y., and Martin Lin. "Principle of Sufficient Reason." Stanford Encyclopedia of Philosophy. Stanford University, September 7, 2016. https://plato.stanford.edu/entries/sufficient-reason/.

Pitts, J. Brian. "Why the Big Bang Singularity Does Not Help the Kalām Cosmological Argument for Theism." *The Kalām Cosmological Argument : Scientific Evidence for the Beginning of the Universe*, 2008. https://doi.org/10.5040/9781501335907.0007.

Plato in Timaeus found in Chapter 1 of Bruce V. Foltz ed, *Medieval Philosophy: A Multicultural Reader*. (London, UK: Bloomsbury Academic, 2019), 21.

71

Rasmussen, Joshua. "From a Necessary Being to God." *International Journal for Philosophy of Religion* 66, no. 1 (2008): 1–13. https://doi.org/10.1007/s11153-008-9191-8.

Reichenbach, Bruce. "Cosmological Argument." Stanford Encyclopedia of Philosophy. Stanford University, October 11, 2017. https://plato.stanford.edu/entries/cosmological-argument/.

Rowe, William L. *The Cosmological Argument*. New York, NY: Fordham University Press, 1998.

Rubenstein, J M. "Cosmic Singularities: On the Nothing and the Sovereign." *Journal of the American Academy of Religion* 80, no. 2 (2012): 485–517. https://doi.org/10.1093/jaarel/lfs012.

Shapiro, Stewart, and Teresa Kouri Kissel. "Classical Logic." Stanford Encyclopedia of Philosophy. Stanford University, March 11, 2018. https://plato.stanford.edu/entries/logic-classical/.

Sorensen, Roy. "Nothingness." Stanford Encyclopedia of Philosophy. Stanford University, August 31, 2017. https://plato.stanford.edu/entries/nothingness/.

Taylor, Richard. *Metaphysics*. Upper Saddle River, NJ: Prentice-Hall, 1991.

Wright, Benjamin G., and Albert Pietersma. *A New English Translation of the Septuagint: and the Other Greek Translations Traditionally Included under That Title*. New York, NY: Oxford University Press, 2007.

Additional Sources/Sources Recommended

Boyer, Robert W. "Did the Universe Emerge from Nothing? Reductive vs. Holistic

Cosmology." *NeuroQuantology* 12, no. 4 (2014). https://doi.org/10.14704/nq.2014.12.4.777.

Cahoone, Lawrence. "Arguments From Nothing: God And Quantum Cosmology." *Zygon* 44, no. 4 (2009): 777–96. https://doi.org/10.1111/j.1467-9744.2009.01033.x.

Craig, William Lane. "Beyond the Big Bang." bethinking.org, January 1, 2007. https://www.bethinking.org/is-there-a-creator/beyond-the-big-bang.

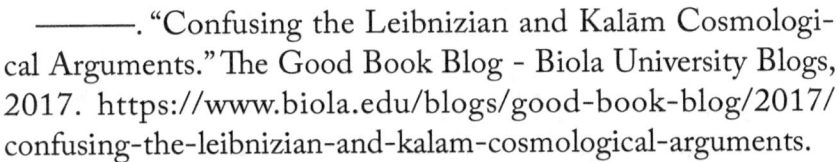

———. "Confusing the Leibnizian and Kalām Cosmological Arguments." The Good Book Blog - Biola University Blogs, 2017. https://www.biola.edu/blogs/good-book-blog/2017/confusing-the-leibnizian-and-kalam-cosmological-arguments.

———."In Defense of the Kalam Cosmological Argument: Reasonable Faith." Reasonable Faith, 1997. https://www.reasonablefaith.org/writings/scholarly-writings/the-existence-of-god/in-defense-of-the-kalam-cosmological-argument/.

———. "On the Argument for Divine Timelessness from the Incompleteness of Temporal Life." *The Heythrop Journal* 38, no. 2 (1997): 165–71. https://doi.org/10.1111/1468-2265.00042.

Craig, William Lane, and Quentin Smith. *Theism, Atheism, and Big Bang Cosmology*. Oxford, UK: Clarendon Press, 2010.

Davey, Kevin, and Mark Lippelmann. "Closed Systems, Explanations, and the Cosmological Argument." *International Journal for Philosophy of Religion* 62, no. 2 (2007): 89–101. https://doi.org/10.1007/s11153-007-9134-9.

Dennis, Dan. "Evil, Fine-Tuning and the Creation of the Universe." *International Journal for Philosophy of Religion* 70, no. 2 (2010): 139–45. https://doi.org/10.1007/s11153-010-9275-0.

Feser, Edward. "The New Atheists and the Cosmological Argument." *Midwest Studies In Philosophy* 37, no. 1 (2013): 154–77. https://doi.org/10.1111/misp.12000.

———. "The New Atheists and the Cosmological Argument." Wiley Online Library. John Wiley & Sons, Ltd, September 16, 2013. https://onlinelibrary.wiley.com/doi/abs/10.1111/misp.12000.

Halvorson, Hans, and Helge Kragh. "Cosmology and Theology." Stanford Encyclopedia of Philosophy. Stanford University, April 5, 2017. https://plato.stanford.edu/entries/cosmology-theology/.

Heller, Michael. "Cosmological Singularity and the Creation of the Universe." *Zygon* 35, no. 3 (2000): 665–85. https://doi.org/10.1111/0591-2385.00303.

Hicks, Stephen R. C. *Explaining Postmodernism: Skepticism and Socialism from Rousseau to Foucault*. Roscoe, IL: Ockham's Razor, 2011.

Hiebert, Paul G. *Transforming Worldviews: an Anthropological Understanding of How People Change.* Grand Rapids, MI: Baker Academic, 2009.

Lewis, C. S. *Miracles.* Nashville, TN: HarperOne, 1978.

Lipton, Peter. *Inference to the Best Explanation.* London, UK: Routledge, 2007.

Lærke, Mogens. "Leibniz's Cosmological Argument for the Existence of God." *Archiv für Geschichte der Philosophie* 93, no. 1 (2011). https://doi.org/10.1515/agph.2011.003.

Metcalfe, Curtis J. "A Defense of the Kalam Cosmological Argument and the b-Theory of Time." Thesis, Graduate Works, 2013.

Moreland, James Porter., and William Lane Craig. *The Blackwell Companion to Natural Theology.* Malden, MA: Wiley-Blackwell, 2012.

Morriston, Wes. "Must the Beginning of the Universe Have a Personal Cause?" *Faith and Philosophy* 17, no. 2 (2000): 149–69. https://doi.org/10.5840/faithphil200017215.

Nadis, Steve. "What Came Before the Big Bang?" Discover Magazine, April 12, 2020. https://www.discovermagazine.com/the-sciences/what-came-before-the-big-bang.

Park, John J. "The Kalām Cosmological Argument, the Big Bang, and Atheism." *Acta Analytica* 31, no. 3 (2015): 323–35. https://doi.org/10.1007/s12136-015-0273-9.

Peacocke, Arthur R. *Creation and the World of Science: The Re-Shaping of Belief.* Oxford, UK: Oxford University Press, 2009.

Poplin, Mary S. *Is Reality Secular?: Testing the Assumptions of Four Global Worldviews.* Downers Grove, IL, IL: Intervarsity Press, 2014.

Ross, Hugh. *Why the Universe Is the Way It Is.* Grand Rapids, MI: Baker Books, 2008.

Strobel, Lee. *The Case For A Creator.* Grand Rapids, MI: Zondervan, 2004.

Stump, James B., ed. *Four Views on Creation, Evolution, and Intelligent Design.* Grand Rapids, MI, MI: Zondervan, 2017.

Wallace, J. Warner. *God's Crime Scene: a Cold-Case Detective*

Examines the Evidence for a Divinely Created Universe. Colorado Springs, CO: David C Cook, 2015.

Weaver, Christopher Gregory. "Yet Another New Cosmological Argument." *International Journal for Philosophy of Religion* 80, no. 1 (2015): 11–31. https://doi.org/10.1007/s11153-015-9534-1.

Worthing, Mark William. *God, Creation, and Contemporary Physics*. Minneapolis, MN: Fortress Press, 1996.

ENDNOTES

20. *Rudy* (TriStar Pictures, 1993).

21. *Doctor Strange* (Walt Disney studios, 2016).

22. Gottfried Wilhelm Leibniz, Paul Janet, and George R. Montgomery, *Discourse on Metaphysics; Correspondence with Arnauld ; and Monadology* (BiblioLife, 2009).

23. Terry Eagleton, *The Meaning of Life a Very Short Introduction* (Oxford, UK: Oxford University Press, 2008), 12.

24. Written by Jason Lee McKinney (Zekers and ZiZi Music (BMI); and Sam Berce

25. Plato in Timaeus found in Chapter 1 of Bruce V. Foltz ed, *Medieval Philosophy: A Multicultural Reader.* (London, UK: Bloomsbury Academic, 2019), 21.

26. John C. Lennox, *Seven Days That Divide the World: The Beginning According to Genesis and Science* (Grand Rapids, MI: Zondervan, 2011), 151.

27. John C. Lennox, *God's Undertaker: Has Science Buried God?* (Oxford, UK: Lion, 2009), 58.

28. Thomas Aquinas, Summa Theologiae found in Chapter 28 of Bruce V. Foltz ed, *Medieval Philosophy: A Multicultural Reader.* (London, UK: Bloomsbury Academic, 2019), 305.

29. Gottfried Wilhelm Leibniz, Roger Ariew, and Daniel Garber, Discourse on Metaphysics and Other Essays: Discourse on Metaphysics, On the Ultimate Origination of Things, Preface to the New Essays, *The Monadology* (Indianapolis, IN: Hackett, 1991), no.45.

30. William L. Rowe, *The Cosmological Argument* (New York, NY: Fordham University Press, 1998), 6.

31. Dan D. Crawford, "The Cosmological Argument, Sufficient Reason, and Why-Questions," *International Journal for Philosophy of Religion* 11, no. 2 (1980), 4.

32. Michael V. Griffin, Leibniz, *God and Necessity* (Cambridge, UK: Cambridge University Press, 2015), 42.

33. Griffin, *God and Necessity*, 47.
34. Gottfried Wilhelm Leibniz, The Monadology found in *The Monadology: and Other Philosophical Writings* (Oxford, UK: Clarendon Press, 1898), no.48.
35. Leibniz, *Discourse*, 42.
36. Brian Leftow, "A Leibnizian Cosmological Argument," *Philosophical Studies* 57, no. 2 (1989): 135-155, https://doi.org/10.1007/bf00354595, 8.
37. Leibniz, *Discourse*, 44.
38. Lennox, *God's Undertaker*, 50-51.
39. Lennox, *God's Undertaker*, 50.
40. Lennox, *God's Undertaker*, 51.
41. Lennox, *God's Undertaker*, 52, 54-56.
42. Yitzhak Y. Melamed and Martin Lin, "Principle of Sufficient Reason," *Stanford Encyclopedia of Philosophy* (Stanford University, September 7, 2016), https://plato.stanford.edu/entries/sufficient-reason/, 1.
43. William Lane Craig, *The Kalam Cosmological Argument* (Portland, OR: Wipf and Stock, 2007), 10.
44. Leibniz, *Monadology*, no. 32.
45. Richard Taylor, *Metaphysics* (Upper Saddle River, NJ: Prentice-Hall, 1991), 103.
46. Taylor, *Metaphysic*, 103–4.
47. Lennox, *God's Undertaker*, 177.
48. Leibniz, *Metaphysics*, 41.
49. J. Brian Pitts, "Why the Big Bang Singularity Does Not Help the Kalām Cosmological Argument for Theism," *The Kalām Cosmological Argument: Scientific Evidence for the Beginning of the Universe*, 2008, https://doi.org/10.5040/9781501335907.0007, 83-84.
50. Pitts, *Big Bang Singularity*, 90.
51. Encyclopaedia Britannica, "Olbers' Paradox," *Encyclopædia Britannica* (January 17, 2018), https://www.britannica.com/science/Olbers-paradox.

52. Encyclopaedia Britannica, ed., "Nucleosynthesis," *Encyclopædia Britannica* (November 7, 2011), https://www.britannica.com/science/nucleosynthesis.

53. Bruce Reichenbach, "Cosmological Argument," *Stanford Encyclopedia of Philosophy* (Stanford University, October 11, 2017), https://plato.stanford.edu/entries/cosmological-argument/, 6-8.

54. Bruce V. Foltz, *Medieval Philosophy: A Multicultural Reader* (London, UK: Bloomsbury Academic, 2019) 305.

55. Craig, *Kalam*, 66.

56. Griffin, *God and Necessity,* 64

57. William Lane Craig, "God and the Beginning of Time: Reasonable Faith," *Reasonable Faith*, 2017, https://www.reasonablefaith.org/writings/scholarly-writings/divine-eternity/god-and-the-beginning-of-time/.

58. Gottfried Wilhelm Leibniz, *Theodicy: Essays on the Goodness of God, the Freedom of Man, and the Origin of Evil* (Whithorn: Anodos Books, 2017), sec.184, 91.

59. Dennis Fried, "Necessity and Contingency in Leibniz," *The Philosophical Review* 87, no. 4 (1978): 575, 582, https://doi.org/10.2307/2184461.

60. Gottfried Wilhelm Leibniz, *Philosophical Texts* (Oxford, UK: Oxford University Press, 2011), 58.

61. Jason McKinney, Final unpublished paper for *Modern Philosophy* PH701. (Summer 2020), 9.

62. Roy Sorensen, "Nothingness," *Stanford Encyclopedia of Philosophy* (Stanford University, August 31, 2017), https://plato.stanford.edu/entries/nothingness/.

63. Igor Douven, "Abduction," *Stanford Encyclopedia of Philosophy* (Stanford University, April 28, 2017), https://plato.stanford.edu/entries/abduction/.

64. Stewart Shapiro and Teresa Kouri Kissel, "Classical Logic," *Stanford Encyclopedia of Philosophy* (Stanford University, March 11, 2018), https://plato.stanford.edu/entries/logic-classical/.

65. Craig, *God and Time*, 2017.
66. Steven Hawking, *A Brief History of Time* (New York, NY: Bantam Books, 1988), 116, 136.
67. Craig, *Kalam*, 117.
68. Ibid.
69. Ibid.
70. Richard Knopp, *Cosmology and Creation* (PH605 Fall 2020), 1.
71. Leftow, *Leibnizian Cosmological Argument*, 136.
72. Leibniz, *Theodicy* sec. 7, 38.
73. J M. Rubenstein, "Cosmic Singularities: On the Nothing and the Sovereign." *Journal of the American Academy of Religion* 80, no. 2 (2012), 487.
74. Griffin, *God and Necessity*, 59.
75. Craig, *The Kalam*, 15.
76. Benjamin G. Wright and Albert Pietersma, *A New English Translation of the Septuagint: and the Other Greek Translations Traditionally Included under That Title* (New York, NY: Oxford University Press, 2007), 705,
77. Leibniz, *Theodicy* sec 180, 89.
78. Joshua Rasmussen "From a Necessary Being to God." *International Journal for Philosophy of Religion* 66, no. 1 (2008): 2.
79. Reichenbach, *Cosmological Argument*, 5.
80. Written by Jason Lee McKinney (Zekers and ZiZi Music (BMI)

Part 2

Worldviews,
the Self, and the Nature of Truth

In *Star Wars: Episode IV - A New Hope* Harrison Ford's character, a younger Han Solo has this exchange with a young Luke Skywalker.

HAN SOLO
Hokey religions and ancient weapons are not a good match for a blaster at your side, kid.

LUKE SKYWALKER
You don't believe in the Force, do you?

HAN SOLO
Kid, I've flown from one side of this galaxy to the other; I've seen a lot of strange stuff. But I've never seen anything to make me believe that there's one all-powerful Force controlling everything. There's no mystical energy field that controls my destiny. Anyway, it's all a lot of simple tricks and nonsense.[81]

Now an old man, Han Solo speaking with Rey and Finn about the force in *Star Wars: Episode VII - The Force Awakens*.

REY
Why did he [Luke Skywalker] leave?

HAN SOLO
He was training a new generation of Jedi. There was nobody

else left to do it, so he took the burden on himself. Everything was going great, until ... one boy, an apprentice, turned against him, destroyed it all. Luke felt responsible. He just walked away from everything.

Finn

Do you know what happened to him?

Han Solo

There were a lot of rumors. Stories. People who knew him best think he went looking for the first Jedi temple.

Rey

[in awe] The Jedi were real?

Han Solo

I used to wonder about that myself. Thought it was a bunch of mumbo jumbo. A magical power holding together good and evil, the dark side and the light. Crazy thing is ... it's true. The Force, the Jedi. All of it. It's all true.[82]

In the 1995 film Mr. Holland's Opus about an aspiring composer who ends up taking a 35 year detour into teaching music has the following exchange with his Vice Principal about cutting the music program in favor of more empirically driven objective subjects.

Vice Principal Wolters

I care about these kids just as much as you do. And if I'm forced to choose between Mozart and reading and writing and long division, I choose long division.

Glenn Holland

Well, I guess you can cut the arts as much as you want, Gene. Sooner or later, these kids aren't going to have anything to read or write about.[83]

Throughout the *Star Wars* anthology Han Solo's worldview deconstructs from a materialist worldview to one that included the metaphysical. Han changed his mind on what could be true and what the nature of truth was. The shift in worldview then re-shaped Han's view of the universe and his place within it. Han deconstructed his initial worldview and reconstructed a new worldview based upon new information and experience.

As I write this part of the book it is winter here in Nashville. We have just been hit with six inches of snow. As is our tradition when the weather turns cold, my wife makes a big pot of chili; slow cooked in the crock pot for six–eight hours. Our tradition, once the chili is ready to eat, is for my wife and I to pour our bowls and then make a peanut butter sandwich to go along with it. We will dip the peanut butter sandwich directly into the chili and eat that while the chili itself is cooling off. My wife and I both were born and raised in southern Indiana, and this is a very normal practice for that region. It is Hoosier normal; it is just the way you eat chili. It is just the way it is. My grown children also enjoy a good peanut butter sandwich dipped into their chili. Their significant others however, who all grew up in the south, think this is insanely bizarre. We discovered this difference in worldview recently when we made chili for the family Halloween pumpkin carving contest. My kids all poured their chili and made a sandwich to go along, not suspecting their sanity to be questioned by my daughter in law Juliana. Juliana polled the other significant others and they agreed with her, that dipping the sandwich into the chili was insane. I chimed in with a challenge to them that this was an opportunity to treat this antithesis as an opportunity to reach a higher synthesis or more plainly spoken, don't know it until you try it. Each of the significant others agreed to try this delicious expansion of their culinary pallets. They each nervously and skeptically dipped their sandwiches into the chili and cautiously took a bite. The results were very humorous and decidedly negative. I find it interesting that it was not just the thought of this food pairing they found to be odd, but they actually found the taste odd. For my family who grew up with this as a part of our food culture, we experience the taste to be very normal and quite delicious. For me and my family it is true that this food pairing is delicious while to my kids' significant others it is true that this food pairing is odd and gross. I guess in the case of food what is true for me may not be true for you, but does this often-used phrase work for matters that aren't individual experience and perception? This new information and experience was an opportunity to deconstruct what I once considered a normal food pairing. It is an opportunity for me to consider just how weird it is to dip a peanut butter sandwich into chili. Is that a culturally confined food pairing or does it stretch beyond southern Indiana? As far back as I can remember I have been eating chili this way. This food pairing was in many ways constructed for me. It goes back so far in my history that I was not really an active participant in it. Mom and dad ate chili this way, the school cafeteria served it this way, friends and neighbors ate it this way, so I did not think through this food pairing it was a given belief. I was indoctrinated into thinking this food pairing was normal. My conception of the world assumed this to be a delicious and normal pairing and I in turn passed this indoctrination down to my children. Their view of this food pairing was constructed for them.

While this example is humorous and trivial its implications go much deeper. Deconstruction can be a very healthy thing to do. I assert we are all deconstructing and reconstructing our worldview constantly. There are some aspects of my worldview today that are the same as I had as an 18-year-old and there are others I have changed in the last year. As we learn and gain exposure and experience our worldview expands. We are in a constant state of a dialectic moving from thesis to antithesis (new information/experience) to synthesis. I would say it is unhealthy if your worldview has not changed at all in your lifetime.

For all of us our initial worldviews were to a great degree constructed for us. At least in the early stages of life our worldview is handed down. We are indoctrinated by our family, friends, schools, churches, culture and even government. I don't say this as a negative. We must begin life with some sort of conception of the world. We begin life without any ability at all to have any conception of the world on our own (not that we are born blank slates, more on that later), it must be constructed for us. Those who are in positions to construct our initial worldview hand down to us that worldview they hold to be the best conception of the world. The worldview that is constructed for us has massive impact on who we view ourselves to be (and how we view the concept of the self), our place in the world, and what it means for us to be in that world.

I was born into a blue collar lower middle-class family in southern Indiana (see above). My first job was detasseling corn. I grew up around these simple but hard-working people who were proud to be American's (even before Lee Greenwood told them to be), loved their families, and held a generally Judeo-Christian view of the world. Folks were predominantly Catholic or non-denominational with some sprinkling of General Baptists, Methodists and various charismatic churches. As a teenager, I adopted a non-denominational (mostly evangelical) worldview. In this view heavy emphasis was placed on literal innerrancy of the Bible (more on this in Part 5), Jesus bearing the punishment for our sins so believers could escape hell (substitutional atonement), and what I would call a strict doctrinal particularism (basically our churches theology is right and everyone else is wrong and going to hell, no matter how small the differences). There was an attitude of McCarthur-ism … I mean McCarthy-ism (Freudian slip) where boogey man heresies could be found around every corner. Much like some of today's celebrity pastors who hand out heresy like Oprah hands out books. During this time there was also the big satanic panic. In short there was a lot of judgment and fear wrapped up in my Christian worldview. When I went off to college, I began to encounter worldviews that challenged my assumptions. I had professors who asserted that my worldview at the time was narrow and limited. In many ways these professors were correct. I often heard it said early on in my Christian faith that we need to get back to the old way of doing church only later to find out the "old way" of doing church only went back a couple of hundred years. There was almost 1700 years of Christianity and church before the "old way" became the "old way." In my naivety I would have never dreamed of reading a Catholic like Aquinas because us Protestants didn't read those heretics. I would have thought this not knowing that Aquinas lived BEFORE the Protestant reformation. I was also introduced to a modern worldview at this time that asserted human reason and objective knowledge was the only kind of knowledge. In this view the world is not enchanted, there is no mystery, no paradox, only objective truth that humans have yet to find. In this view humans aren't made in the image of God; humans are purely biology. I was encountering a antithesis to my worldview. My college professors were trying to get me to dip the peanut butter sandwich in the chili. At first, I resisted. I dug in my heels and recited "Onward Christian Soldier" in my head. But eventually I began to doubt.

A little after college I was introduced to the new paradigm of the time- postmodernism (deconstruction as a philosophy was birthed out of this, i.e. see Derrida in the intro of the book). This new antithesis told me that I had my truth and someone else had their truth but there was no truth that we shared other than by coincidence. Postmodernism relegated meaning to the individual and eventually in this view there is no meaning at all. I went from believing I was a child of God to being told I was only biology that had no meaning at all. I was encountering new forms of indoctrination and I had to deal with them. These were the prevailing philosophies of the time and like I said they had some points. In many ways the worldview I grew up with was narrow and limiting but did it fairly represent the real Christian worldview? I needed to deconstruct, I needed to wrestle through my doubts. I could no longer assume the version of Christianity I grew up with represented the Christian worldview most fully. I also needed to deal with how the modern and postmodern worldviews rubbed against the Christian worldview. What did this mean for meaning? What did it mean for me as a person in the world? What did it mean for truth itself? I don't blame my parents, school, or the state of Indiana for this indoctrination and I don't blame my college professors and people I encountered as I traveled who brought me new information and experiences of the modern and postmodern worldview.

We are all indoctrinated, and we indoctrinate. I indoctrinated my children about peanut butter sandwiches and chili. I also indoctrinated my children about a great many other things, basketball, music, philosophy, faith, etc. My eight-year-old already has a book of philosophy that is written for kids, that I read with him. He and I also read the Bible together every night. We also watch basketball together and he plays year-round. His mom played rugby in college and now he plays rugby in the spring and fall. Our whole family is musicians and so he plays drums (he is savant level good too, its crazy). He is being indoctrinated into all those things. In many ways his worldview up to this point has been constructed for him. As he gets older, he will more and more take agency over his worldview. He will inevitably deconstruct to a degree (maybe very little, maybe some, maybe much of it) his initial worldview that has been constructed for him. While I maintain our initial worldviews being constructed for us is necessary as it is the only option, I also maintain deconstructing that initial worldview can be healthy.

DECONSTRUCTION IS NOT A DIRTY WORD

In many religious circles deconstruction is painted with a negative hue. This is reductionist and largely fear based. I have heard many a pastor says something like, "when I meet with someone and they say they are deconstructing, I ask them what sin are they committing, or who are they sleeping with." I covered in the intro of the book that this is for sure a possibility, maybe even a likely one, as there are different reasons for deconstructing. I would challenge those same pastors by asking them if their theology has changed at all from the point of their salvation until the moment they made that statement. If the answer is yes (and I would assume it would be) then they themselves have deconstructed. As we grow we will for sure deconstruct certain views in favor of others. We may start out biasing one view of (insert theological topic) and holding it to be true but then as we study more, we deconstruct that view in favor of another. The process of construction (thesis), deconstruction (antithesis), and reconstruction (synthesis) is the path a disciple takes. Romans 12:2 states, "Do not conform any longer to the pattern of this world but be transformed by the renewing of your mind. Then you will be able to test and approve what God's will is—his good, pleasing and perfect will." The renewing of the mind is an ongoing and lifetime process for a disciple. Colossians 3:10 also states, "And have put on the new self, which is being renewed in knowledge after the image of its creator." Finally in the Wisdom of Solomon 8:8 it states, "And if anyone longs for wide experience, she [lady wisdom] knows the things of old and infers the things to come; she [lady wisdom] understands the subtleties of speech and the solution of riddles." As our experience widens our wisdom grows and expands which in turn means our worldview will change and expand as well. This is how a disciple grows. This does not mean, and I am not saying that leaving old beliefs behind is always a move towards wisdom. It can be but it can also mean abandoning wisdom for foolishness. Wisdom knows the things of old which indicates a holding on to that which is orthodox in a worldview but also infers the future. It is in the tension of holding tight to what we know to be true while also searching for truth in what is to be learned.

Our initial worldview is given to us, and historically most people did not move outside of this worldview. The sense of self given to the individual was sustained throughout life. A person's family, church and the community gave someone their sense of self and their meaning. Meaning being assigned from the community is proved out in that if your father was a blacksmith, you were likely to either be a blacksmith, join the military or join a monastery.

Your options were limited by the meaning created for you. While this was indeed limiting, it firmly put meaning outside of the individual. Today this has shifted. Tim Keller in *Making Sense of God* states, "The meanings that secular people have are not discovered but rather created. They are not 'objectively' there."[84] Keller asserts that while assigned meanings (as was the case historically) are confining, meanings created by an individual are fragile, which is worse. You can be confined but still be sturdy. All buildings are limited in space but not all buildings are fragile. You might feel claustrophobic in a small, confined room but you aren't in any real danger by being confined, however if you are in a fragile building you could be in real danger of the whole thing collapsing upon itself. When an individual tries to create themselves by themselves meaning is shifting sand because individuals often have competing desires. The competing desires of individuals are at times mutually exclusive or opposed places for meaning. If there is no meaning beyond what the individual creates for themselves, they ultimately have no meaning. An example is that I want to be alive and in good health to see my grandkids (when I have them) grow up, but I also really like key lime pie. I wish to eat as much key lime pie as I can all the time. These desires are competing and most likely in the long run mutually exclusive.

A warning. In the deconstruction process it should be made clear that we never move from a worldview to no worldview. The move from one worldview always means adopting or moving toward another worldview. Humans do not and cannot function without a conception of the world, so the deconstruction process is a move from one worldview to another worldview. Additionally, humans are incapable of deconstructing objectively. As long as you are you and cannot detach yourself from yourself then you cannot deconstruct in true objectivity. One of the criticisms of Descartes aim to doubt everything is that he concluded he was a thinking thing. He ultimately could not remove himself from himself and this was evidence that he existed. It is also evidence that humans cannot detach from the self that is us. Humans are predictably irrational.

The danger in this goes back to the why of the deconstruction. Are you moving toward something or just away from something? The overwhelming tendency is to be much more critical on the worldview you historically held over the one you are deconstructing to; this is a mistake. This is why we should spend as much effort and be as critical on our doubt as we are on our faith. The deconstruction process is trading one bias for another, one indoctrination for another, one worldview for another. This should not be done without a critical eye on what you are deconstructing towards. Tim Keller in his book *Making Sense of God* puts forth the following challenge:

"Rather than unfairly asking only religious people to prove their views, we need to compare and contrast religious beliefs and their evidences with secular beliefs and theirs. We can and should argue about which beliefs account for what we see and experience in the world. We can and should debate the inner logical consistency of belief systems, asking whether they support or contradict one another. We can and should consult our deepest intuitions."[85]

The preceding quote is obviously on a macro level, but I think the principle applies on a micro level. If you are deconstructing a worldview that included a theonomous indoctrination you should be just as critical in assessing the evidences of a material naturalist or atheistic worldview as you are in the theonomous. The reverse could also be said, if you are deconstructing from a material naturalist worldview to one that includes a metaphysical reality you should be just as critical on the evidences (new information, experiences). Regardless of what worldview you are deconstructing from or to a critical eye and equal weight should be placed upon the evidence. A mistake most disciples of a worldview make when deconstructing is that they are only critical of what they are leaving and much more willing to overlook inconsistencies, counter evidences, and counterfactuals of the worldview that is being constructed.

Your initial worldview that was constructed for and handed

down to you provides much of the instruction manual for how you develop a sense of self (again this is not necessarily a bad thing). Your worldview and sense of self provide much of the instruction manual for how you see truth. Someone who holds a material naturalist view of the world will see truth much more from an objective standpoint. Truth is that which is observable and can be measured. While someone with a relativist worldview will obviously view truth as relative. Someone with a postmodern or existentialist worldview will be far more likely to view truth from a subjective standpoint. Someone with a religious worldview is far more likely to see truth as transcendent or divinely revealed. All worldviews give priority and are biased to a certain view of truth. In *Is Reality Secular?*, author Mary Poplin compares worldviews to computer operating systems.[86] To change the way a computer primarily functions, an entirely new operating system may need to be installed. Installing a new operating system requires over-riding the old system. It requires a deconstruction. Poplin states that worldviews, or our operating systems, determine processing, decision making, actions, interpret reality (subjectively of course), and orient our lives daily.[87] All truth claims are exclusive, truth excludes that which is not true (even the claim there is not absolute truth is an exclusive truth claim.) Therefore, for anything to be truth something else must not be true. This does not mean to reduce truth to binary propositions as that would be a category mistake. If worldviews are making truth claims about ultimate reality this cannot be discerned without understanding the nature of truth. This also cannot be discerned without understanding what a worldview is and what it means for the individual, the self.

From a Christian perspective should we not want people to deconstruct? I would say yes. Did the disciples not deconstruct their worldview of the expectation and theology of what the Messiah would be when they accepted Jesus as Messiah? Did they not trade biasing one conception of the world for another? If someone grew up in a cult, their conception of the world is through the eyes of that cult. They have been indoctrinated into that worldview. As a Christian, I don't want them to have a conception of the world that is not found on ultimate reality. I want them to deconstruct to a conception of the world that I believe corresponds to ultimate reality and truth. If someone grew up in the church don't we want them at some point to make their faith their own and not just have their parents faith? For the individual to make their faith their own they must in fact deconstruct. In both examples here I as a Christian want them to truly encounter for themselves and adopt what I believe to be the worldview that connects to the whole truth and ultimate reality which is found in the one who claims in John 14:6, "Jesus answered, "I am the way and the truth and the life. No one comes to the father except through me."

I grew up being read the Bible by and going to church with my grandparents. My worldview on the character of God was shaped from them, however there was conflicting messages. At home the God my grandmother read to me was one of justice but also mercy. A God who was neither Robin William's Genie in *Aladdin*, ready to grant my every wish, nor the distant Emperor Palpatine who was ready to use his Sith power at the slightest misstep. The God my grandparents presented was a Father, firm and wise yet kind and loving. However, this was contrasted by the God presented in their Hell Fire and Brimstone Baptist church. I remember being so afraid of Brother Mayne (the pastor). He yelled and screamed from the pulpit to the congregation about the fiery pits of hell and how we were all surely going there if we did not get our act together. Away from the pulpit he was a stern, distant, unfriendly man. As a child to me he was God's representative in church. One Sunday when I was three or four years old, I remember being so frightened by his message that I hid under the pew behind my grandmother's legs until the end of his message when I ran upfront crying to receive Jesus so that I would not have to burn in fire and be tormented by Satan, eaten by worms forever. I did not pray this prayer because I felt Jesus loved me or that I was an ill patient who needed a physician. I prayed and "converted" solely out of fear and not wanting to go to hell. The conflicting worldview I received from these two versions of God left me confused and always with a looming feeling that somehow no matter what I did I would never be good enough to receive God's grace (poor theology I know). What I did not do for a long time was question the truth of that message. That was presented as the divine truth, and I accepted it a so, it was my worldview about God. Eventually I had a real experience and encounter with God (more on this in the final part of the book) that changed all this and I did truly become a Christian.

However, in adulthood I heard messages from many Christians and non-Christians who act as if the truth is reducible to the objective. Truth is objectively the Word of God (and their interpretation of it) or truth is found in that which is measurable (as if science doesn't itself change as new discoveries are made). Then there were others who just asserted either what is true for you is true for you, or that what you feel is the truth. All three of these perspectives seemed to be lacking to me, so I set out to deconstruct my worldview of truth and then reconstruct it with a higher synthesis. I will unpack what I reconstructed into in the rest of this part of the book. In short Is truth objective? Yes. Is truth subjective? Also, yes. Is truth relative? Also, yes. Is there transcendent truth? Absolutely. Is there such a thing as the whole truth (truth that connects and encompasses all other truth and perfectly connects to ultimate reality)? Yes. Do humans have access to the whole truth? Emphatically No! 1 Corinthians 13:9, "What we know now is not complete. What we prophesy now is not perfect."

Old Pews

V.1
My first memory was being 3 years old
with my grandma at the church of hell fire and brimstone
I didn't know what was so wrong with my soul
But hell was a place I didn't want to go

CH.1
I went down down, between those old pews
said a prayer at the altar the preacher lead me through
and the holier than thou's all raised their hands
and sang "ye must be born again"

V.2
When I was 18, I didn't know who to be
I didn't think of God or what he thought of me
Until I knocked up my girl and hit my knees
"God I'm scared do you care for me"

CH. 2
I fell down down, didn't know what else to do
said a prayer in my car, swore I'd see it through
she cried on shoulder I vowed to (always) hold her hand
I promised to be a man

V.3
Me and my guitar watched life through a windshield
I lost who I was, forgot how to feel
Until I lost my Dad, marriage and record deal
When I ran out of options, I picked up my cross for real

CH. 3
I went down down, between those old pews
Said a prayer on the altar, the Lord lead me to
and the weak, poor sinners all raised their hands
and sang, "in Christ alone I stand"

REFRAIN
Wade in the water that satisfies
Washed by the blood of sacrifice
Drowned in the terrible price
Paid that I might
Be free from sin through Jesus Christ[88]

A Deeper Understanding of Worldview

The term worldview is bantered about as often as a tennis ball at Wimbledon but with little cohesion in the definition. Up until now we have used the definition of worldview as a conception of the world. This is not incorrect at all, but I would like to deepen our understanding by drilling into a more thorough definition. A worldview is a set of mores by which paradigms of life are oriented, ordered, and operated. Further, Paul Hiebert defines worldview as, "The foundational cognitive, affective, and evaluative assumptions and frameworks a group of people makes about the nature of reality which they use to order their lives."[89] Theologian N. T. Wright's description of worldview is "the basic stuff of human existence, the lens through which the world is seen, the blueprint for how one should live in it, and above all the sense of identity and place which enables human beings to be what they are."[90]

One of the biggest factors in what shapes our worldview and conceptions of truth is the culture in which we are in. For a culture to function, there must be certain shared presuppositions held in congruence. It is akin to a band, which is a system and culture unto itself. If all the tonal instruments are of the view, the song is in G♭; then, tonally, the view is integrated. The band is auditorily playing in G♭. However, if the drummer is counting time in 5/4 time instead of 12/8 time, the feel of the song will be off and will cause issues. The band agrees about certain assumptions, but singular disagreement causes tension. A person or culture's view on the existential meaning and relational order affect the way that person or culture will process values, behaviors, and views. Terms that rally betwixt newsreels, Facebook posts, and water coolers like "protestant work ethic," "American spirit", "pull yourself up by your bootstraps" and "don't tread on me," aren't just fodder for memes but reveal an undercurrent of what the American culture holds dear—rugged individualism, toughness, liberty, and upward mobility. These factors weave into every aspect of American life without consciousness of their effect and presumption of their existence. It is hard for someone in a culture not to imagine the ethos of his or her culture not being the way things are for everyone. Paul Hiebert argues that a worldview is the "most fundamental and encompassing view of reality" that a group of people shares.[91] Hiebert further states that worldviews (perception of the world) provide the baseline suppositions for culture.[92]

Another one of the major factors in understanding worldviews is that all worldviews require faith; whether it is material naturalism, secular humanism, pantheism, or the Judeo-Christian worldview, the adopter has to make some leap of faith in order to accept that worldview.[93] Poplin states that worldviews do not conclude with a commitment to faith but begin with it.[94] Remember that when we are talking about the big issues we are dealing with plausibility and probability not provability. If something is not provable then it requires faith. In order to change a person's perspective, often, there must be a fundamental shift in worldview. Within society, the large number of shared views allows communication between sub-cultures.[95] Tim Keller puts it like this, "All reasoning is based on prior faith commitments to which one did not reason."[96] Everyone's worldview has presuppositions through which certain aspects of the lived world are taken on faith.

- Culture- According to the Routledge Encyclopedia of Philosophy, culture is "those aspects of human activity which are socially rather than genetically transmitted." The beliefs, behaviors, and bonds of a group of people.
- Material Naturalism- the mind is no more than the physiology of the brain, and therefore, humans have no autonomy of thought that is not pre-programmed in DNA.
- Secular Humanism- The belief that humanity is capable of morality and self-fulfillment without belief in god.

- Monotheism- The belief in one God.
- Pantheism- The universe itself is god. Everything is god and god is everything.
- Polytheism- The belief in more than one god.
- Judeo-Christian- Relating to the worldview held in common by Judaism and Christianity.

MEANING AND HUMANITY

Humans have an innate and imprinted need for meaning. Meaning for humans is intrinsically tied to the self. Meaning can be divided in global meaning and local meaning. Local meaning is centralized to one's own life and relationships. Anyone human regardless of worldview can find local meaning in their life. This is the type of meaning that is discovered in social constructs (family, community, friends etc.) Local meaning is meaning in close proximity. Global meaning in an individual's life is tied to the individual's relation to all creation.[97] This is only available to the theists, be they Muslim, Jew, Christian, or even Pantheist. Global- meaning is best and perhaps only found in religion.

If we no longer receive meaning from God or our culture/community and each individual is left to construct their own meaning, then shared values and shared meaning are an impossibility. There is either meaning or there is not, it is a binary proposition. Self-created meaning has no value, eventually even to the self who created it. In the theist worldview meaning is divinely and communally given. Ecclesiastes 1:3 states, "'Smoke! Mist!' says the Teacher. 'Utterly meaningless! Everything is Vapor. What do people gain from all their labors at which they toil under the sun?" Later in Ecclesiastes 4:9-12 it states, "Two people are better off than one, for they can help each other succeed. If one person falls, the other can reach out and help. But someone who falls alone is in real trouble. Likewise, two people lying close together can keep each other warm. But how can one be warm alone? A person standing alone can be attacked and defeated, but two can stand back-to-back and conquer. Three are even better, for a triple-braided cord is not easily broken." Still later in 9:9 it states, "Enjoy life with your wife, whom you love, all the days of this meaningless life that God has given you under the sun—all your vaporous days. For this is your lot in life and in your toilsome labor under the sun." Finally in Ecclesiastes 12:13 it states, "That's the whole story. Here now is my final conclusion: Fear God and obey his commands, for this is everyone's duty." In the Christian worldview meaning is discovered not created. Meaning is inherent. It is found in God (Macro-meaning) and community (Micro-meaning). A life where someone tries to create meaning in anything other than God and others can't be grasped and doesn't last. It is smoke, it disappears as fast as it appears. In the Christian worldview the meaning of life is found in Mathew 22:37–40, "'Love the Lord your God with all your heart and with all your soul. Love him with all your mind.' (Deuteronomy 6:5) This is the first and most important commandment. And the second is like it. 'Love your neighbor as you love yourself.' (Leviticus 19:18) Everything that is written in the Law and the Prophets is based on these two commandments.'"

Paperback Novels

V.1
For 20 years I've been out on this road
Bleeding into strings Using words as swords
Trying to create something great
To show we all share the same pain
but in a different way

Chorus
Were all paperback novels
Here today and gone tomorrow
We get used, discarded and resold
Were all paperback novels
We get dog eared and tattered
But each with a story of their own
paperback novels

V.2
We all chase our tails for meaning
Like Pavlov's dog we salivate when we here the bells ringing
Love's the dividing line
The only thing that satisfies
Redemption came through sacrifice
Through the broken bread and the blood red wine

Bridge
It's all smoke
It's all mist
Only time and death are certain
(So give your kids a hug and your wife a kiss)
It's all smoke
It's all mist
So worship the Lord
With every second that you get[98]

THE ENLIGHTENMENT, MODERNITY AND ITS INFLUENCE ON THE WORLDVIEW OF THE WEST

According to Stephen Hicks, "any intellectual movement is defined by its fundamental philosophical premises."[99] The modern worldview, birthed out of the Enlightenment, prioritizes reason, logic, and empirical truth. The modern worldview orders truth mechanistically and reduces truth to digital sets like Turing's binary code. In a modern worldview, myth is not reality because the specific facts about myth cannot reduce to a true/false equation. If story cannot be logically reduced to facts, it is discarded on the pile of refuse. In the modern worldview, only empirically knowable truth is the truth.[100]

The modern worldview (not to be confused with contemporary but rather modern as coming out of the modern philosophy and the time period of modernity) was birthed out of the Enlightenment. The enlightenment was a philosophical worldview movement of the 17th and 18th centuries that moved away from the more classical synthesis of the world. One of the primary triggers for this movement was the aftermath of the reformation period of the church. Prior to the reformation the Church (catholic- little c at this point) had fallen into corruption. The church which was the trusted disseminator of truth for centuries could no longer be trusted. In the classical synthesis of Christianity exposited by Dr. Christopher Simpson in his book, *Modern Christian Theology*, there is a deep interrelation between distincts (almost Trinitarian in essence).[101] An interrelated communion and relation between man, God, and nature. Man is not only natural but is related to nature. God is related to the world but is not the world. Nature is created by God and therefore is good. Nature has inherent value and meaning in itself- not out of what it can do for humanity. The material world does not stand in opposition to the spiritual world (no Gnosticism to be seen here). Nature reflects the wisdom and goodness of God. In the classical synthesis worldview, all is connected but not reducible to homogeny. This is not pantheism but connection. God is everywhere at all times but everywhere is not God. God, nature, and humanity were held together, understood together, ordered together as a community. The reformation unintentionally broke this togetherness. There is a change in the conditions of belief. When the reformation happened, the assumption was that because every Christian had the Holy Spirit dwelling in them and every Christian could now (assuming they could read) read the Bible for themselves, the Christian world would unite without the need for the hierarchy and corrupt bureaucracy of things like indulgences and simony. Instead, this led to division amongst believers and the 30 Years War. Out of the disillusionment from this along with advances in science, there was a shift toward man's ability. God was removed from the center of meaning and man took center stage. Modernism reduced God to "a distant architect" rather than a God who is concerned with creation, a move from theism as essential to theism as one option along with deism and atheism.[102]

I want to take a brief sidebar to distinguish the difference between deism and theism with a cooking analogy. As opposed to atheism which asserts there is no God, both deism and theism do assert that there is a God. However, there is a distinction between the two. Deism's God is like making a pizza from scratch. You roll the dough, put on the sauce, the cheese and the toppings. You set your oven for the appropriate setting and once the oven has pre-heated, you put the pizza in the oven, set the timer and walk away. Once the pizza is cooking you do not need to be involved. You just wait. You let the cheese bubble where it may, the crust rises in the way that has been set in motion by the creation of the crust. Theism's God however is making risotto. The beginning steps are the same, you bring the water to a boil, add broth, put in the rice and seasoning along with butter but you have to constantly stir the ingredients so they will cook thoroughly and with the desired consistency. When cooking risotto, the chef has

101

to stay involved the whole time. The chef is constantly active in his creation so that it turns out the way the chef desires. Deism's God is making pizza while theism's God is making risotto. The existence of suffering cause many to doubt whether humanity is at a dinner where risotto is being made or if it is risotto, it is bad enough that Gordon Ramsey would throw it against the wall and curse the chef out. Is a theistic God possible given that there is so much suffering in the world? Is a theistic God required to intervene sometimes to remove some suffering or would a theistic God, in order to be a good God, be required to remove all suffering at all times? Is humanity in a position to know or judge what a theistic God would or would not do? I have had my own doubts about this and will address this issue extensively in Part 3 of the book.

The shift brought on by modernity was the shift from an epistemic assumption of the limitations of human knowledge to the assumption that human knowledge is ascending ever further and eventually achieving complete synthesis. The confidence in human knowledge is a significant shift and one that creates several issues. For instance, while contemporary humanity questions why God would or would not do certain things, this was not the case in ancient times. Tim Keller posits:

> "Ancient people did not assume that the human mind had enough wisdom to sit in judgment on how an infinite God was disposed of things. It is only in modern times that we get 'the certainty that we have all the elements we need to carry out a trial of God.' Only when this background belief in the sufficiency of our own reason shifted did the presence of evil in the world seem to be an against the evidence of God."[103]

No one comes to the table tabula rasa but instead has presuppositions that color how evidence for or against God is ascertained. Modern philosophy began to leave the cohesiveness of the classical synthesis for the yellow lines and armadillos of the paradoxical middle. Modern thought moved to the ditches of empiricism and rationalism. Philosophy in modernity began to assert man could get to all knowledge through reason. Even Hegel's dialectic system of thought asserted this while others, like Immanuel Kant, questioned the reach of reason. The limits of reason lead some towards transcendence (see Romantics) while others to Nihilism (see Nietzsche, even though he didn't think he was a Nihilist) or it's partying cousin absurdism. Nihilism is the emo version of meaninglessness; it is all meaningless and nihilism is really depressed about it. While absurdism is the Nu metal version of meaninglessness. It is all meaningless so let's just party and break stuff. This shift in worldview is not too far off from the extremes of early Gnosticism. Like Elvis, in nihilism once meaning has left the building it will not come back for an encore. We cannot construct our own meaning if meaning does not exist. A nihilistic worldview is not rationally compatible with any meaning much less self-created meaning.

There were significant philosophical paradigms brought about during the Enlightenment. The impact of this paradigm on western worldviews was a loss of transcendence and skepticism of the supernatural even within the church. Additionally, the movements of knowledge and reason relegated metaphysics such as transcendent truth to its own category. Philosophers and theologians such as Hume, Schelling, and Schleiermacher, asserted reason and rationalism are separate from God. The effect is that the classical holistic view of God, man, nature, is further separated. The nature of knowledge (epistemology), ethics, and even what constituted an idea was reduced during the enlightenment. I will outline those shifts briefly below:

KNOWLEDGE

The ground began shifting what was once counted on for order. The reason for that order, God, was now being brought into question. It began to be asserted that there are things we can reason but cannot know experientially; God was placed into this category (Kant,

Hobbes). We cannot know there is a God by experience; therefore, God's existence was shifted from certainty to the probability of eventual non-existence. The existence of God was no longer a given and thus had to be argued. "If a criterion for knowledge can be changed or even reasonably disputed, then the criterion itself cannot provide the certainty required for knowledge."[104] The idea of paradox began to be eliminated. Knowledge began to be reduced to only that which can be observed and measured.

ETHICS

In the medieval period, ethics were assumed to have a theonomous foundation or, at the very least, a virtue foundation. During modernity, religion philosophically was reduced to universal ethics. The foundation for ethics was questioned; for instance, social contract theory (Hobbes, Locke) where morals have no self-existence but are instead agreed upon by the members of society. This paradigm removed morals and ethics from scripture, God, or the Church and to man himself to decide. God's goodness began to be questioned (Descartes's evil genius, for example), which lead to Leibniz's modality. The effect was that it was no longer assumed that the Bible has moral authority or that God was good.

IDEAS

The very nature of ideas began to be questioned. Whether ideas and concepts come only from experience or whether some come from innate places began to be questioned. Kant believed man had some a priori ideas, as did Leibniz. It is in the paradigm of questioning ideas that metaphysical questions such as "why is there anything?" can be asked. Before the modern age, this was not a question that would have been asked.

Modernity eventually reduced knowledge and therefore truth only to the objective. Truth only resided in that which can be observed and measure such as math and nature. A further reduction took place that reduced objective truth down to empirically measured scientific truth. "Scientific truth has become recognized as the only objective truth. Science speaks, and most people listen and believe."[105] The reduction of truth to scientific truth eventually leads to scientism (elevation in the belief of science as the sole source of all actual knowledge), displacing transcendence and theism as either nonsense or, at best, a matter relegated to private experience.[106] Huston Smith says through the modern worldview, "[we have] erased transcendence from our reality map."[107] Scientism asserts to know all truth or at least be searching for it, but in reality, it is a reduction to place truth into the box of empiricism. Additionally, it is often asserted that science approaches truth without bias but since the transcendental ego of scientists who have their own presuppositions of a naturalist worldview makes science being unbiased phenomenologically impossible. "The essential point to be made is that when we exercise our rationality, when we act as agents of truth and meaning. We become involved in activities that cannot be treated from a merely empirical point of view."[108]

Poplin argues the elimination of spiritual transactions ignores and excludes any truth beyond the empirical.[109] Science is reductionist in nature (this does not mean science is bad or that it does not reveal truth). Science by nature imposes categories and reduces wholes to their parts. Science isolates particulars in order to experience and study natural phenomena which can tell us much about not only the parts but also the whole. The assertion that science is somehow conducted without bias is wholly false. While science studies the objective world the person conducting the science is a singular subjective self. The event or occurrence of scientific study is always experienced by someone (or group of someone's); experiments/studies are conducted by subjective consciouses. In the plainest terms, science is conducted by scientists (people) so it is biased by their worldview. Even the scientific method, double blind and all functions like this. Science is an all too human affair filled with presuppositions that are assumed by a worldview. Science as a discipline in contemporary culture holds a predominantly material naturalist worldview. Philosopher Thomas Nagel in his book *The Last Word* states, "It isn't just that I don't believe in God and, naturally, hope that I'm right in my belief. It's that I hope there is no God! I don't want there to be a God; I don't want the universe to be like that.[110]

The elimination of the metaphysical is the worldview of material naturalism. When transcendence, metaphysical, and metanarrative are excluded, truth is reduced to the empirical and observable. Speaking of a God who became man and performed miracles becomes fodder for fools and fairytales. The modern reduction of humanity to only the material is an important philosophical factor that contributes to worldviews and how truth is viewed. Material naturalism asserts that the mind is no more than the physiology of the brain, and therefore, humans have no autonomy of thought that is not pre-programmed in DNA. Material naturalists have faith that not only is reality only the material and scientifically verifiable, but consciousness itself does not exist. By contrast, Hiebert notes, "The biblical worldview calls us to reject the dualisms of natural and supernatural."[111] The fact is also that no one lives as if material naturalism is true. The atheist scientist lives as if his consciousness is real. She lives as though she really loves her children, and that love is more than a chemical evolutionary process. They act as though moral actions matter; they ache when a child gets cancer. They ask why God allows so much suffering and use that as evidence against there being a God. But implicit in that is them not living out their worldview as if it is true, so if naturalists do not live as though their worldview is true, should it be assumed to be true? If it is all a delusion and they are willingly living in the delusion, then why assume their assessment is correct? It seems to me that the experience of being human leads us all to believe it is more than biology so perhaps it is.

Han Solo came to conclude there is more to the universe than the material. Humans must be more than material naturalists assert, otherwise free will is an illusion and personal identity is a delusion. We are more than our bodies, so pure empiricism is impossible. Conversely, we cannot detach ourselves from being a thing within the world so pure rationalism is impossible as well. We are always conscious of something. Therefore, there is not a clear connection between stimuli and perception. The empirical can only be seen through the rational. Thus when "we" describe the world through the senses we are describing the objective through the subjective, or the empirical through the rational. It's like when you have a bad cable plugged into your amp, no matter how awesome you play the sound will be bad. It's not the amp's inability to perceive the signal but the communication between the guitar and the amp is not clean. Empiricism seeks to reduce things to their categories, and this does not allow for nor explain our perceptions. Our perceptions cannot be reduced to anything but an interconnected whole. We actually see a whole with a foreground and a background. We need both foreground and background to see something distinct. It's like the concept of evil, we can only know what is evil by knowing also what is good. We perceive the "bits" that empiricism wants to reduce in order to measure only against the backdrop of the whole but then we have to perceive it, which is done through association. Finally, the problem with empiricism is that there is no way to "double-blind" the world enough to truly be empirical because we are always in the world. We are in the perception.

There is much irony in material naturalists' claims that belief in God is from a "God-gene" or "spiritual brain."[112] The assertion itself is coming from consciousness—the very thing the material naturalist dismisses as non-existent. Even if a chemical process was identified in the brain that correlates with faith, that does not mean the process caused belief; in fact, science itself tells us correlation does not equal causation. There is the synapses and neurons interplay when a person falls in love, but that does not explain the experience and reality of love. This reduction to the material also leaves no room to question ethics (not even social contract, deontological, or utilitarian).

- Simony- the buying or selling of ecclesiastical privileges, for example pardons or benefices. Paying the church or church leader to get a certain position of leadership or for certain bad behaviors to be overlooked.
- Deism- Belief in the existence of an impersonal God, who set the laws of nature in motion at creation but does not/has not intervened since creation.
- Theism- belief in the existence of a personal God, who intervenes and sustains the universe.
- Classical synthesis- the worldview that holds that there is deep interrelation and communion between God, nature, and humans. Each is related to the other two but not reducible to either.
- Hegel's dialectic- From the Stanford Encyclopedia of Philosophy, ""Dialectics" is a term used to describe a method of philosophical argument that involves some sort of contradictory process between opposing sides. "Hegel's dialectics" refers to the particular dialectical method of argument employed by the 19th Century German philosopher, G.W.F. Hegel, which, like other "dialectical" methods, relies on a contradictory process between opposing sides"; some assertible proposition (thesis) is necessarily opposed by an equally assertible and apparently contradictory proposition (antithesis), the mutual contradiction being reconciled on a higher level of truth by a third proposition (synthesis).
- Theonomous ethics- Ethical view that a divine being is the ground of man's being, and, therefore, ethics are governed transcendently; man should not separate decisions from divine principles.

- Heteronomous/Social contract ethics- Ethics are decided by what each individual society agrees upon and has no grounding in innate principles. Mob rule ethics.
- Autonomous ethics- According to the encyclopedia Britannica, a system of ethics based on ethics being independent of principle or from external moral demands. Ethics are solely up to the individual free from cultural constraints.
- Deontological ethics- Ethical view places special emphasis on the relationship between duty and the morality of human actions. The term deontology is derived from the Greek deon, "duty," and logos, "science."
- Tabula Rasa- Humans being born having no innate ideas or selves. The view that humans are born as a clean slate. In this view the individual is completely constructed through nurture; nature plays no role.
- Material naturalism- The worldview that holds that there is nothing but the natural elements and governing principles that are studied by the natural sciences. Holds the view that all properties related to consciousness and the mind itself are reducible to nature. The mind is nothing more than the naturalism processes of the brain.
- Scientism- The belief of science as the sole source of all actual knowledge.
- Biologism- The interpretation of human life from a strictly biological point of view.
- Psychologism- a tendency to interpret events or arguments in subjective terms, or to exaggerate the relevance of psychological factors.
- Conflicting conditions fallacy- The definition is self-contradictory.
- Utilitarian ethics- Ethic that asserts an action is right or wrong based upon the criteria of what does the greatest good for the greatest number of people.

- Deontological ethics- Ethic based upon duty. An action is deemed ethical based upon what one "ought" to do. Unlike utilitarianism, the outcome is irrelevant. Ethics are based upon the action itself not the outcome.
- God Gene/Spiritual Brain- The theory that religious belief is determined by heredity.
- Nihilism- there is no meaning in life, all morals are baseless. Nothing can be known or communicated.
- Absurdism- Existence is irrational and seeking meaning is damaging to humans. Here may be meaning in life but humans are not capable of finding it.

THE IMPACT OF MODERNITY ON WORLDVIEWS

Those who hold a modernist worldview have an algorithmic and reductionist approach to truth. The algorithmic view processes units of analysis and works with digital sets.[113] This reductionist view of truth leaves little room for paradox or what Hiebert calls "fuzzy logic."[114] "Traditional" cultures, like the classical synthesis Christian worldview, take an analogical view of logic and hold mystery and paradox as reality.[115] The classical Christian worldview also asserts a metaphysical aspect to the transcendent truth. A Christian worldview believes God transcends digital sets. Paul reasoned with the Athenians in Acts 17, so a Christian worldview does not dismiss or devalue reason, logic, or science. I'll use an analogy here to help clarify by comparing worldviews in terms of sound waves. A modern worldview "treats [sound] as a single category and overlooks infinite variety."[116] In no way is digital sound "fuzzy." Digital sound waves are binary code, while a classical Christian worldview (traditional) is like analog sound waves. Analog sound waves are more like hills, and the sound is saturated and warm. For many who hold a modern worldview (particularly material naturalists and secular humanists), there is no room for analog sound waves that are like rolling hills without the sharp turns. A Christian worldview to someone who is a modernist can get mired down in whether the evidence precisely correlates to the story instead of whether the belief system itself is true. This fact makes communicating the Christian worldview of an active, loving God baffling. Reducing knowledge, ethics and ideas to binary digital sets greatly reduced the ability of what that worldview can accept as truth. The modern worldview played out to the end eliminated the need for God and placed human reason on the throne of existence. Friedrich Nietzsche, through the protagonist, Zarathustra stated, "What does this whole world know today?' asked Zarathustra. 'This perhaps, that the old God no longer lives, the one in whom the whole world once believed?' 'You said it,' answered the old man gloomily. 'And I served this old God until his final hour."[117] In the end the worldview of material naturalism not only kills off the concept of God but also kills off humanities belief in an identity at all. In contemporary culture we spend so much time arguing about identity when if we are accepting of material naturalism as a worldview there is no self to have identity, so there is nothing to argue about. If there is a conscious self (if I am indeed me) and if there is a world out there to be experienced, then there must be an interplay between I and the world. This interplay suggest that I cannot construct my own meaning apart from the world. I experience life in a lived world that I am only a part of AND I am a singular conscious self. Immanuel Kant famously said, "the most important fact about reason is that it is clueless about reality."[118]

POSTMODERNISM AND ITS IMPACT ON WORLDVIEWS

While the enlightenment led to the treatment of any phenomena not naturally occurring or empirically explainable to the playground of imagination and fairytale, the ultimate result being the reduction of the human spirit to mechanistic explanation. Postmodernism is a direct reaction against—but an extension of—modernity. Postmodernism accurately calls out modernity's worship of science and reason. However, instead of reducing truth to the objective and empirical, postmodernism reduces truth to an individual "cognitively constructed" endeavor full of human presuppositions.[119]

Postmodernism eradicates objective truth all together in favor of contextualization. The postmodern worldview values every individual's subjective way of interpreting the world over any attempts to universalize or codify truth. Postmodernity ultimately rejects ultimate reality. Postmodernity even rejects the belief that humans live in an agreed upon shared authenticity reality. Both of these reductions make communicating any shared meaning (intersubjectivity) difficult. Communicating meaning to an individual who does not view truth as anything inherent or shared is very difficult. Postmodernism's critique of modernity's reduction is fair and much needed but the ultimate result was a further reduction of knowledge, ethics, and ideas. Modernity eliminated the metaphysical (transcendent truth), postmodern thought eliminated anything other than subjectivity from the arena of truth. Eliminating all truth other than subjective truth is self-refuting. Postmodernism ends in relativism and a lack of shared meaning or even the ability to communicate with one another. Claims by postmodernists that there is no truth, or there are no moral absolutes, or that humans cannot have access to reality is by logical necessity self-refuting.[120] Postmodernism makes a habit of conflicting conditions fallacies. Claim X is made, which is impossible, as demonstrated by all or part of claim X. While it is accurate and fair to say that every human is subjective, postmodernism inevitably goes too far.

Postmodernism asserts that humans cannot know anything of truth (or that truth does not exist) or reality (if reality exists at all). It is true that human perceptions cannot be trusted. Humans can perceive something, which is not there, which kind of proves the subjectivity of perception. An example of this is the old putting a pencil in a cup of water trick. The water refracts the light making the pencil look bent. In this case, our senses (vision) tell us that the pencil is bent, but reason allows us to intellectually know that it is an illusion caused by the water refracting the light. However, human perceptions are generally accurate enough for us to reasonably function in the lived world (objective) and communicate to other humans about the lived world (objective). How purple is perceived through my eye and interpreted through my synapses may indeed mean that purple looks different to me than another individual. However, the way I perceive purple looks similar enough that when I speak of seeing the purple guitar, the other person (subjective individual) knows which guitar I am speaking of (unless they are color blind). Paul Copan puts it this way, "The commonsense principle of credulity affirms that the everyday world is generally how we experience it to be."[121] I would only add that each subjective human's interaction with the real objective lived world has common enough shared intersubjectivity that humans can communicate about the objective world with reasonable accuracy. Thus, Ockham's razor would dictate we conclude there is indeed reality and truth. The further reduction of the postmodern movement on worldviews is that we are living in a "post-truth" world. This just like the modern movement ends in nihilism. If there is no truth then there is no shared meaning, if there is no shared meaning there is no meaning at all. The interplay of worldview, the self, and truth is vital. Both the modern worldview and the postmodern worldview did not and do not satisfy my doubts, they do not answer my questions in a way that at all convinces me either of those worldviews infer the best conclusion. From my doubting perspective, they each reduce what I rationally think and experience. The individual self that I am reasons there must be more, that exostence cannot be reduced beyond the complexity and paradox.

- Postmodernism- According to Britannica, "in Western philosophy, a late 20th-century movement characterized by broad skepticism, subjectivism, or relativism; a general suspicion of reason; and an acute sensitivity to the role of ideology in asserting and maintaining political and economic power.

- Ockham's razor- the principle (attributed to William of Occam) that in explaining a thing the simplest explanation is often the correct one.

THE ETHICS OF WORLDVIEWS AND LOVE

From *I, Robot*

[Flashback]
ROBOT
You are in danger!
DETECTIVE DEL SPOONER
Save her, save the girl!
[End of flashback]]
But it didn't. It saved me.
SUSAN CALVIN
A robot's brain is a difference engine, it must have calculated—
DETECTIVE DEL SPOONER
It did. I was the *logical* choice. It calculated I had a forty-five percent chance of survival, Sarah only had an eleven percent chance. That was somebody's baby. Eleven was more than enough. A human would have known that. But robots, no, they're just lights and clockwork. But you know what: You go ahead and trust them if you wanna.[121]

In the movie *Interstellar*, Ann Hathaway's character is asking to try and go to a world to reunite with a person she loves even though scientifically the likelihood of her making it is absurd.

COOPER

You're a scientist, Brand.

BRAND

So listen to me when I say that love isn't something that we invented. It's ... observable, powerful. It has to mean something.

COOPER

Love has meaning, yes. Social utility, social bonding, child rearing ...

BRAND

We love people who have died. Where's the social utility in that?

COOPER

None.

BRAND

Maybe it means something more—something we can't yet understand. Maybe it's some evidence, some artifact of a higher dimension that we can't consciously perceive. I'm drawn across the universe to someone I haven't seen in a decade, who I know is probably dead. Love is the one thing we're capable of perceiving that transcends dimensions of time and space. Maybe we should trust that, even if we can't understand it. All right Cooper. Yes. The tiniest possibility of seeing Wolf again excites me. That doesn't mean I'm wrong.

COOPER

Honestly, Amelia ... it might.[123]

After my grandfather passed away from lung cancer my grandmother had to be moved into my father's house as she was bedridden and unable to care for herself. My father was newly re-married (man I am really not trying to bag on my dad's wife over and over but this is all true) and taking care of her was putting a strain on the marriage. The decision was made to put her in a home because she was only a drain on the family. My grandmother told my dad she would not live long in a home and to please let her stay. My dad's new wife made the decision to go forward and put her in a home instead of hiring in-home care. Even as a child this seemed to be a decision made from utility and not love. There was something innate in me that screamed internally that this was wrong, my grandmother's value was not based upon what she contributed to the family at that point. My grandmother was put in the home and died very shortly thereafter.

If the creator created out of love, then perhaps the chief end of human existence is to love. Human awareness of that mission and the ability to choose to live it out is what makes humans particular. Deep-down humans long for meaning and purpose and to know why they exist. Perhaps it really is love and humans have the will, volition, and opportunity to choose to love or not to love.

Voice for the Voiceless

V.1
Oh we have to be the voice for the voiceless
Whose life meant more than someone else's choices
Oh we have to be the grace for the graceless
Whose soul is more than the crowd of faces

Chorus
We're all widows and orphans
Travelers who need a hand
Every now and then
We're knit together in our mothers womb
But it wasn't meant to be a tomb
Souls transcend
Every woman, child, and man
Is worthy to defend
To lend a helping hand

V.2
Oh we have to speak for those with weakness
Whose heart beats but held speechless
Every humans worth is infiniteness
Like the savior showed when he died for all of us

Bridge
Everybody every where
Be their voice Show you care
Everybody every where[124]

In traditional cultures whose worldview is shaped by a classical synthesis ethics are theonomous; ethics are innate, shared, internal and external, necessary, and metaphysical. Brad S. Gregory in his book, *The Unintended Reformation* states, "Christian morality was irreducibly communal and social."[125] In the classical synthesis ethics were institutionalized. The church provided a canopy (though an imperfect one for sure). Belief in God was individual and communal, it was political, personal, occupational. The church, the culture, your family told you the individual who you are and what was ethical. What was considered ethical was believed to have come from God and not the places that disseminated the virtues of ethics. In a classical worldview ethics are virtue based. Ethics are transcendent and come from God. From a modern worldview ethics are heteronomous, consensual, and come from social contracts. Heteronomous ethics place morality as solely external, thus making morality subject to changes in the external environment. If the individual disagrees with the consensus, the individual must comply with the larger group, which in reality is not complete and true consensus. This leaves morality in the hands of the majority. The implication is that if much of the world regarded slavery as moral than it is in fact moral. The major flaw in consensual ethics is how it treats truth. Consensual ethics treat objective truth the way physics describes force, only by its effects. In other words, there is nothing transcendent and unchanging about truth. As opposed to subjective human beings dealing with transcendent, objective, and intersubjective truth like in theonomous societies, consensual ethics takes the majority of subjective human beings' moral conclusions on a particular ethic issue and elevates that as the whole truth.

Understanding the flaws of heteronomous consensual social contract ethics are very important as it is the equivalent to living on top of an active fissure, the ground is always subject to the whims of the mob. In heteronomous consensual social contract-based ethics there is nothing firm as a foundation. If the majority of people all of a sudden started to believe that killing puppies was a moral good, then it would indeed be a moral good. If morality is determined by majority vote, then nothing is permanently immoral. Immoral cannot exist because there is nothing innately wrong in and of itself. Heteronomous ethics view morality as a human construction. Ethics are needed for a healthy society, but the idea of wrong is not rooted in anything permanent. Prior to modernity the condition of man's heart was assumed to be selfish, and many philosophers of this period agreed that man was selfish (Kant, Hobbes) but what came into question was whether man's selfishness was an altogether negative thing. As man ascended to the throne of the focus his selfish began to be seen as either neutral or an all together positive thing. Hobbes for example treated man's self-interest as a good thing.

Morality in postmodernism shifted even further from a theonomous ethical view. Postmodernity shifted from asserting a herd instinct where morality was led by society to an autonomous view of ethics. Nietzsche in *Thus Spoke Zarathustra* states, "My brother, if you have one virtue, and it's your virtue, then you have it in common with no one."[126] In an autonomous view of ethics the individual intimidates the herd by their ability to stand beyond the norms and mores of any given morality. In the autonomous view of ethics obedience equals weakness, whether that is obedience to God or the mob. The postmodern worldview asserts that morality like meaning is self-created, self-virtues are ingrained into the self, thus they cannot be named. Virtues are not innate and given by God. They are not needed for a healthy society. Virtues are contingent down to the singular instance; they are not necessary at all.

Contemporary western culture asserts to value autonomy but only as far as that autonomy agrees with the majority- heteronomous. There is irony in contemporary western cultures mix of heteronomous (modern worldview) and autonomous (postmodern worldview) ethics. On the one hand our society believes the individual should have the freedom to live how they see fit as long as that freedom does not disagree with the majority of people. This is relativism and it is self-refuting. Contemporary western culture combines either material naturalism or pantheism combined with asserting autonomy but as long as that autonomy does not disagree with the majority rule. This means there really is no grounding for human rights. Rebecca McLaughlin in her book *Confronting Christianity* states it this way, "If we are no more than the features that can be described by science, and our only story is the evolutionary story, we have no grounds for insisting on human equality, protection for the weak, equal treatment of women, or any other ethical beliefs we hold dear."[127] If nature is all there is, why should humans protect children, or the disabled, or the elderly? Those that are subjugated, disenfranchised, other-abled, poor, weak, uneducated are in a purely pragmatic sense a drain on society and the survival of the fittest would dictate they should be eliminated. If no human has innate and intrinsic value, then the issue of human rights boils down to utility. In scientism, biologism, and material naturalism (which ever branch of the same tree) there is no grounds to call murder or rape wrong. Those acts are simply the strong in nature asserting their autonomous dominance over the weak and if most people decided this was upright and moral there is nothing innate about the acts, nothing intrinsic about the victims that would make it wrong. The virtue based theonomous view of ethics is different. It asserts morality is beyond utility but comes from a divine decree (*revisit the lyrics for the song Freedom). As Detective Spooner said a human would have known to save the girl and not the adult. Humans are capable of making altruistic self-sacrificing decisions because of love. Love is more than utility. Love is more than kindness (more on that in the next part of the book), love is more than a feeling. Love is the ultimate ethic.

Morality is either delusion or revelation. It really comes down to that. The overriding ethical principle is love (not kindness... again more on that in the next part of the book). Love is the privation of selfishness. Love is the denial of self and one of the biggest evidences of the divine. Humans ability to love from time to time is evidence of us being made in the image of the divine. Soren Kierkegaard says of love in his book *Works of Love*, "To love another in spite of his weaknesses and errors and imperfections is not perfect love. No, to love is to find him lovable in spite of and together with his weakness and errors and imperfections."[128] In his work *The Elements of True Piety*, Gottfried Leibniz says of love, "To love is to be delighted by the happiness of someone, or to experience pleasure upon the happiness of another. I define this as true love. Those who think they can love only the people they prefer do not love at all. Love discovers truths about individuals that others cannot see."[129] The ethic of love cannot be autonomous because it is about denying the self. The ethic of love is not about heteronomous utility either as love is about serving the minority. The Christian view of the ethic of love is about leaving the 99 to find the 1. It is about taking care of the fatherless and the widow. Thomas Aquinas says in the Summa Theologiae, "And therefore man is reckoned to be good or bad chiefly according to the plea-sure of the human will; since that man is good and virtuous, who takes pleasure in the works of virtue; and that man evil, who takes pleasure in evil works."[130] I want to be the kind of person who loves those I disagree with, even those I think are full of hate, even those whom I think are bigoted, even the serial killer, that is an ethic I have no need to doubt. This does not mean I think loving them means to remove consequences, it just means I find value in their existence anyway.

No matter how many doubts I have had over the years about existence itself, my faith, the Bible, or evil I have never doubted the Christian view of what love is. I am not talking about how Christians throughout history or even today live this ethic out. I grieve like a lot of other doubters Christians poor track record in living out the Christian ethic of love, but this does not take away the beauty of that ethic. The most famous verse in the New Tes-tament is John 3:16 "for God so loved the world that he gave his only son that whosoever believes in him shall not perish but have eternal life." Next to that is probably 1 John 4:8" … God is love." Finally, 1 Corinthians 13:4–7 is the most beautiful descriptor of what love is:

Love is patient and kind. Love is not jealous or boastful or proud or rude. It does not demand its own way. It is not irritable, and it keeps no record of being wronged. It does not rejoice about injustice but rejoices whenever the truth wins out. Love never gives up, never loses faith, is always hopeful, and endures through every circumstance.

The apostle Paul in Romans 12:13–20 beautifully articulates the Christian philosophy regarding the ethic of love:

Share with the Lord's people who are in need. Practice hospitality.

Bless those who persecute you; bless and do not curse.

Rejoice with those who rejoice; mourn with those who mourn.

Live in harmony with one another.

Do not be proud but be willing to associate with people of low position.

Do not be conceited.

Do not repay anyone evil for evil.

Be careful to do what is right in the eyes of everyone.

If it is possible, as far as it depends on you, live at peace with everyone.

Do not take revenge, my dear friends, but leave room for God's wrath, for it is written: "It is mine to avenge; I will repay," says the Lord.

On the contrary: "If your enemy is hungry, feed him; if he is thirsty, give him something to drink. In doing this, you will heap burning coals on his head."

Regardless of where my doubts or beliefs have been at different times in my life. No matter what I am currently deconstructing from or reconstructing to I have always known that if I could live out 1 Corinthians 13:4–7 I could make both my life and others lives better. I think Christians, Atheists and Agnostics alike would agree that the world would be better if the principles outlined above could be lived out in each of us. The Christian ethic of love is obviously theonomous, it isn't something we invented, it's not about social utility; it is an artifact of a higher dimension (a transcendent metaphysical dimension); love transcends space, time and matter. In her work *Revelations of Divine Love*, 14th century Christian Mystic Julian of Norwich said, "there is a force of love moving through the universe that holds us fast and will never let us go."[131] In fact, the Christian view of the ethic of love not only is a beautiful call to how I should love but it also categorizes me as infinitely loved. Brennan Manning in his book *Abba's Child* details it in the poetic fashion when he says, "being the beloved is our identity, the core of our existence. It is not merely a lofty thought, an inspiring idea, or one name among many. It is the name by which God knows us and the way He relates to us."[132]

The Self and The Nature of Truth

In the movie *Transcendence*

Max Walters

I spent my life trying to reduce the brain to a series of electrical impulses. I failed. Human emotion, it can contain illogical conflict. [Humans] can love someone, and yet hate the things that they've done. Machine can't reconcile that.

Later in the movie the following dialogue takes place.

Evelyn

We can upload his consciousness. We can save him ...

Max Walters

Not like this ... Assuming that this works, if we miss anything, a thought, a childhood memory, how would you know whom we're dealing with.

DR. WILL CASTER

You're surprised to see me, Joseph?

JOSEPH TAGGER

Hmmm, that depends. Can you prove that you are self-aware?

DR. WILL CASTER

Well that's an interesting question. Can you prove to me that you are?[133]

The movie *Dead Man Walking* deals with Matthew Poncelet who is sentenced to death for committing murder. He writes to Sister Helen Prejean to privately talk to her. While Poncelet's co-murderer avoided the death penalty thanks to good lawyers, Matthew did not. Sister Helen and Matthew form a deep bond as he awaits his execution. The following dialogue speaks to selfhood and the soul.

SISTER HELEN PREJEAN

Show me some respect, Matthew.

MATTHEW PONCELET

Why? 'Cause you're a nun?

SISTER HELEN PREJEAN

Because I'm a person."

†††

CLYDE PERCY

How can you stand next to him?

SISTER HELEN PREJEAN

Mr. Percy, I'm just trying to follow the example of Jesus, who said that a person is not as bad as his worst deed.

CLYDE PERCY

This is not a person. This is an animal."

†††

SISTER HELEN PREJEAN

You are a son of God.

Matthew Poncelet

Thank you. I've never been called a son of God before. I've been called a son of a you-know-what plenty of times, but I've never been called a son of God."

†††

Sister Helen Prejean

"I want the last face you see in this world to be the face of love, so you look at me when they do this thing. I'll be the face of love for you."[134]

Who am I? That is a question humans have asked since we began to ask questions. There is a question behind the question of "who am I?" The more foundational question is what it means to be an "I." What does it mean to be a self? If consciousness is a farce, then so is the self. If humans are just biological material, if we are just mammals, then how can that mammal reasonably use first-person pronouns? Scientifically there is no "I" or "me," the individual is not real. Only the physical matter of "I" that is leading "me" to believe there is "I" (a "me" the material naturalist denies is real); "I" does not exist. "My" brain is lying to "me"; "I" has no mind. In other words, material naturalism eliminates the idea of the self by which all humans daily operate. The mind is a construct of the brain. Without the metaphysical, there is no consciousness. The existential and moral implications of material naturalism are dire and, therefore, significant in terms of unfavorable influence on contemporary mindsets.[135] For example, when Daniel M. Wegner writes in his book *The Illusion of Conscious Will,* "contrary to each individual's own introspective feeling that he/she consciously initiates such voluntary acts" as a statement out of his own individual consciousness about a book he (as a self) wrote, I would posit he does not know what the word consciousness means.[136] Is it not fair to assume that if Mr. Wegner's hypothesis is correct then every time, he uses the word "I" in reference to himself is he not being self-refuting to his own assertions? This begs the question what is the self. What is selfhood? Some might say that selfhood is simply consciousness, but this cannot be the case otherwise every time I go to sleep or lose consciousness (due to anesthesia or low blood sugar, or fear, etc.) I lose selfhood. If selfhood is simply consciousness, then every time I lose consciousness, I am no longer a self. I am no longer an individual. The implications of this false equivalence fallacy also mean humans in a coma are no longer people and newborn babies are not yet people. The concept of the self and selfhood are much more complex and deeper than being reduced to consciousness. Some may also define a self as a living person, but this reduces selfhood to laws of nature. Material naturalism renders true actual selfhood as impossible. If material naturalism's reduction is wrong and the mind is more than the brain, then the mind is more than biology. If the singular self (me, you) is indeed a self, then is it not reasonable to think there that selfhood is a metaphysical reality? Would there not be the potential for the self to go beyond temporality? Phenomenologically I have never experienced self as anything other than embodied. My embodied self will obviously die. Death of the body is objectively true. If however there is an actual "me" beyond the brain that is a metaphysical reality. If natural law is all there is then I am confined to space, time, and matter (biology) and there is no actual "me." Richard Dawkins wrote of the God delusion, if he and other material naturalists are correct there is also a "me" delusion. However, if I am an actual self then that is a metaphysical reality. Metaphysical reality is not confined by space, time, or matter. The self would be beyond material biology. If I have or am a self which is separate from space, time, and matter then do I have the potentiality of being immortal? I think it is reasonable to believe so. If the self is a metaphysical reality and yet all selves (you and I) are contingently existing, then the self transcends physical being and has the potential to be immortal. The self is the soul, a contingent soul that is made in the image of a prototype. Replicas are not exact, but they are reasonable facsimiles of the prototype. The contingent self being non-physical must be made in the image of a necessarily existing causal agent, who is non-physical, has volition, and whose essence is soul. In the Septuagint the book Wisdom of Solomon 2:23 states, "For God created man to be immortal, and made him to be an image of his own eternity. The righteous, because they are made in the image of God, can rest in the full hope of eternal life." C.S. Lewis in his fictional work the *Screwtape Letters* says the following through the demonic mentor character Screwtape to his mentee Wormwood, "Humans are amphibians ... half spirit and half animal ... as spirits they belong to the eternal world, but as animals they inhabit time. This means that while their spirit can be directed to an eternal object, their bodies, passions, and imaginations are in continual change, for to be in time, means to change."[137] Humans are both physical and spiritual, an embodied soul that exists within the material world but is not reducible to the material world. This does not mean nor am I asserting a permanent disembodied existence of souls beyond the material world. There is a symbiotic and reciprocal relationship between the self and the body. I am only stating the self is a metaphysical reality that is not reducible to the material world. If there is a higher order it is the metaphysical self and not the physical body. The self is of higher order because it is metaphysical, but this does not mean the body is evil or bad. The body and the soul are inextricably linked, and both are good, i.e. the classical synthesis.

THE PHENOMENOLOGY OF THE SELF

Humans cannot reduce ourselves to the scientific/objective world as we are both things in the world and experience the world from within ourselves. Science is always conducted by a scientist. There is no way to reduce reality to its parts which is the flaw of empiricism (modern worldview) and rationalism (postmodernism). Phenomenology is clarifying the balance of rationalism and empiricism. We both experience the world as well as sense the world that is objective. The overarching theme of the world is the interaction between these two. We should resist reducing consciousness to one or the other.

Where rationalism can easily drift into the ditch of total subjectivity or relativism (what is true for you is your truth and what is true for me is my truth) and empiricism drift into the ditch of reducing the mind to brain with the out there world being the only truth (material naturalism). Phenomenology is philosophical middle ground. Phenomenology is a method for talking about the human experience and perception. Phenomenology asks can we step back from the experience of experience to think about what it means to experience the experience? How can we reflect upon the subjective experience of being an individual while not denying objective reality? In modern culture truth has been reduced to the objective (even while being conducted by subjective beings) or to complete subjectivity. Truth is more than objective or subjective. Phenomenology is acknowledging humans are singular in consciousness and therefore subjective while maintaining there is a real objective world to be known. So how does a finite singular consciousness make sense of an objective world without falling into either ditch of empiricism nor the ditch of rationalism? "[Phenomenology] recovers the wider whole, the greater context... it considers dimensions the other sciences abstract from."[138] Phenomenology uses suspension of belief as opposed to Cartesian doubt in order to help stay away from the ditches. It attempts to avoid the solipsism of the self only being able to know the self. "The most important contribution phenomenology has made to culture and the intellectual life is to have validated the truth of prephilosophical life, experience, and thinking."[139]

We are never conscious without being conscious of something. When someone states they are an "objective person" this is false,(even when it is Richard Dawkins or Neil Tyson Degrasse), yet there are objective conditions on which self-perception depends. Maurice Merleau-Ponty in his book *Phenomenology of Perception* has this to offer, "From this, it follows that there is, in principle, a point-by-point correspondence and a constant connection between the stimulus and the elemental perception." Consciousness is always relating to something. Consciousness is always conscious of, even Descartes determined that he was because he was conscious of having thought. While consciousness is always singular and individual and thus subjective, consciousness is conscious of an objective real world. "If we do not have a real world in common, then we do not enter into a life of reason, evidence and truth."[140] Your consciousness is subjective because it is made up of your perspective, perceptions, memories anticipations, imagination, personality, and soul BUT you must be conscious of something objective otherwise there is not collective reality. The mind and brain are distinct but not separate.

We, no matter who "we" are, are never free of the self. The psychology of perception is loaded with philosophical presuppositions. The self is the interplay between remembered, perceived, and projected. Displacements of self- where one can imagine, remember, or anticipate the self-free of the constraints of time or place. We are never free of what Merleau-Ponty calls the lived world. Even science cannot ontologically escape this subjectivity. Science is a second-order expression. It is analogous (loosely but still) to Aristotle's concept of first and second mover. In this case, the first mover is the mind, the self. The first mover in human endeavors is always subjective. In other words, no matter what endeavor of knowledge we must move through the subjective to get to the objective. The empirical can only be seen through the rational. Thus when "we" describe the world through the senses we are describing the objective through the subjective, or the empirical through the intellectual. This does not mean "we" can know nothing beyond our own subjectivity, as Merleau-Ponty states in his book *Phenomenology of Perception*, "This is to acknowledge that sensation must be sought beneath all qualitative content, since in order to be distinguished as two colors, red and green—even if lacking a precise location—must already form some scene before me and thus cease to be part of myself."[141] Reality is the interplay of the objective world being perceived by the subjective self, always already. It has "never not" been this way and "we" can never rise above or escape it. We cannot escape the singularity of our consciousness in which we analyze the world and yet there is an objective world that comes at us and has always been speaking to us, impressing upon us. C.S. Lewis in *The Screwtape Letters* through demonic mentor Screwtape to his mentee Wormwood states, "Always remember, that they are animals and that whatever their bodies do affects their souls."[142]

Dr. Christopher Ben Simpson offers, "The world is not what I think, but what I live; I am open to the world, I unquestionably communicate with it, but I do not possess it, it is inexhaustible."[143] I have my experience with the world, the signs and symbols of connections I find in it. There are, however, significations and meanings which I cannot fully understand empirically through the senses. I can rationally understand through historical recounts and imagine what that must have been like, but I did not and cannot experience it through my body, so the reduction cannot be complete. I cannot wholly take a philosophical attitude. We do interact with an objective world, and we communicate about it analogously with each other in our intersubjectivity but never in a completely univocal way for two primary reasons:

1. The world/universe in inexhaustible. We will never fully understand nor be able to communicate the universe to one another. This does not mean there is no knowledge or that knowledge cannot be communicated at all.

2. We are contained by the nature of being a subjective self. Our experience of truth will never fully coincide with another subjective selves interaction with it. This does not mean there is not truth only that we each interact with truth as ourselves and thus we can never communicate it wholly to one another.

Once there is shared meaning and signification, the symbolism to a degree becomes shared, which creates a cultural identity. There is a historical context to the meaning. Merleau-Ponty claims that the "most important lesson of the reduction is the impossibility of a complete reduction."[144] I cannot escape my subjectivity. I am historically sedimented by demographics (race, gender, geography), family of origin, and cultural history and influences that frame my 'lived world.' "We must recognize a sort of sedimentation of our life: when the attitude toward the world has been confirmed often enough, it becomes privileged for us."[145]

While you and I may share a great deal of intersubjectivity being from the same culture, living in the same time of history, and speaking the same language, and have many aspects of shared meaning, that meaning never reaches harmonious univocality. There will always be limits to the shared meaning. There will always be points where a word, picture, song, phrase… any aspect of your lived world, where you and I cannot view the truth the same. Simply because we cannot rid ourselves of ourselves. While this may seem like a negative, I believe God actually made us all as individuals so that we can inform the collective.

I cannot truly complete the epoch of phenomenology and block biases and assumptions to explain a phenomenon in terms of its inherent system of meaning. This is where the self and worldview collide, this is where subjective truth and objective truth intermingle. I cannot rid myself of the meaning it has to ME. If I take a philosophical attitude, it shifts focus away from what I have when reflecting upon all the intentionalities that occur within a given truth in the lived world and yet I still cannot wholly depart from myself. I can never engage with ultimate reality apart from myself. To summarize the two sections on the self, the self is metaphysical and cannot be reduced to the body. The self is transcendent and made in the image of God, but the entire human experience is as an embodied soul. Therefore, humans are not in an epistemic position to speak of the self as anything but embodied. We have only lived as metaphysical selves in a physical world, but we are not reducible to the physical world. As Sting wrote when he was still in the Police, "we are spirits in the material world." I/we should aim to step back and "transcend the world ... [while] remaining part of it."[146]

THE SELF AND THE SOUL

For all intents and purposes the soul (as I defined it) and the self are univocal. The understanding of the soul has had a number of interpretations throughout philosophy. The way I am going to use the term soul it will be synonymous with immortal essence. Immortal essence is the metaphysical reality that makes someone fundamentally who they are. Paul Copan in *Loving Wisdom* describes the soul as, "a substance with characteristics that just can't be physical; thoughts, feelings, intentionality, the 'first person' experience."[147] Aquinas describes a soul through an Aristotelian lens, "The soul is the first act of an organized body having life potentially within it." The soul is the reason humans have innate value beyond utility. Simon Weil in *Gravity and Grace* says, "the soul is the human being considered as having a value in itself."[148] Since God is simple and not reducible to the divine attributes and since God is the prototype of the soul, human selves/souls are a facsimile of the prototype soul thus it stands to reason those human souls are simple as well. Saint Augustine says that God is the "life of the soul." Phenomenologically the soul/body union is direct. We experience our soul and our body simultaneously as ourselves. It is analogous to the hypostatic union in Christ. While He is perfectly human and perfectly divine at the same time, our selfhood is both the metaphysical soul and the physical body. This happens while not reducing the body or the soul to one another. Humans share our physical realities with all living things, we grow, we need nutrition, we reproduce. Humans share movement, sense perception and appetite with other animals. Humans do not share free will, the need for meaning, or imagination with any other animal on earth. Humans do not share an immortal essence with anything else in creation. There is something unique and distinct about humans from all other creation, this is the classical synthesis, it is human exceptionalism (see discussion questions for Part 1).

Maurice Merleau Ponty states, "the body is the acquired dialectic soil upon which the higher 'formation' is accomplished, and the soul is the meaning which is then established."[149] The soul gives the meaning to existence. Body and soul together are what we think of when we think of ourselves. They form a whole of our existence in the lived world. Our souls are embodied and interact with an objective world. In our interactions with the world, we encounter others, and we recognize other autonomous selves or souls because of the kinship of one immortal nature recognizing another. I am not asserting a collective soul (philosophically or a terrible '90s grunge band) but rather a singular subjective self or soul recognizing a likeness of another subjective self. This opens up an intersubjectivity, we share common ground. Humans share the fact that we are made in the image of God. Maurice Merleau-Ponty in his work *Signs* puts it this way, "others are not fictions (like hyper-rationalism) but 'my twins' 'flesh of my flesh'; though we have different lives, different thoughts, we share something of the world of perception."[150] In the simplest terms I share a soul with no one, my soul is singular in nature but the fact that I have a soul (made in the image of God- the prototype) means every soul and myself share a likeness that I share with nothing else in all of creation.

- Phenomenology- According to the Cambridge Dictionary of Philosophy phenomenology is "the study of essences, but also attempts to blend essences back into existence" (Audi, 665). According to the Stanford Encyclopedia of Philosophy, "Phenomenology is the study of structures of consciousness as experienced from the first-person point of view."

- Second-order expression- Extrapolation of a qualitative first order expression and reducing it to its quantifiable bits.
- Epoch- According to Edmund Husserl the father of phenomenology, it is the negative move whereby we bracket the world.
- Immortal Essence- The metaphysical reality that makes someone fundamentally who they are.
- Hypostatic Union- Jesus Christ as being fully God and fully man. Christ having two natures.

THE NATURE OF TRUTH

Truth as a general concept can be defined as accurately aligning with the actualized state of affairs or the property of agreeing with what is the case. Humans have been wrestling with what truth is as far back as can be traced. The questioning of what truth actual is, is not a new phenomenon. Socrates taught that truth is relative while Plato taught that truth is objective. Aristotle said of Plato, "Plato is dear to me, but dearer still is truth." Pilate and Jesus had the following dialogue in John 18:37–38,

"So, you are a king, then!" said Pilate.

Jesus answered, "you say that I am a king. In fact, that's the reason I was born. I was born and came into the world to be a witness to the truth. Everyone who is on the side of truth listens to me."

"What is truth?" Pilate replied.

People have questioned the nature of truth for so long and with such veracity because it is so very important and so very complex. Aristotle in *On the Heavens* said, "the least initial deviation from the truth is multiplied later a thousand-fold" (Aristotle, 10). The consequences of not reaching for truth are substantial. We must do our best to understand truth. All forms of truth by nature exclude false options. In chapter three of *Mere Christianity*, C.S. Lewis states, "As in arithmetic—there is only one right answer to a sum, and all other answers are wrong: but some of the wrong answers are much nearer being right than others."[151] All truth claims have innated and necessary to them the exclusion of aspects.

There are different kinds of truth: subjective, relative, objective, transcendent and the whole truth (or what I will use synonymously with 'ultimate reality', what Maurice Merleau-Ponty called translucent truth or truth from every angle).[152] It is correct to assert that truth is not always reducible to binary options and is far more nuanced than many people treat it. However, truth is never all-inclusive, not everything is true. Once you get beyond personal perception and experience, what is true for you is no longer your truth. A concept or thing can be subjectively true to you but that does not make it true for everyone else. Subjective truth is yours, all other forms of truth are shared. For example, if I do not like chocolate, that is not in relation to anything else. My dislike of chocolate is an absolute truth for me as an individual. Even subjective truth is necessarily exclusive and narrowed to the individual, as all truth is perceived through the body. It is correct that all truth is perceived subjectively but just because all truth is perceived subjectively by the individual does not mean all truth is subjective. Subjective truth is just one kind of truth and one aspect of the whole truth (ultimate reality). A couple of very basic examples are that you may be convinced that 2 + 2 is 5. Subjectively that is true for you, but this does not make it true in any other way. Every other kind of truth (even transcendent) is shared. It may be true to you that 2 +2 equals 5 but it is not objectively true. A subjective truth can (and often is) absolute truth to the individual but objectively false to everyone else. The man in the mental hospital who believes he is Santa Claus is convinced of the absolute nature of his identity and in that regard, it is true for him but to the rest of the world he is rightly committed under permanent psychiatric care. It is important that subjective truth is not relegated to merely the trivial however as this robs each of us of the truth of our lived experience. If subjective truth is of no importance, then our testimonies, our romances, our mountain tops and valleys aren't true. Subjective truth is much more than opinion, subjective truth is our experiences and our perceptions (Part 5 of the book will focus on just this part of truth.) My life and lived experiences are my truth and they are absolutely true in my perception of it. Conversely truth cannot be reduced to the subjective. The reduction of truth down to individual experiences and instances fails as subjective truth is absolute only to the individual. Transcendent truth comes through revelation from God to the individual soul but because God is one and the same and does not change transcendent truth is also a shared truth though it is perceived subjectively. Transcendent truth can be perceived through nature and other individuals as indirect divine revelation, but ultimately transcendent truth is always communicated through divine revelation whether direct or indirect.

Yes, even transcendent truth is perceived subjectively. In the classical synthesis of the Christian worldview the Holy Spirit communicates to the Christian directly to the soul, as well as through the Bible. This however is still ultimately filtered through the Christians body (the mind, senses, etc.) and is subjective. If this were not the case all Christians would agree perfectly on doctrine and theology. If God does not change and God's character is the same always then theology that is based in ultimate reality is in agreement at all times. If transcendent truths where perfectly understood, then all Christians everywhere would agree on all doctrines and theology. Paul affirms this when he says in 1 Corinthians 13:9–12, "What we know now is not complete. What we prophesy now is not perfect. But when what is complete comes, the things that are not complete will pass away."

Objective truth is perceived through the body and therefore encountered subjectively. However, this does not change the fact that those individual selves live in an objective world. Intersubjective truth and objective truth come to the individual from the world. There is a lived world in which all individuals treat as though it is there. The lived world is the individuals encounter with the objective word or other subjective individuals.

Nature of Truth

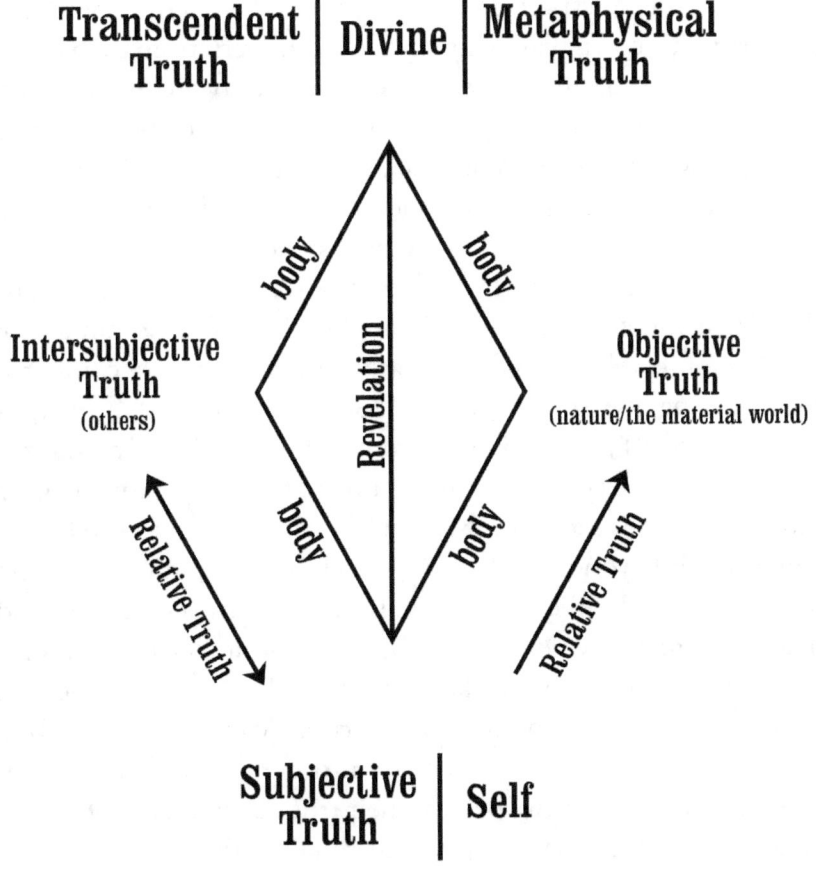

Relative truth compares the intersubjectivity between variables. For example, the notion of what is true for me may not be true for you works if you are talking about relative comparisons, like whether ketchup should go on a hot dog or not. I may find it true that ketchup goes on a hotdog (subjective truth) while you may not (subjective truth for you). The connection between these two subjective truths is a relative. There is intersubjectivity between subjective perspectives, which is relational. Relative truth is very valuable. Intersubjectivity, potentially and often does, allow for a comparison of a thesis or relation. The comparison gives rise to antithesis (deconstruction) and then perhaps higher synthesis (reconstruction). In plain language humans learn from each other. We can obtain a higher understanding of truth by interacting with other subjective selves. There is nothing negative about relative truth. However, this does not mean that all truth is relative. That is relativism. Relativism holds the idea that truth claims have an implicit relationship to a domain or instance.[153]

A relativist might agree that truth excludes but would deny this exclusion could be broadly applied beyond the domain or instance of its relation. While relative truth exists only compared to something else, subjective truth belongs to the thinking subject (the individual) and is distinct from a thing itself.[154] Therefore a relative truth is exclusive only in relation to the comparative, while a subjective truth is exclusive to the individual perspective. A relativist denies truth beyond the domain, which is both reductionist and self-refuting.[155] While worldviews from religious perspectives and material naturalistic perspectives both (including scientism, biologism, and psychologism) stake claim to THE truth; a postmodern relativism worldview counters these claims with the assertion that all truth is only true in the instance it occurs. While modernism and religious worldviews believe their truth claims to be absolute, relativists believe those truth claims to be particular to a cultural framework and thus ultimately false.[156] Tim Keller states, "they do the very thing they forbid other communities to do."[157]

Copan advances that relativists are hypocritical in claiming there is no truth beyond the instance or domain. This view takes away regard for the absolute nature of subjective truth to the individual and eliminates objective truth (and transcendent truth) entirely. When claiming that there is no objective truth, relativists are making an objective truth claim. It is correct that each person interacts with objective truth subjectively and only subjectively (as long as humans are singular selves, humans only have the option of being subjective individually and intersubjective with each other), but this does not mean there is no objective truth. Paul Copan demonstrates the reduction of truth down to only relative truth as hypocritical when he states, but "relavist(s) insist that no one is wrong (unless you disagree with the relativist)."[158] Copan elaborates, "If truth is just a matter of perspective, the relativist is either saying something trivial or self-contradictory."[159] In summary objective truth is from the world to the individual body, perceived subjectively. Objective truth is measurable, observable, replicable, and shared by all of nature.

Intersubjective truth is two or more subjective singular individual bodies communicating about their subjective view of truth through their body (relative truth; relating to one another) AND about objective truth through their bodies (senses, brain, etc.). Transcendent truth is metaphysical and directly communicated from God to the individual's soul AS WELL AS through other subjective individuals' bodies (words, thoughts, touch, etc.) OR the objective truth of the world (nature) to the individual subjective body. Even more plainly, I can learn an aspect of the whole truth/ ultimate reality from observing the world (science, nature, etc.) I can learn an aspect of the whole truth/ultimate reality from other people (their experience, stories, books, movies, hugs, etc.). I can learn an aspect of the whole truth/ultimate reality by my own perceptions, reasoning, thoughts, etc. I can learn an aspect of the whole truth/ultimate reality from the direct revelation of God through the Holy Spirit to my soul. God can also speak through nature (objective truth) or other people (scripture (the authors), other books, movies, my wife, kids, friends, sermons, TED talks, etc. All of these different kinds of truth are a part of the whole truth/ultimate reality. Humans will never be in a situation where we can see or understand the whole truth/ultimate reality, only a causal agent who is omniscient can understand the whole truth/ultimate reality. The whole truth is absolute, there are no gray areas in the whole truth.

The problem is that humans will never be in an epistemic position to be able to ascertain the whole truth/ultimate reality. Again, when we are dealing with the big questions, we humans are dealing in plausibility and probability, we should not reduce truth to one kind of truth as we are not omniscient. We should always be humble and respect someone's beliefs. However, respecting someone's beliefs does not require that we affirm that person's beliefs as corresponding to the whole truth/ultimate reality. This is especially the case considering the whole truth/ultimate reality. Remember just as there are different kinds of truth, all truth necessarily excludes beliefs that are false options in comparison to the ultimate reality. I am not advocating universalism nor religious syncretism (more on this subject in Part 4 of the book). Going back to the C.S. Lewis quote at the beginning of this section, some answers are nearer right than others, but there can only be one correct answer in matters where the options are mutually exclusive regardless of our experience and perceptions. The interplay of subjective truth, relative truth, objective truth, and transcendent truth all play a role in the connection to ultimate reality/whole truth. The whole truth/ultimate reality is truth from every angle, the highest form of truth, having the necessary condition of self-evidence. The whole truth IS ultimate reality, absolute in nature and self-evident. The whole truth/ultimate reality is what accurately aligns with the actualized state of affairs once all other kinds of truth are reported completely. Maximus the Confessor in *Ambigua* puts it this way, God "who is and who becomes all for all beings, through whom everything is and becomes but who by himself never is nor becomes." Ultimate reality is not contained by any form of truth but contains all of them and the only one who could possibly access the whole truth is an omniscient God.

- Truth- accurately aligning with the actualized state of affairs; the property of agreeing with what is the case.
- Subjective truth- an inward truth based upon a person's perspective, feelings, or opinions Soren Kierkegaard defined subjective truth as, "it is an uncertainty that cannot be solved objectively."
- Intersubjectivity- Conscious attribution of intentional acts between two or more individuals. It is when we learn from, empathize with, or put ourselves in someone else's shoes.
- Relative truth- Compares the intersubjectivity between variables. Relative truth is in relation to instances.
- Relativism- there are no universal truths or intrinsic characteristics to the lived world.
- Objective truth- Things in the material natural world that are true for everyone. Found in mathematics and science. Ex. 2 + 2 is 4 no matter what anyone thinks. This is objectively true.
- Transcendent Truth- Metaphysical truth; truth discovered through divine revelation. In Christendom truth that is revealed through the Holy Spirit and Holy Scripture.
- Whole truth (ultimate reality)- Truth that is ultimate, final, complete and supreme over all knowledge and any other minds of truth.
- Omniscient- having unlimited understanding or knowledge.

The Nature of Truth graph illustrates the workings of the nature of truth. There are the four points of the subjective self (subjective truth), the natural world (objective truth), other subjective selves (intersubjective truth), and then Transcendent metaphysical truth (divine revelation). The lines connecting the points represent the human body. Other than direct revelation and subjective truth, all other forms of truth are perceived through the body (i.e. the five senses, the brain). We perceive objective truth through the body. A tree is objectively there but we still perceive it subjectively through the eyes. Or a math equation is true whether our brain can apprehend it or not, but we comprehend math through the brain as seen through the eyes or heard through the ears. We experience the objective world relatively. We relate to the objective world subjectively. The natural world does not speak back relatively, as this would be contrary to its essence. We perceive intersubjective truth through the body as well. We relate to other subjective selves through the senses and through the brain. Intersubjective truth happens in a reciprocal manner of relating and comparing subjective perspectives. Notice that for both objective truth and intersubjective truth we can indirectly receive transcendent truth. We can learn about divine reality (God) through nature as well as through others. I have quoted a number of authors, philosophers and theologians here that I have learned a great deal from (even though I have never met them in person). I would assert many of them have communicated transcendent truth. For those who believe the Bible contains transcendent truth, is this not partially what happens when we read Paul's epistles? Are we not learning transcendent (divine) truth through Paul's words and the Holy Spirit's direct revelation to Paul? Nature speaks of transcendent truth as well. Second century Christian writer and early apologist Tertullian once said, "We conclude that God is known first through nature, and then again, more particularly, by doctrine; by nature in His works, and by doctrine in His revealed word." Additionally, the Psalms speak to this as well, Psalm 19:1 says, "The heavens

declare the glory of God; the skies proclaim the work of his hands."
Psalm 104: 24–25 states, "O Lord, what a variety of things you
have made! In wisdom, you have made them all. The earth is full
of your creatures. Here is the ocean, vast and wide, teeming with
life of every kind, both large and small."

Transcendent truth is indirectly communicated through objective truth (the natural world) and through intersubjective truth
(other people, books, movies, music) but it is also communicated
directly to the individual through divine revelation (God) and this
is not through the body but directly to the self (the soul). It may
seem at first transcendent truth is purely subjective, but this is not
the case because transcendent truth can also be indirectly communicated through the natural world and through other people.
It is this triple constraint that makes sure that transcendent truth
can be discerned clearly. If a person tells you proposition X about
divine reality (God) but it does not seem right to you, and it does
not fit with the objective world, plus it does not align with what
other people you trust are saying then it is prudent to red flag
proposition X until further information is gained. The same triple
constraint applies if you feel God has told you something directly
but it does not line up with what others who share your worldview
believe, and it does not line up with the natural world it might be
a good idea to question if what you felt you heard from God was
from God. This does not mean that God does not speak directly
to people but there are checks and balances that the objective
world and other people provide to confirm direct revelation. This
is confirmed even in the Bible. The apostle Paul states in Galatians
1:11–12, "Dear brothers and sisters, I want you to understand that
the gospel message I preach is not based on mere human reasoning.
"I received my message from no human source, and no one taught
me. Instead, I received it by direct revelation from Jesus Christ." He
is confirming that the message was from divine revelation, but he
goes on to say (even he says he did not hurry to do it. 14 years later)
in Galatians 2:2, "I went there because God revealed to me that I

should go. While I was there, I met privately with those considered to be leaders of the church and shared with them the message I had been preaching to the Gentiles. I wanted to make sure that we were in agreement, for fear that all my efforts had been wasted and I was running the race for nothing." Transcendent truth is not completely subjective as some would assert, there are checks and balances to ensure transcendent truth can be discerned accurately.

The totality of the graph is the whole truth and ultimate reality. The totality of the graph is all truth, from every angle, not bound by time, space, or matter. Truth that is not hindered by perspective or aspect or interpretation.

CONCLUSION

In *The Abolition of Man*, C.S. Lewis declares, "If nothing is self-evident, nothing can be proved. Similarly, if nothing is obligatory for its own sake, nothing is obligatory at all."[160] Omniscience is reserved for a causal agent that is necessary, self-evident and self-existing, i.e. God. God is the only one who could be cable or have access to all the data, to every kind of truth at all times even separate from time, space and matter. Either there is no ultimate cohesive reality or there is God. Either there is no meaning or there is God. Truth is either only that which can be empirically proven, making consciousness, love, meaning, etc., a farce or there is God. Either there is not truth at all or there is God. St. Bonaventure says of God and his connection to the whole truth/ultimate reality, "By God's power, presence, and essence, God is the One whose center is everywhere and whose circumference is nowhere. God exists uncircumscribed in everything." Truth cannot always be reduced to binary options, it is often much more nuanced and complicated than binary options, but then there are other times once you get to the end of things that it is binary. The truth is there is either nihilism or there is God. The more we experience our worldviews the more they expand. The more we understand our perceptions of ourselves, both our perceptions and our understanding of truth should expand as well. Like Han Solo we may start with the limited worldview that was constructed for us but find ourselves through experience and new information deconstructing that worldview for a more expansive one. Too often we allow our doubts to cause us to run from the complex nature of truth and we end up reducing our worldview, our concepts of the self and the nature of truth instead of expanding them. Falling into modernism or postmodernism as a worldview reduces how we perceive the self and the nature of truth. Instead of being a soul that relates to both nature and God, we become purely material and biological. Instead of truth being physical and metaphysical, truth is reduced to either only the physical or to not existing at all. I ultimately reject this as too narrow and limited of a view. Meaning is inevitable. Like Mr. Holland if there is no meaning then what are we reading and writing about? We all live as if there is truth, we all live as if there is meaning, we all live as though there is an ultimate reality (the whole truth) so I conclude there is, living in the paradox and mystery of this reality is not always comfortable but it is the most comprehensive worldview. G.K Chesterton said this in his book *Orthodoxy*,

"Mysticism keeps men sane. As long as you have mystery you have health; when you destroy mystery you create morbidity. The ordinary man has always been sane because the ordinary man has always been a mystic. He has permitted the twilight. He has always had one foot in earth and the other in fairyland. He has always left himself free to doubt his gods; but (unlike the agnostic of today) free also to believe in them. He has always cared more for truth than for consistency. If he saw two truths that seemed to contradict each other, he would take the two truths and contradiction along with them. His spiritual sight is stereoscopic, like his physical sight: he sees two different pictures at once and yet sees all the better for that. Thus, he has always believed that there was such a thing as fate, but such a thing as free will also. Thus, he believes that children were indeed the kingdom of heaven, but nevertheless ought to be obedient to the kingdom of earth. He admired youth because it was young and age because it was not. It is exactly this balance of apparent contradictions that has been the whole buoyancy of the healthy man. The whole secret of mysticism is this: that man can understand everything by the help of what he does not understand. The morbid logician seeks to make everything lucid and succeeds in making everything mysterious. The mystic allows one thing to be mysterious, and everything else becomes lucid." (Chesterton, 16–17)[161]

The conflicting worldviews I received as a young child between the God my grandmother read me about and the one I saw at the hell fire and brimstone church left me confused. Always with a looming feeling that somehow no matter what I did I would never be good enough to receive God's grace. What I did not do for a long time was question the truth of that message. That was presented as the divine truth, and I accepted it as so, it was my worldview about God. In the hell fire and brimstone message of legalism God is mad, nature is bad, and humans are worse. There's no mystery, no beauty, no romance, no grace in the hell fire and brimstone image of God. As a child Brother Mayne was the disseminator of truth and there was no room for truth or perspective apart from him. As I grew and my worldview too my experience expanded, and the hell fire and brimstone God became problematic for me. I didn't like that God much and I knew that God didn't like me. I had to deconstruct and reach a new conclusion about the relationship between God, the world and me. The God I found is a God of justice but justice out of love not justice that is hoping for and finding pleasure in the failure of his beloved. I had to reconstruct that humans are made in God's image and have a divine spark, sons and daughters of Abraham, and that nature is fallen but good.

I concluded and reconstructed to the classical synthesis of Christianity that holds the tension of the mystic nature of things is the more comprehensive and expansive worldview and also that a peanut butter sandwich is delicious when dipped into chili.

Without End

V.1
You're uncreated and undefeated
Words can't contain your transcendence
While everything else is wasting away
You hold the darkness, and you are the day

V.2
You're universal and you are unique
You're absolute but in everything
You are unknowable but make yourself known
You have no rival you are God

Ch.
The greatest thing about you is you came to save
The greatest thing about you is you defeated the
The greatest thing about you is you call by name
You're the Center and the Circumference
Love with no beginning and without end

V.3
You are the Cause and the effects
Bigger than reason beyond intellect
The only true creative, with no need fill
Father, Son, Spirit you create out of will

V.4
You pre-exist the nothing and eternity
You're infinite and your right here with me
You are self-existing and self-evident
Time does not have you no you have it[162]

Discussion Questions

1. What are the implications of what Han said regarding a "power holding together good and evil?"

2. How does Han's worldview evolve over time? Do you think his worldview expands or contracts?

3. How does Mr. Holland's quote speak to the nature of what it means to be human? How do he and Principal Wolters display a different worldview?

4. Why do you think the church often portrays deconstruction in a negative light? Should the church want people to deconstruct? What about people who have faith in Christ? Give your reasoning as to why or why not.

5. What types of values were explicit and implicit in your initial worldview?

6. When you think of the "old way" of doing church what comes to mind? Research where that tradition started and why? Where the reasons for starting the tradition good? Are they still good reasons to continue the tradition today? Why or why not?

7. What are the ditches of modernism and postmodernism in your own words?

8. What is the difference between proof and evidence? Do you agree with Tim Keller that a higher standard is put on religious beliefs?

9. Carl Sagan famously said that "extraordinary claim require extraordinary evidence." Which is a more extraordinary claims that the universe came to exist by accident or that there is a God?

10. Have you experienced a fear-based faith like the author described encountering at his grandparents Baptist church as a child? If so, does this experience still impact how you think about faith and God?

11. In the song *Old Pews* what is the primary difference

between the author's first conversion experience and his second?

12. Which definition of worldview do you feel is the strongest? Why?

13. Describe the difference between theonomous cultures, deontological cultures, and autonomous cultures? What type of culture is asserted in the West?

14. Does the cultural ethics system asserted match the reality?

15. Is America, or the country you live in, today more influenced by a modern or postmodern worldview?

16. In the bridge of *Paperback Novels*, where is the human search for meaning found?

17. Do the lyrics of *Paperback Novels* proclaim a more modern worldview, postmodern, or classical Christian synthesis worldview? Why?

18. In your initial worldview (the one that was primarily constructed for you), was God making pizza or risotto? Or was the food just making itself (atheism)? How did this shape the way you saw the world?

19. How are Hegel's dialectic and deconstruction related?

20. Describe in your own words what phenomenology is?

21. Did the author's discussion on the nature of truth expand your worldview of the nature of truth? If so in what ways?

22. Can you articulate the differences between the kinds of truth in your own words?

23. Why is ultimate reality and the whole truth treated by the author as synonyms?

24. Is omniscience required to know the absolute nature of ultimate reality? How does the line in *Without End* that quotes Saint Bonaventure about God being the center and circumference play into the need for omniscience as a requirement for knowledge of ultimate reality?

25. Compare the Chesterton quote about mysticism keeping men sane to the nihilism found in Nietzsche.

Which one offers a wider more holistically constructed worldview?

Bibliography

Aquinas, Thomas. *Summa Theologica*. New York, NY: Benziger Brothers, Inc, 1948.

Chesterton, Gilbert Keith. *Orthodoxy*. S.l.: BROADMAN & HOLMAN PUB, 2022.

Copan, Paul. *Loving Wisdom: A Guide to Philosophy and Christian Faith*. Grand Rapids, MI: William B. Eerdmans Publishing Company, 2020.

Dead Man Walking. United States: Gramercy Pictures, 1995.

Gregory, Brad S. *Unintended Reformation: How a Religious Revolution Secularized Society*. Boston, MA: Belknap Harvard, 2015.

Hicks, Stephen. *Explaining Postmodernism: Skepticism and Socialism from Rousseau to Foucault*. Roscoe, IL: Ockham's Razor Publishing, 2011.

Hiebert, Paul G. *Transforming Worldviews an Anthropological Understanding of How People Change*. Grand Rapids, MI: Baker Academic, 2009.

I, Robot. United States: 20th Century Fox, 2004.

Keller, Timothy. *Making Sense of God: Finding God in the Modern World*. New York, NY: Penguin Books, 2018.

Kierkegaard Sören Aabye, Howard Vincent Hong, and Edna Hatlestad Hong. *Works of Love*. Princeton, NJ: Princeton University Press, 1995.

Lewis, C. S. *The Abolition of Man*. New York, NY: Exciting Classics, 2013.

Lewis, C. S. *The Screwtape Letters*. Uhrichsville, OH: Barbour Book, 1990.

Lewis, Clive Staples. *Mere Christianity*. New York, NY: Simon and Schuster, 1996.

Manning, Brennan, John Blase, and Jonathan Foreman. *ABBA's Child: The Cry of the Heart for Intimate Belonging*. Colorado Springs, Co: NavPress, 2015.

Martinich, A. P., Fritz Allhoff, and Anand Jayprakash Vaidya.

Early Modern Philosophy: Essential Readings with Commentary. Malden, MO: Blackwell Publishing, 2007.

McLaughlin, Rebecca. *Confronting Christianity: 12 Hard Questions for the World's Largest Religion.* Wheaton, IL: Crossway, 2019.

Merleau-Ponty, Maurice, and Colin Smith. *Phenomenology of Perception.* Las Vegas, NV: Franklin Classics, 2018.

Merleau-Ponty, Maurice. *Signs.* Evanston, IL: Northwestern Univ. Press, 1995.

Mr. Holland's Opus. Burbank, CA: Hollywood Pictures Home Video, 1995.

Nagel, Thomas. *The Last Word.* New York, NY: Oxford University Press, 2006.

Nietzsche, Friedrich. *Thus Spoke Zarathustra.* La Vergne, TN: Antiquarius, 2020.

of Norwich, Julian, and Clifton Wolters. *Revelations of Divine Love.* London, UK: Penguin Books, 1966.

Poplin, Mary S. *Is Reality Secular?: Testing the Assumptions of Four Global Worldviews.* Downers Grove, IL: Intervarsity Press, 2014.

Robbins, Tim, Tim Robbins, Susan Sarandon, Sean Penn, and Robert Prosky. *Dead Man Walking.* United States: Gramercy Pictures, 1995.

Simpson, Christopher Ben. *Merleau-Ponty and Theology.* London, UK: Bloomsbury T & T Clark, 2014.

SIMPSON, CHRISTOPHER BEN. *Modern Christian Theology.* London, UK: T & T CLARK, 2020.

Sokolowski, Robert. *Introduction to Phenomenology.* Cambridge, UK: Cambridge University Press, 2017.

Star Wars IV: A New Hope. United Kingdom: Lucas Film Ltd, 2008.

Star Wars VII: The Force Awakens. USA: Lucasfilm Ltd., 2015.

Strickland, Lloyd. *Shorter Leibniz Texts: A Collection of New Translations.* Continuum International Publishing Group, 2010.

Toadvine, Ted. "Maurice Merleau-Ponty." Stanford Encyclopedia of Philosophy. Stanford University, September 14, 2016. https://plato.stanford.edu/entries/merleau-ponty/#PhenPerc.

Transcendence. Milano: Mondadori, 2014.

Wegner, Daniel M. *The Illusion of Conscious Will*. Cambridge, MA: The MIT press, n.d.

Weil, Simone. *Gravity and Grace*. London, UK: Routledge, 2004.

White, James Emery. *The Rise of the Nones: Understanding and Reaching the Religiously Unaffiliated*. Grand Rapids, MI: Baker Books, 2014.

Wright, N. T. *The New Testament and the People of God*. London, UK: SPCK, 2013.

ENDNOTES

81. *Star Wars IV: A New Hope* (Lucasfilm Ltd, 2008).

82. *Star Wars VII: The Force Awakens* (Lucasfilm Ltd., 2015).

83. *Mr. Holland's Opus* (Hollywood Pictures Home Video, 1995).

84. Timothy Keller, *Making Sense of God: Finding God in the Modern World* (New York, NY: Penguin Books, 2018), 65.

85. Timothy Keller, *Making Sense of God: Finding God in the Modern World* (New York, NY: Penguin Books, 2018), 50.

86. Mary S. Poplin, *Is Reality Secular?: Testing the Assumptions of Four Global Worldviews* (Downers Grove, IL: Intervarsity Press, 2014), 27.

87. Ibid.

88. Written by Jason Lee McKinney (Zekers and ZiZi Music (BMI); and Scott Fairfloff (Scott Fair Music (ASCAP)

89. Paul G. Hiebert, *Transforming Worldviews an Anthropological Understanding of How People Change* (Grand Rapids, MI: Baker Academic, 2009), 25-26.

90. N. T. Wright, *The New Testament and the People of God* (London, UK: SPCK, 2013), 123–124.

91. Paul G. Hiebert, *Transforming Worldviews an Anthropological Understanding of How People Change* (Grand Rapids, MI: Baker Academic, 2009), 84.

92. Paul G. Hiebert, *Transforming Worldviews an Anthropological Understanding of How People Change* (Grand Rapids, MI: Baker Academic, 2009), 85.

93. Mary S. Poplin, *Is Reality Secular?: Testing the Assumptions of Four Global Worldviews* (Downers Grove, IL: Intervarsity Press, 2014), 15.

94. Mary S. Poplin, *Is Reality Secular?: Testing the Assumptions of Four Global Worldviews* (Downers Grove, IL: Intervarsity Press, 2014), 30.

95. Mary S. Poplin, *Is Reality Secular?: Testing the Assumptions of Four Global Worldviews* (Downers Grove, IL: Intervarsity

Press, 2014), 30.

96. Timothy Keller, *Making Sense of God: Finding God in the Modern World* (New York, NY: Penguin Books, 2018), 34.

97. Rebecca McLaughlin, *Confronting Christianity: 12 Hard Questions for the World's Largest Religion* (Wheaton, IL: Crossway, 2019), 23,30,31.

98. Written by Jason Lee McKinney (Zekers and ZiZi Music (BMI)

99. Stephen Hicks, *Explaining Postmodernism: Skepticism and Socialism from Rousseau to Foucault* (Roscoe, IL: Ockham's Razor Publishing, 2011), 5.

100. Mary S. Poplin, *Is Reality Secular?: Testing the Assumptions of Four Global Worldviews* (Downers Grove, IL: Intervarsity Press, 2014), 16.

101. Christopher Ben Simpson, *Modern Christian Theology* (London, UK: T & T CLARK, 2020), 13.

102. Stephen Hicks, *Explaining Postmodernism: Skepticism and Socialism from Rousseau to Foucault* (Roscoe, IL: Ockham's Razor Publishing, 2011), 25.

103. Timothy Keller, *Making Sense of God: Finding God in the Modern World* (New York, NY: Penguin Books, 2018), 37.

104. A. P. Martinich, Fritz Allhoff, and Anand Jayprakash Vaidya, *Early Modern Philosophy: Essential Readings with Commentary* (Malden, MO: Blackwell Publishing, 2007), 20.

105. Paul G. Hiebert, *Transforming Worldviews an Anthropological Understanding of How People Change* (Grand Rapids, MI: Baker Academic, 2009), 145.

106. Stephen Hicks, *Explaining Postmodernism: Skepticism and Socialism from Rousseau to Foucault* (Roscoe, IL: Ockham's Razor Publishing, 2011), 26.

107. James Emery White, *The Rise of the Nones: Understanding and Reaching the Religiously Unaffiliated* (Grand Rapids, MI: Baker Books, 2014), 47.

108. Robert Sokolowski, *Introduction to Phenomenology*

(Cambridge, UK: Cambridge University Press, 2017), 115.

109. Mary S. Poplin, *Is Reality Secular?: Testing the Assumptions of Four Global Worldviews* (Downers Grove, IL: Intervarsity Press, 2014), 207.

110. Thomas Nagel, *The Last Word* (New York, NY: Oxford University Press, 2006), 130.

111. Stephen Hicks, *Explaining Postmodernism: Skepticism and Socialism from Rousseau to Foucault* (Roscoe, IL: Ockham's Razor Publishing, 2011), 269.

112. Mary S. Poplin, *Is Reality Secular?: Testing the Assumptions of Four Global Worldviews* (Downers Grove, IL: Intervarsity Press, 2014), 53.

113. Paul G. Hiebert, *Transforming Worldviews an Anthropological Understanding of How People Change* (Grand Rapids, MI: Baker Academic, 2009), 39.

114. Ibid.

115. Paul G. Hiebert, *Transforming Worldviews an Anthropological Understanding of How People Change* (Grand Rapids, MI: Baker Academic, 2009), 39.

116. Paul G. Hiebert, *Transforming Worldviews an Anthropological Understanding of How People Change* (Grand Rapids, MI: Baker Academic, 2009), 39.

117. Friedrich Nietzsche, *Thus Spoke Zarathustra* (La Vergne, TN: Antiquarius, 2020), 208.

118. A. P. Martinich, Fritz Allhoff, and Anand Jayprakash Vaidya, *Early Modern Philosophy: Essential Readings with Commentary* (Malden, MO: Blackwell Publishing, 2007), 29.

119. Paul G. Hiebert, *Transforming Worldviews an Anthropological Understanding of How People Change* (Grand Rapids, MI: Baker Academic, 2009), 213–214.

120. Paul Copan, *Loving Wisdom: A Guide to Philosophy and Christian Faith* (Grand Rapids, MI: William B. Eerdmans Publishing Company, 2020), 108.

121. Paul Copan, *Loving Wisdom: A Guide to Philosophy and*

Christian Faith (Grand Rapids, MI: William B. Eerdmans Publishing Company, 2020), 111.

122. *I, Robot* (20th Century Fox, 2004).

123. *Interstellar* (Paramount Pictures, n.d.), accessed December 31, 2021.

124. Written by Jason Lee McKinney (Zekers and ZiZi Music (BMI); and Sam Berce

125. Brad S. Gregory, *Unintended Reformation: How a Religious Revolution Secularized Society* (Boston, MA: Belknap Harvard, 2015).

126. Friedrich Nietzsche, *Thus Spoke Zarathustra* (La Vergne, TN: Antiquarius, 2020), 24.

127. Rebecca McLaughlin, *Confronting Christianity: 12 Hard Questions for the World's Largest Religion* (Wheaton, IL: Crossway, 2019), 122.

128. Kierkegaard Sören Aabye, Howard Vincent Hong, and Edna Hatlestad Hong, *Works of Love* (Princeton, NJ: Princeton University Press, 1995).

129. Lloyd Strickland, *Shorter Leibniz Texts: A Collection of New Translations* (Continuum International Publishing Group, 2010), 189.

130. Thomas Aquinas, *Summa Theologica* (New York, NY: Benziger Brothers, Inc, 1948).

131. Julian of Norwich and Clifton Wolters, *Revelations of Divine Love* (London, UK: Penguin Books, 1966).

132. Brennan Manning, John Blase, and Jonathan Foreman, *ABBA's Child: The Cry of the Heart for Intimate Belonging* (Colorado Springs, Co: NavPress, 2015).

133. *Transcendence* (Mondadori, 2014).

134. *Dead Man Walking* (Gramercy Pictures, 1995).

135. Mary S. Poplin, *Is Reality Secular?: Testing the Assumptions of Four Global Worldviews* (Downers Grove, IL: Intervarsity Press, 2014), 50.

136. Daniel M. Wegner, *The Illusion of Conscious Will* (Cambridge,

MA: The MIT press, n.d.), 51.

137. C. S. Lewis, *The Screwtape Letters* (Uhrichsville, OH: Barbour Book, 1990).

138. Robert Sokolowski, *Introduction to Phenomenology* (Cambridge, UK: Cambridge University Press, 2017), 54.

139. Robert Sokolowski, *Introduction to Phenomenology* (Cambridge, UK: Cambridge University Press, 2017), 63.

140. Robert Sokolowski, I*ntroduction to Phenomenology* (Cambridge, UK: Cambridge University Press, 2017),10.

141. Maurice Merleau-Ponty and Colin Smith, *Phenomenology of Perception* (Las Vegas, NV: Franklin Classics, 2018), 3.

142. C. S. Lewis, *The Screwtape Letters* (Uhrichsville, OH: Barbour Book, 1990), 25.

143. Christopher Ben Simpson, *Merleau-Ponty and Theology* (London, UK: Bloomsbury T & T Clark, 2014), 9.

144. Ted Toadvine, "Maurice Merleau-Ponty," *Stanford Encyclopedia of Philosophy* (Stanford University, September 14, 2016), https://plato.stanford.edu/entries/merleau-ponty/#PhenPerc.

145. Maurice Merleau-Ponty and Colin Smith, *Phenomenology of Perception* (Las Vegas, NV: Franklin Classics, 2018), 466.

146. Robert Sokolowski, *Introduction to Phenomenology* (Cambridge, UK: Cambridge University Press, 2017), 196.

147. Paul Copan, *Loving Wisdom: A Guide to Philosophy and Christian Faith* (Grand Rapids, MI: William B. Eerdmans Publishing Company, 2020), 298.

148. Simone Weil, *Gravity and Grace* (London, UK: Routledge, 2004), 66.

149. Maurice Merleau-Ponty and Colin Smith, *Phenomenology of Perception* (Las Vegas, NV: Franklin Classics, 2018).

150. Maurice Merleau-Ponty, *Signs* (Evanston, IL: Northwestern Univ. Press, 1995), 15.

151. Clive Staples Lewis, *Mere Christianity* (New York, NY:

Simon and Schuster, 1996), 43.

152. Maurice Merleau-Ponty and Colin Smith, *Phenomenology of Perception* (Las Vegas, NV: Franklin Classics, 2018), 71.

153. Maria Baghramian and J. Adam Carter, "Relativism," *Stanford Encyclopedia of Philosophy* (Stanford University, September 15, 2020), https://plato.stanford.edu/entries/relativism/#HidParDef.

154. "Subjective Definition & Meaning," Dictionary.com (Dictionary.com), accessed November 7, 2021, https://www.dictionary.com/browse/subjective.

155. Paul Copan, *Loving Wisdom: Christian Philosophy of Religion* (Grand Rapids, MI: Chalice Press, 2012), 115.

156. Ibid,115.

157. Timothy Keller, *The Reason for God: Belief in an Age of Skepticism* (New York, NY: Penguin Books, 2018), 258.

158. Ibid., 114.

159. Ibid., 115.

160. C. S. Lewis, *The Abolition of Man* (New York, NY: Exciting Classics, 2013), 53.

161. Gilbert Keith Chesterton, *Orthodoxy* (S.l.: Broadman and Holman Pub, 2022), 16–17.

162. Written by Jason Lee McKinney (Zekers and ZiZi Music (BMI)

Part 3

Appearance, Actualization, Attributes
and Analogy in the Problem of Evil

INTRODUCTION

I am taking a little different approach to the integration of movie characters and lines in this part of the book. For the problem of evil, I am taking lines these characters did deliver in movies and paraphrasing them for our purposes. The essence of the characters traits remains intact even if the lines are paraphrased.

EXT. POE'S BAR (TYPICAL MIDWESTERN DIVE) - JUST PAST DINNERTIME

Dig if you will the picture of a scene where Dr. STRANGE, LOKI god of mischief, Buffalo news reporter BRUCE NOLAN, DOC BROWN, and INIGO MONTOYA pile out of a DeLorean and walk into the bar. INT. Each man bellies up on the left side of the bar, all sitting save for LOKI. They begin to talk about how an omnipotent, omniscient, and wholly good God could coexist with evil in the world.

DR. STRANGE

It is plausible that the universe, as it is, is the only way a good God could make souls ascend and for justice to win.

[The guy at the other end of the bar named Gottfried stops mid-complaint about how Isaac Newton stole calculus from him to raise his glass and nod affirmingly to Strange as if to say, "well said young man."]

LOKI

No matter how many universes that could potentially be that an omnipotent, omniscient, wholly good God could make, the essence, nature, and depravity of free creatures would be the same, so it is plausible that this is the only world that could obtain and maintain libertarian freedom!

[In the corner of the bar, a patron named Alvin chimes in with an "Amen" to Loki but gives Gottfried the side-eye.]

BRUCE NOLAN

An omnipotent, omniscient, wholly good God would not prevent all the evils in the world, would not grant all human requests, or make the world a hedonist perfect state of affairs as that would make things worse. Humans would not have the chance to become truly and fully human without the opportunity to overcome evil.

[The table by the Jukebox—that happens to be playing Hurt's So Good by John Cougar Mellencamp—who are eavesdropping at this point comprised of Marilyn, Alston, Wykstra, Lewis, Allen, and Hick give a baker half dozen "right on brother!" right after Wykstra walks to the Jukebox, drops a quarter in and pushes P2 which of course is Snap!'s 1990 hit "I've Got The Power."]

DOC BROWN

Even if an omnipotent, omniscient, wholly good God would remove the most minor evil, which is to say what negative effect that may have on the rest of the universe.

[Diogenes Allen and Simone Weil give Doc a tip of the hat.]

INIGO MONTOYA

You keep using those words omnipotent, omniscient, wholly good; I do not think they mean what you think they mean.

[Vizzini shouts from the pool table room "inconceivable" while the bartender, who goes by the nickname the Dumb Ox, says "Exactly" as he is checking on the latest brew he is creating.]

AND SCENE

Are Evil and the Nature of God non-compatible?

In this part of the book, I am tackling the problem of evil. There are two approaches in addressing the problem of evil, a defense, and a theodicy. The approach I am taking is one of a theodicy. I will argue that God does not actualize any moral evil. I will argue that while some evil may appear pointless, it is plausible that it does have a point humans cannot understand. I will argue that humans can only understand the divine attributes (omnipotence, omniscience, and goodness) by analogy, so it is plausible that our lack of understanding is why evil seems so incongruent with God.

I will be making a theodicy and not merely a defense. Before I dive into the theodicy, I will give some background on understand what all of the fuss is about with God and the problem of evil. The problem of evil is not a contemporary issue. Rising out of potential absoluta into the enlightenment was a reassessing of God's nature in terms of morality. How do God and evil co-exist? What does the existence of evil say about the nature of God?

David Hume states, "The idea of God, as meaning an infinitely intelligent, wise, and good Being, arises from reflecting on the operations of our mind, and augmenting, without limit, those qualities of goodness and wisdom. We may prosecute this inquiry to what length we please; where we shall always find, that every idea which we examine is copied from a similar impression."[163] This statement not only calls into question the existence of God but if God does exist, is he good. Hume states in *Dialogues Concerning Natural Religion* (1779), "Is [God] willing to prevent evil, but not able? Then is he impotent? Is he able, but not willing? Then is he malevolent? Is he both able and willing? Whence then is evil?"[164]

The underlying assertion is that if God does exist, and it is known that evil exists, then either God is all-powerful, and wills for evil or God is not all-powerful. It challenges the existence of evil with an all-powerful God. More plainly, but analogously it is like the triple constraints in business- quality, time, and cost; a project can have two of the three but never have all three. A project can be done cheaply and quickly, but the quality will lack. This argument by Hobbes frames God's goodness, omnipotence, and evil in this same triangulation. God can be good, and there can be evil, but if those constraints are lifted, the third cannot stand. God cannot be omnipotent. Another example that contrasts this triple constraint can be found in the reader Leibniz *On God and Religion* translated and edited by Lloyd Strickland. In this Leibniz gives the example of an artist stating,

> "An artist produces two paintings, one of which is large in order to serve as a model for a tapestry, while the other is only a miniature. Let us take the miniature one and say that there are two things to consider in it; firstly, its positive and real aspect, which consists of the board, the background, the colors, and the brush-strokes; and secondly, its privative aspect, which is the disproportion to the large painting, or its smallness. Therefore, it would be absurd to say that the artist is the author of all that is real in the two paint-ings, without also being the author of the privative, or of the disproportion between the large one and the small one. For by the same reason, or rather by a stronger reason, one could say that an artist can be the author of a copy or of a portrait, i.e. without being the author of this flaw. For, in fact, the privative is nothing other than a simple result or infallible consequence of the positive and does not require a separate author."[165]

To Leibniz, it is not that God does not have foreknowledge of sin or that he is the "author" of sin but that in his wisdom, he allows for such with a purpose. The question becomes, does God's foreknowledge make him sinful or make him culpable?

Does God's foreknowledge of sin make him an accessory to sin? Just because God can prevent sin does not mean that He ought to. Is God preventing sin always the wisest thing to do? This idea hints at Leibniz's concept that perfection and perfect are not inextricably linked. Additionally, God's foreknowledge is not a deception akin to Descarte's question of whether there is anything real outside the mind. Leibniz God could not deceive for that would not be the best nor indeed infinitely good. God does nothing out of order.[166] Things may seem extraordinary to us, but from God's perspective in how he in actuality made creation, they are ordered. Created things might just misunderstand things that may seem as though they are evil or disordered. If it is assumed, there is a God and that He created humans, He also created morality and humanities' sense of it, leaving man without moral grounds to question his creator about morality, which his creator also created. It is analogous to when I found a mistaken chord sheet on a chord website for one of my songs. A fan of the song had uploaded a chart of the song. I found it endearing, but there was a mistake. The chart listed a chord in the bridge to be a C# minor when in fact, it is an A major chord in first inversion. I sent a note thanking the fan for caring enough to upload the chart but wanted to help them out and correct the mistake. The fan indignantly fired back that I was incorrect, and it was indeed a C# minor. I replied, "I was there when the song was written; I know it is an A/C#. I wrote it that way." So one of the arguments theists make is that humans are not in an epistemic situation to question God if the divine attributes given are indeed held by God. He is the songwriter he knows the chords far better than humans do.

The problem reminds of God's dialogue with Job in chapter 38, verses 4–7,

"Where were you when I laid the earth's foundation? Tell me if you understand. Who marked off its dimensions? Surely you know! Who stretched a measuring line across it? On what were its footings set, or who laid its cornerstone—while the morning stars sang together, and all the angels shouted for joy?"

The dialogue between Job and God makes perfect sense if God is infinitely good and infinitely wise.

- Problem of Evil- logical or evidential challenge questioning the congruence of the divine attributes with the existence of evil and suffering in the world.
- Theodicy- A logical argument for the plausibility even probability of God despite the presence of evil and suffering in the world.
- Defense- A logical argument for the possibility of God despite the presence of evil and suffering in the world.
- Epistemic situation- the level of validity of humanity's knowledge about a given state of affairs.

2006 was a rough year for me. As I mentioned in the introduction of the book my father passed away from a lengthy battle with cancer. We had a complicated relationship and yet he was still my hero. That same year my first marriage ended. After years of putting up with my neglect, selfishness, and constant quarrelsomeness, my first wife snapped. My family fell apart and it was my fault. Because of the marriage ending, I had to come off the road, ask to be released from my recording contract and start a new career. In a sixth month period my world had fallen apart. I questioned how God could allow so much suffering in my life at one time? I knew some of it was due to my own poor but freely made choices yet some of it seemed unfair. During this time, I think because of my own suffering I became hyper aware of the suffering of others. I was deeply aware of every kid on the St. Jude's commercials and asked myself why a good and all-powerful God would allow that kid to go through that? I would often think I may have deserved my suffering; it may be well earned but that kid dying of cancer? That seemed gratuitous. There was a story about puppies that were stuffed in a pillowcase and thrown off a bridge into the river and it crushed me. It didn't make sense.

I am writing this part of the book as our family dog of 12 years is dying. Our wolf hybrid has been the most amazing, loyal and loving pet I have ever owned. On some level suffering never makes sense. Suffering always stings of something being off. Is that sting evidence that God is guilty of or complicit in suffering or is it a sign to humanity that existence itself is not as it was intended to be? I vacillated during this time between being closer to God than ever and doubting there was a God at all almost daily. I was feeling the heavy weight of not only what I was going through but also what others who were more innocent like my own children who suffered greatly by all that occurred and did nothing wrong. My children suffered the loss of their grandfather, their parents split up and their dad lost his job all in a sixth month period. While there are certainly families who have gone through worse than me and my children did, death, divorce and financial destruction could be considered gratuitous for innocent children to go through. I know I often questioned how a good God would allow my kids to suffer as they did. I deconstructed from the assumption of God being good, all knowing and all powerful. Maybe God actually lacked in one or all of these attributes, otherwise why does suffering like this occur. I got it for me I could see how I earned it so to speak, but not kids, not puppies, not when it came to things like genocide or hurricanes and earthquakes. I decided to try and reconstruct my belief in the divine attributes before I abandoned them completely. If I could make both an intellectually cogent argument for not only the possibility of the divine attributes but also their plausibility and probability and I could reconcile it emotionally, then perhaps I could stay in my worldview. Honestly the alternative is that there is no meaning, there is no evil. So like the inverse of Thomas Negel I didn't want there not to be a God, I didn't want to live in a world where I couldn't reconcile evil and suffering with God. That universe, that worldview would take away the very comfort I was seeking. But I didn't know if I could build a case intellectually and emotionally that would allow me to reconstruct my belief. In this part of the book I walk you through the process I undertook and what the results were for this disciple.

French enlightenment philosopher Pierre Bayle's book *Dictionnaire Historique et Critique* asserted there is no rational reason for an infinitely good and all-powerful God to not be the cause of evil. Bayle separated theology from reason and religion from ethics, much like Kant and Jacobi.[167] Bayle argues it would not be possible for Adam and Eve to sin unless God authored it. If Adam and Eve were created in God's image and wholly good, how could they sin unless God willed it to be?[168] Bayle's idea, along with Descartes's deconstruction into questioning reality itself, fundamentally changed the potential view on God's nature from that of medieval and classical times towards an impotent or morally questionable God. Leibniz's book *Theodicy* makes a rationalist argument of why evil co-exists with a good and wise God. God did not have to create at all, and his nature of being good is not dependent upon him willing anything good. The necessary causal agent if good must be good within its own nature. The goodness must be by necessity and not contingent upon behavior or acts of will. A necessarily existing causal agent is not good because it created a good universe, but because it is simply good; indivisibly, intrinsically, and essentially good, independently in every sense of creation.

In *The Four Loves*, C.S. Lewis states, "God, who needs nothing, loves into existence wholly superfluous creatures in order that he may love and perfect them."[169] The question is often asked why would a good God allow evil and suffering. However, implicit in this question is two presuppositions. One that a perfect world would be a better world and two that a good God always prevents all evil, including the evil choices of man and yet still be accountable to maintain conserving man's liberty of will. On why God allows evil, Leibniz states, "God has a far stronger reason [than men do], and one far more worthy of him, for tolerating evils. Not only does he derive from them greater goods, but he finds them connected with the greatest goods of all those that are possible: so that it would be a fault not to permit them."[170]

In my own life 2006 was my face to face reckoning with the problem of evil. In a six-month time, frame, I lost my first marriage, my dad to cancer and my record deal. Newly single, without my dad and without a job I was reeling. I cannot in all honesty say for sure that if I did not have my children and my own responsibilities of being a father that I would not have attempted suicide. I was a broken man. Spiritually speaking I vacillated wildly during this time. There were days and weeks I experientially felt a closeness with God that I never had before and then there were other days I was depressed and drank too much (much more on the divorce in Part 5 of the book). During this time, I was extra sensitive to other's sufferings as well. Every instance of suffering seemed magnified. I questioned God's goodness some days and his existence on other days. In the days in between I would feel a closeness to God like I have never felt before or since. I questioned a lot. Why did God not change my ex-wives heart and give me a chance to prove myself? Why did God not wake me up sooner to my failings as a husband? Why did my dad who was simultaneously my hero and my greatest source of wounding have to die right as my life was falling apart? Why did I not forgive my dad when I had the chance? Why did God not reward me walking out on my record deal to save my marriage? Isn't that how the Kirk Cameron movie script goes? I asked all these questions and more. Why did God allow all this evil in my life? Why did he allow kids to be abused and sold, murdered? Why allow the holocaust of his own people? I did not understand. So, I began to deconstruct my blind belief in the attributes of God and see if I could form a theodicy to rebuild them. I doubted mightily during this time, but I tried to make sure I did not trade a bias towards one worldview for another. I decided to doubt my doubt and give the views of the divine attributes I had been holding the same footing as not keeping them. Here is the conclusion I came to.

Lord Knows

V.1
Too many dimes in the wishing well
Too many times I could not tell
What it was that she needed from me
Was it flowers that I sent in vain?
One more kiss in the pouring rain
I just don't know

Pr.
Was there anything that could've changed her mind
Ch.
Lord knows that I've been wrong
Living out some old country song and
I don't want to be part of a world where she don't belong
Lord knows how I've tried to get her back into my life
And I don't understand why she won't take a chance let it go
(There's a reason why life makes us turn on this long winding road)
Lord knows

V.2
Another mile one more step
Away from the girl that I almost let get away from me
All those years ago
Is there a way back to when love was good?
And if there was, I wish I could find that road
Back home

Pr.
Is there any way anything but good bye Lord knows

Bridge
Is there a reason why a kid gets cancer?
What's the meaning of old folks dying alone?
So much pain so many questions without answers
Just have to trust that he knows, and his loving hand has it
under control
And I have to let her go
Lord knows[171]

In this theodicy, I will argue:

1. God could not have created a world of free creatures where evil could not exist. God created the potential for evil when He created beings with free will (angelic and human), but He did not actualize the privation of evil. The actualization of evil is necessitated only by the free choices of beings with free will.

   i. Possible Worlds (Dr. Strange)

   ii. Essence and Free Will, Actuality and Potentiality (Loki)

2. It is plausible that evil (pain and suffering) has a beneficial impact on the ultimate good, but humanity's epistemic situation is such that humans cannot fully comprehend it.

   i. The Benefit of Suffering and Divine Goodness (Bruce Nolan)

   ii. Human Epistemic Situation (Doc Brown)

3. Humanity's epistemic situation is such that humans cannot fully comprehend the divine attributes as applied in the definition of God in the context of the problem of evil. Humans can only comprehend the divine attributes by analogy and therefore cannot judge whether God lives up to the definition.

   i. Human Limitations in Defining Divine Attributes (Inigo Montoya)

The three arguments above are used to show why evil and an omnipotent, omniscient, and wholly good God is not merely possible but probable using the backdrop of contemporary cinematic storytelling that illustrates the points for those who are unfamiliar with philosophy and the problem of evil.

STATEMENT OF THE PROBLEM

What is the Problem of Evil? The problem of evil stems from the position that the existence of evil creates an obstacle to belief in God. If God is all-powerful, all-knowing, and all good, then evil would not or could not exist. If God (if such a being exists) does not have the power to stop evil, then God is not all-powerful. If God has the power but not the foreknowledge to prevent evil, then God is not all-knowing. If God possesses the power and the knowledge to prevent evil but does not do so, then God is not wholly good. The problem in its essence is that the existence of evil (something no one argues does not exist) means God is limited in some capacity or God does not exist. There are two primary versions of the problem of evil, the logical problem of evil and the evidential (or probabilistic) problem of evil. The first contends that it is logically inconsistent for God and evil to both exist. For the most part, even atheists agree this version of the problem has been solved by Alvin Plantinga's free will defense (discussed further in this theodicy). The evidential problem of evil is still highly debated. The difference between the two is:

- Logical Problem of Evil- The existence of evil makes it impossible for an omnipotent, omniscient, wholly good God to exist.
- Evidential Problem of Evil- The existence and amount of evil is evidence against the probability of an omnipotent, omniscient, wholly good God existing.
    i. The 'amount' of evil in the world here refers to both the intensity of evil in the world and the number of instances of evil.

WHAT THE CRITICS ARE SAYING

Imagine the old Siskel and Ebert theme song playing as the camera zooms in; only sitting in the empty theater are not Gene and Robert but rather Oxford philosophy professor J.L. Mackie, Purdue philosophy professor William L. Rowe, fellow Purdue philosophy professor Paul Draper, and Wayne State philosophy professor Bruce Russell. They are set to give their reviews on the probability of both God and evil existing. Mackie comes in first (and the graphics show a thumbs down), saying that evil and the existence of God are incompatible. Much like the triple constraints in project management of time, scope, and cost, you cannot have all three. Mackie rejects what he calls fallacious solutions as he maintains these solutions try to have all three propositional constraints. Mackie's big claim is that a wholly good God would always eliminate every evil it could in every circumstance.[172] Mackie rejects any usefulness of evil for the greater good. Mackie asserts that a good God would necessarily eliminate every evil God could if God were to exist.[173]

William Rowe gives his review next, and once again, the graphic shows a thumbs down (though Rowe is friendly and kind in his criticisms). Rowe centers his criticism on appearance and rationality. If evil appears to be gratuitous or pointless, how rational is it to conclude that it is indeed gratuitous or pointless?[174] Rowe uses the example of a fawn being burned in a forest fire and suffers (apparently pointlessly) for several days before dying as a type of animal suffering that cannot be justified. Rowe asserts it is rational even reasonable to believe that because the suffering appears pointless, it is indeed pointless, although he admits this does not prove it is pointless.[175] Rowe asserts, "there exist instances of intense suffering which an omnipotent, omniscient being could have prevented without thereby losing some greater good or permitting some evil equally bad or worse" therefore, it is rational to assume the appearance of that particular suffering is pointless and God does not exist.[176]

After a quick commercial break, Paul Draper gets to have his say. However, again the graphic displays a thumbs down (this picture may be nominated for a Razzie). Draper focuses his review on validity. Draper acknowledges that the argument is one of probability, not provability.[177] Draper asserts a hypothesis of indifference.

174

The hypothesis of indifference is that if a deity or supernatural beings exist, they are indifferent to human and animal suffering. Further, this is a better explanation of the existence of suffering than theism.[178] Draper asserts that the biological function of both pleasure and pain favors indifference over divine benevolence. Draper rejects that there is moral value in pain. Draper questions whether humans have free will and, if they do, are they worthy of such freedom morally.[179] Is free will of absolute value? Draper and others conclude not.[180]

Finally, Bruce Russell gets to close the show, and he virtually guarantees God and Evil will get several Razzie awards. Russell makes it a clean sweep of thumbs down. Russell asserts there is sufficient evidence for humans to conclude that there is no point for certain instances of suffering.[181] Russell also concludes that any instances of what appears to be a miracle are more likely due to simple chance. Russell posits that the instances of potential goods that would give sufficient reason to allow gratuitous evil that humans know of is a representative sample of all the potential reasons. Russell posits that if God (should he exist) is not expected to intervene to relieve or prevent evils, then why should humans be expected to intervene. Russell concludes that theism is defenseless in light of the amount of evil that exists in the world.[182]

- Hypothesis of indifference- Argues not against the divine attributes of God nor the existence of evil but argues that if God(s) exist they do not lack the ability to end suffering but are indifferent to suffering.

Possible Worlds (Dr. Strange)

In the 2019 Marvel comic film *End Game*, the following scene plays out:

TONY STARK
Strange, are you all right? You're back; you're all right.
DR. STRANGE
I went forward in time. To view alternate futures; to see all the possible outcomes of the coming conflict.
PETER QUILL
How many did you see?
DR. STRANGE
Fourteen million six hundred and five.
TONY STARK
How many do we win?
DR. STRANGE
One![183]

In this section of the theodicy, I am referencing the work and philosophies of Alvin Plantinga, John Hick, and Gottfried Leibniz.

God could not have created a world of free creatures where evil could not exist. God created the potential for evil when He created beings with free will (angelic and human), but He did not actualize the privation of evil. The actualization of evil is necessitated only by the free choices of beings with free will.

What worlds are possible? Could God create a world where creatures are free but would never choose to do wrong? Is this the best version of the universe that there could be? Is God to blame for moral evil? These are all questions people ask, especially when trying to understand how God could be omnipotent, omniscient, and wholly good.

First, the question must be asked what a possible world is? Then followed by what worlds are possible?

A possible world, according to Alvin Plantinga, is synonymous with a possible state of affairs. *The Cambridge Dictionary of Philosophy* defines a state of affairs as "a possibility, actuality, or impossibility of the kind expressed by a nominalization of a declarative sentence."[184] The world (our reality) is a state of affairs that has obtained (it has happened in reality, in actuality). Some states of affairs that do not obtain are impossible, and others are possible even though they do not obtain.[185] According to the *Stanford Encyclopedia of Philosophy*, "States of affairs are similar to thoughts. Thoughts are true or false; states of affairs obtain or not. There are also similarities between facts and states of affairs. Both facts and states of affairs are supposed to be complexes that contain (in a sense to be explained further) objects and properties."[186]

So what worlds are possible? A possible world is a state of affairs that is complete. So all possible worlds are states of affairs (maximal ones), but not all states of affairs are possible worlds.[187] In potentiality, any number of worlds is possible, but only one world has been actualized. Plantinga is not asserting a multiverse here. What he is asserting is that God cannot actualize any world he wishes. God is limited to logical possibilities. Plantinga asserts that God cannot grant humans libertarian choice (free will) and yet intervene or prevent humans from making wrong choices. If the choice is between A and B, but every time B is chosen, it becomes A, then B is never truly an option, and thus it is a faux choice. Humans have to have the ability to choose wrong in order for humanity to maintain its status as morally free beings. John Hick asserts that if God intervened at all points of evil/moral choices, man would cease to be free and cease to be a morally capable being. Freedom to Hick is essential to human moral development.[188]

Plantinga asserts there are possible worlds that God cannot actualize. God could not have actualized a world in which God did not exist. God can actualize any possible world in which God exists but not one that God does not exist.[189] Of the worlds, God can actualize by logical possibility, which ones by divine attributes would God actualize? In his work *Theodicy*, Gottfried Leibniz posits,

> "Now this supreme wisdom, united to a goodness that is no less infinite, cannot but have chosen the best. For as a lesser evil is a kind of good, even so a lesser good is kind of evil if it stands in the way of a greater good; and there would be something to

correct in the actions of God if it were possible to do better. As in mathematics, when there is no maximum nor minimum, in short nothing distinguished, everything is done equally, or when that is not possible nothing at all is done; so it may be said likewise in respect to perfect wisdom, which is no less orderly than mathematics, that if there were not the best (optimum) among all possible worlds, God would not have produced any."[190]

This all points to the fact that God cannot (Plantinga) or would not (Leibniz) actualize a world where humans are free but do not have libertarian freedom.[191] In potentiality, God can conceive of a world where humans are free but will always choose what is right, but he cannot actualize that world. For God to actualize, a world is partially dependent upon the free choices humans make.[192] Thus God creates the potential for evil by endowing free will upon humans, but God does not actualize any moral evil.

When Doctor Strange tells Tony Stark of all the possible worlds where the Avengers battle Thanos, only one possibility obtains where the Avengers win the victory, further, there was no way to actualize a version where the Avengers won, and half the universes population was not wiped out for five years. There was no way for the Avengers to win and take away the free will of Thanos.[193] I argue that God does not actualize any moral evil and thus cannot be blamed for human choices.

- State of Affairs- Analogous to thoughts of how things are or might possibly be or cannot be in reality.
- Multiverse- a hypothetical and infinite number of alternate universes beyond the observable known universe in which we exist in our present forms.
- Privation- the absence of something necessary and good. A privation is not a thing in and of itself but only the absence of the thing.

ESSENCE AND FREE WILL, POTENTIALITY AND ACTUALITY (LOKI)

In episode five of the Disney+ and Marvel partnered series *Loki*, Loki (the version common to the MCU universe to date) discovers that there are many variant versions of himself, a sort of transworld Loki within the multiverse. One of the variants is classic Loki, who states the following:

CLASSIC LOKI

We lie, and we cheat, we cut the throat of every person who trusts us, and for what? Power. Glorious power. Glorious purpose!

We cannot change. We're broken, every version of us. Forever. And whenever one of us dares try to fix themselves, they're sent here to die.[194]

In this section of the theodicy, I am referencing the work and philosophies of Alvin Plantinga, C.S. Lewis, and Thomas Aquinas.

In P1 Q3 Article 3 of the *Summa Theologiae*, Aquinas asserts that God is the same as His nature as God is not composed of matter and form. Humans, however, do have matter and form, and thus humans could look different, have different origins and backgrounds, have different temperaments and emotions in other worlds should they exist. Given these different attributes, would humans be different in essence? Is there a world where humans have free will yet would never choose to do evil? Is choosing evil in the matter and form of humanity, or is it an essential property?

C.S. Lewis states in *The Problem of Pain*, "Christ takes it for granted that men are bad. Until we really feel this assumption of His to be true, though we are part of the world he came to save, we are not part of the audience to whom His words addressed."[195] Theism asserts (particularly the Christian version of theism) that depravity (the penchant to choose wrong) is a part of the essence of humanity. The bent to choose evil is a part of what Plantinga

179

would call a world-indexed property; it would exist in every world that humans exist. The property of depravity is either essential to humanity, or the inverse is essential.[196] The limitation does not say anything of God's omnipotence. C.S. Lewis asserts that God does not have the power to do what is intrinsically or absolute impossible (meaning the impossibility is carried within itself instead of borrowing it from others). In intrinsic impossibilities, there are no unless clauses. It is impossible for all times in all worlds and all causal agents.[197]

Alvin Plantinga writes of his concept of transworld depravity. It is possible that, for all we know, in any world of humans that can be actualized and where humans have libertarian freedom, each human would sin (i.e., each person's freedom would inevitably go wrong). The reason for this is that essence would not change. Loki is Loki. There may be female Loki, Alligator Loki, Arrogant Loki, but the essence is the same, and depravity is in the essence of every human.[198] By God creating creatures whose essence (at least partially) is free will (libertarian freedom), then the potential for depravity that comes with it means no world without evil can be actualized.[199] Therefore like Loki, humans are broken; every potential version of us will choose wrong, so God could not actualize a world where humans are free but never choose evil.

- Essence—the properties that make a thing what it is.
- Free Will- the ability to choose or not to choose to take an action.
- Transworld Depravity- central to human free will is in any possible world in which humans exist and have free-will, each human will choose at least one morally reprehensible action.
- Theism- belief in a God or gods that are active within nature and humanity as opposed to

- Deism- the belief in a creator who set in motion the laws of nature and does not interact of intervene with nature or humanity.

THE BENEFIT OF SUFFERING AND DIVINE GOODNESS (BRUCE NOLAN)

In the Universal Pictures movie *Bruce Almighty*, main character and news reporter Bruce Nolan says in frustration
BRUCE
God is a mean kid sitting on an anthill with a magnifying glass, and I'm the ant. He could fix my life in five minutes if He wanted to, but He'd rather burn off my feelers and watch me squirm.
[Later in the film, God replies:]
GOD (MORGAN FREEMAN)
Do you want to see a miracle? Be the miracle.
[After manipulating and trying to get his girlfriend to come back to him when God asks Bruce what he wants, Bruce replies:]
BRUCE
I want her to be happy, no matter what that means. I want her to find someone who will treat her with all the love she deserved from me. I want her to meet someone who will see her always as I do now, through Your eyes.[200]

In this section of the theodicy, I am referencing the work and philosophies of Marilyn Adams, Richard Swinburne, William Alston, Stephen Wykstra, C.S. Lewis, Diogenes Allen, and John Hick.

Would a good God not give humans what they want? Would a good God not want his children always to be happy? Are kindness and love not the same thing? Allow me one more movie reference.

In the marvel movie *Eternals*, the character Sersi, who is a member of an extraterrestrial race bestowed with powers and abilities, has the following conversation with her human boy-friend Dane about the Eternals mission to protect humanity from Deviants (genetic offshoots of celestial beings)

DANE

Why Didn't you guys' help fight Thanos? Or any war? Or all the other terrible things throughout history?

SERSI

We were instructed not to interfere in any human conflicts unless Deviants were involved

DANE

Why?

SERSI

If we protected humanity from everything for 7,000 years, you'd never have had the chance to develop.[201]

William Alston posits that a reason God may allow evil is punishment for sin or virtue development. This is the same reason Sersi gives for why The Eternals did not interfere in human atrocities. Even natural evils can push humans toward God and toward eternal salvation, which is the ultimate good and finally, the fulfillment of ultimate good to the sufferers or if not for the sufferer to humanity and creation itself.[202] Charles Spurgeon in *Sermons on Great Prayers of the Bible* states, "I am certain that I never did grow in grace one half so much anywhere as I have upon the bed of pain."[203]

What humans deem as good and what God calls good are wholly different. Converting to God's idea of good is not a reversal (going one direction and then the opposite) but more of a perfection. Lewis makes the point that humans (particularly modern humans) confuse kindness for love.[204] Kindness and love are not the same things. Lewis says love is much more stern as it cares for whether its object is becoming good. Love demands the object becomes better, not in a comparative way to any other object but that the loved object reaches for perfection of itself.[205]

Richard Swinburne asserts that good states of affairs are not reducible to pleasures and bad states of affairs are not reducible to suffering. Good states of affairs will have suffering within them. For compassion to occur, there must be a bad state of affairs where a compassionate response is needed. Making wise choices requires the option of choosing wrong options, serving others requires they have a need, and finally, the humility of making amends can only happen after wronging another.[206] Swinburne's assertions align with John Hick's soul-making theodicy. Hick posits that most critics of the Christian view of the world assume that God would create a hedonistic paradise for humans to get what they want when they want. God's purpose is not "immediate pleasure but the realizing of the most valuable of human potentialities."[207]

William Alston, John Hick, Marilyn Adams, and Stephen Wykstra all utilize a parental analogy in one way or another. God's cognitive situation is more beyond humans than a parent's cognitive situation from their infant child. A child will not understand the pain of the surgeon's scalpel nor why his father allowed the surgeon to hurt her. The father knows the pain is for the ultimate good of fixing a heart issue. Adams posits that the cognitive understanding of the good will not comfort the child or take away the pain but the father's "intimate care and presence through the experience."[208] Most children run to the parent when pain and suffering come. It is plausible that God analogous to a parent might allow a lack of goodness (pain and suffering) in part, that there may be an increase of goodness in the whole.[209] The suffering needs to occur to fix the heart issue and to cause the child to run into the embrace of the father. The parent does not maximize pleasure, but it does maximize good. God is a good maximizer, not a pleasure maximizer.

Is the pain allowed by a parent or friend perceived differently than that of one who intends harm? Diogenes Allen utilizes the analogy of the intense grip of a friend that you have not seen in a while compared to the suffering God allows. The grip hurts and causes pain, yet it is not perceived as harmful. The pain itself does not change but the perception changes based upon the intention of the one causing the pain.[210] "This is the final perfection of the soul: to be so grounded in the love of God as to be able to respond with faithful obedience when all joy is absent and no favorable consequences are foreseen as flowing from the suffering."[211]

Bruce Nolan begins the film angry at God for not granting him all Bruce wants out of life. Bruce is unwilling to accept any meaningful purpose for the pain of life. Bruce is allowed to be God for a time and takes the approach of being a pleasure maximizer. This approach leads to chaos and not the greater good. Bruce comes to realize and ultimately longs for what is best. I argue that while some evil may appear pointless, it is plausible that it does have a point humans cannot understand.

- Epistemic access- You know what you are thinking and your thoughts in a way and to a degree that you will never have with anyone else.
- Epistemic probability- the belief in one variable given the degree to which another variable supports or makes it plausible. The belief takes in the total body of evidence.
- Omnipotent- possessing infinite power.
- Omnipresent- possessing no limitations of presence. Can be everywhere all at once.
- Omni-good (wholly good)- possessing infinite goodness.

Human Epistemic Situation (Doc Brown)

In *Back to The Future part two*, Doc Brown and Marty McFly have the following exchange regarding their epistemic situation:

Doc Brown

They're taking her home, to your future home! We'll arrive shortly thereafter, get her out of there and go back to 1985.

Marty

You mean I'm going to see where I live? I'm gonna see myself as an old man?

Doc Brown

No, no, no Marty, that could result in a ... [gasps] Great Scott! Jennifer could conceivably encounter her future self! The consequences of that could be disastrous!

Marty

Doc, what do you mean?

Doc Brown

I foresee two possibilities. One: coming face to face with herself thirty years older would put her into shock, and she'd simply pass out. Or two, the encounter could create a time paradox, the result of which could cause a chain reaction that would unravel the very fabric of the space-time continuum and destroy the entire universe! Granted, that's worst-case scenario. The destruction might in fact be very localized, limited to merely our own galaxy.

Marty

Well, that's a relief.[212]

In this section of the theodicy, I am referencing the work and philosophies of William Alston, Stephen Wykstra, and Alvin Plantinga.

Alvin Plantinga defines epistemic probability as the probability of a belief in one variable given the degree to which another variable supports or makes it plausible. The belief takes in the total body of evidence.[213] Wykstra puts forth his CORNEA argument. CORNEA stands for Conditions Of Reasonable Epistemic Access. The basic argument is within a specific situation; a person is entitled to claim "It appears that " only if it is reasonable for that person to believe that, given their cognitive abilities, that if what appears is not the case, the situation would likely be different than it is in some way so far as the person could/would recognize. Alternatively, more fundamental, would the situation seem any different if what appears to be the case were not, in fact, the case.[214] Alston puts forth his CORNEA theory, which aims to assess the reasonable seeability requirement.[215] An illustration that might clear up epistemic situation is the following: when I got my first car the gas gage did not work properly. The gage did not read accurately after it passed a half a tank. I would have to fill up at the beginning of the week (Monday). I knew for a normal week I would not have to fill up again until the following Monday. I knew that driving around town to places I normally drove such as school and work that I could reasonably assume the car would not run out of gas. I did not however actually know for certain at any time how much gas was in the tank after it passed a half a tank (between half a tank and empty the gage did not work). Now if I drove to the town an hour away on Friday night to see my girlfriend was I in a reasonable position to assume I had enough gas to make it to next Monday just because the gage was not on empty? Keep in mind on the one hand cars get better mileage on the highway than in town but I was adding an additional 100 miles to my normal usage. Now if the tank read a quarter of a tank it would appear to me that I still had some gas. I also would not normally have to fill up between Mondays but I had used the car in a "gratuitous" manner so would I be in a reasonable position to know whether I needed to fill up or not? I would say the amount of gas left in the tank was not accessible to me and therefore my seeability was such that I could not trust what appeared to be true, either by data or inference from the past.

My ignorance of the situation does not mean there is not gas in the tank. One other analogy, ignorance does not mean something has no meaning (no gas in the tank). I have spent most of my life as a professional songwriter, when I end a song on a minor six chord instead of the major one chord my mom is uncomfortable and uneasy with how it sounds but she (not being a musician) is ignorant to the fact that this is exactly the desired effect I am aiming at for a number of potential reasons: how the song flows into the next song on the album or to emphasize the mood of the lyrics.[216] Any reason she might give would be groping in the dark, the same as humanity's knowledge of reasons why God might allow evil. This analogy also functions on the level of just because everyone listens to music does not mean the majority of people (even really smart) understand music, even though humans live and experience the world with its goods and evils does not mean we hold a valid opinion on what the reasons may be for God to allow them. Humans do not possess epistemic access for the interconnectedness.[217]

The question is that if an omnipotent, omniscient, wholly good God had reasons for allowing evil, are humans in a position to assume the knowledge or reasons why would be accessible to humans? Are the goods, which would provide morally sufficient reason for God to allow gratuitous evil that humans are aware of or could conceive of, provide enough data to be a representative sample of the morally sufficient reasons God may have to permit gratuitous evil? I argue that if God is as defined in the problem of evil, all-powerful, all-knowing, and wholly good, humans are not in and should not expect to be in a position to know what God could or could not, would, or would not do. Nor are humans in a position to know what sufficient reasons God may have for allowing evil. It cannot be shown by the available data or epistemic situation that any evil is gratuitous; thus, it is plausible there is a sufficient and good reason for it.[218]

As Doc Brown communicates to Marty about their epistemic situation; Not knowing how Marty seeing his older self would affect the space-time continuum. Doc is only able to see two possibilities. Humans are not in an epistemic situation to assess the possible reasons God may have for allowing instances of evil that seem pointless. I argue that while some evil may appear pointless, it is plausible that it does have a point humans cannot understand.

Human Limitations in Defining Divine Attributes (Inigo Montoya)

In the movie *The Princess Bride,* the characters Inigo Montoya and Vizzini have the following exchange when there is repeated failure to cause the Dread Pirate Roberts to fall off a cliff, and Vizzini repeatedly uses the word Inconceivable:

Vizzini
He didn't fall? Inconceivable!
Inigo
You keep using that word. I do not think it means what you think it means.[219]

In this section of the theodicy, I am referencing the work and philosophical work of Thomas Aquinas, Stephen Wykstra, and Eleonore Stump.

Throughout this theodicy I have made ample use of analogy. An analogy illustrates correspondence between two situations, which clarify a similar truth between the situations. Analogies are an amazing tool of communication. However analogies also break down. Analogies are meant to show correspondence, but that correspondence is a always limited. For instance in the previous section I used the analogy of the broken gas tank in my car to illustrate humanity's epistemic situation when it comes to reasons why God would allow seemingly pointless evil. While it worked to show that I probably would have a hard time knowing how much gas was in the tank given the extra use, I could have easily found out. I could have researched that the tank in my car was a 15 gallon tank and that in the city my car got 24 miles to the gallon while it got 28 miles to the gallon on the highway. I could have reset the trip setting on the odometer and by simple math gained reasonable epistemic access to whether my car would run out of gas or not. The analogy breaks down.

I will argue in this final section what I believe to be the most important charge against the critics. The charge is that the human definition used in the argument of the problem of evil by theist and atheist alike is not sufficient to describe God (should such a being exist). The definition of God commonly used in the problem of evil are the divine attributes of an omnipotent, omniscient, wholly good being. This definition like all analogies is a reduction. It breaks down and distorts God as God is. When humans try to make God accountable to the human understanding of these terms, humans neither error down to false equivalence nor reach anywhere near a reasonable facsimile. As Aquinas says, "God is more distant from creatures than any creatures are from each other."[220] Thomas Aquinas says in the Summa Theologiae P1 Q13,

> "It seems that no word is applied literally to God.... No word can be said literally of something if it is more truly denied of it than predicated of it. But all such words as 'good,' 'wise,' and the like are more truly denied of God than predicated of him, as is clear from what Dionysius says in The Celestial Hierarchy, (chap. 2, no. 3). Therefore none of these names belong to God in their literal sense."[221]

Aquinas asserts that humans speak and know about God by analogy. The human understanding of God as omnipotent, omniscient, wholly good is neither univocal nor equivocal. God's goodness and God as the center and circumference of good are more unlike human good and goodness than the same (literal). The human conception of God is a gesture towards or a shadow of God's power, knowledge, and state of good, but it is neither utterly unrelated nor precisely the same. Aquinas asserts that human understanding of omnipotent, omniscience and wholly good is more, unlike God's simplicity, than it is alike. God as the center and circumference of omnipotence is more unlike the human conception of

189

unlimited power than it is alike. Thus, humans can only conceive of omnipotence by analogy. Finally, God's being the center and circumference of omniscience, the state of God as all-knowing, is conceptually something humans can only grasp by analogy and not literally for "language as we use it, will fail to represent adequately what God is."[222]

Aquinas states, "no name belongs to God in the same sense that it belongs to creatures."[223] Conversely, Aquinas also asserts, "neither, on the other hand, are such names applied to God and creatures in a purely equivocal sense, as some have said. If true, it follows that nothing could be known or demonstrated about God from creatures, for the reasoning would always be exposed to the fallacy of equivocation."[224] Aquinas speaks of shades of likeness and the analogy of being. There is correspondence and partial similarity between God and humans. In Aquinas' teachings, there is the horizontal and the vertical analogy of being. In the horizontal analogy of being, Aquinas discusses the categories humans encounter across the world's horizon. In Aquinas, with the vertical analogy of being, everything in creation has good; goodness is inherent there. The vertical analogy of being is dealing with the very different realities of substances and accidents. If God is the cause of all that exists, then the effects must possess analogous goodness to the cause. Humans infer from creation the goodness of God. In this way, marriage, parenting, even nature itself is analogies that point humanity to the goodness of God.

The difference between God and man is qualitative, not quantitative. God's power is not human power on steroids. It is qualitatively other. God's knowledge is not human knowledge on crack; it is qualitatively other; God's goodness is not human goodness with the high beams on. Therefore when humans define God as an omnipotent (all-powerful), omniscient (all-knowing), and wholly good (perfectly good), the qualitative otherness of those attributes cannot be reduced to or ascended from human attributes and cognitive understandings of power, knowledge, and goodness.[225]

To think humans can reduce the existence of God or hold God accountable to a human analogically gestured definition is inadequate at best and more likely asinine. God is the "source and goal of all things," the center and circumference. God is unknowable yet makes himself known both by reason and revelation.[226]

THE SIMPLICITY AND GOODNESS OF GOD

In P1 Q3 A4, Aquinas discusses the simplicity of God. The unity between God's essence and existence. Avicenna is quoted as saying, "In God alone essence (what he is) and existence (that he is) coincide." God's simplicity and perfection are intrinsically tied to one another. God is simple in that God is whole, not a composite of individual substances. Humans have a body, a mind, and a soul; humanity is, therefore, a composite. Because God is whole, God is simple in that God is both immaterial and indivisible. Humans share a nature with other humans, where God shares a nature with none other. God shares no kind while humans receive examples of what it means to be good from each other.

When humans speak of God as wholly good, how does the simplicity of God change the meaning of that word? When applied to God, good does not mean that God possesses the attribute of good like humans learn good from each other. Merriam Webster defines good in the human sense as "of a favorable character or tendency."[227] Human constructs of good, though accurate, are reductionist to understand what good is in its perfect and simple form. Rather, good when applied to God includes the human understanding of good but also means God *IS* good. God is the very nature or essence of goodness. God is the center and circumference of good. Even the most comprehensive combination of understanding God's good is still reduced as God's goodness is not cumulative as humans' conception of good and goodness is. God is undivided and whole. God *IS* good. All the goodness of humanity are divided and multipllicious diluted parts of the whole of God's goodness. In the Q13 A2 Reply to O2, Aquinas states, "And as God is simple, and subsisting, we attribute to Him abstract names to signify His simplicity, and concrete names to signify His substance and perfection, although both these kinds of names fail to express His mode of being, forasmuch as our intellect does not know Him in this life as He is."

God's knowledge is an eternal simple gaze. God is omnipresent. God first knew himself before creation. God foreknew that He would create the world. God knew He would create secondary causes, persons with free will. God foreknew our choices. Analogously like a songwriter has the idea of a song (melody, rhythm, lyrics) before recording the song. Unlike a songwriter, God does not have lots of parts (ideas) in his head. Therefore things in the world are modeled on the whole of God himself. In a phenomenological sense, God knows all the angles and aspects at once. Humans can participate, but in parts, not the whole; humans are subjective, God is not.

Aquinas asserts that even our concept of God cannot grasp his essence because human experience is entirely linear and temporal; God is not limited by time, space, or matter. God's knowledge is not limited to experience, the present, or the past. God is not confined in temporality. Robert Sokolowski states, "temporality is the condition for perceptions, memories, and anticipations and for the self that lives in them."[228]

GOD'S OMNISCIENCE/HIS KNOWLEDGE

Merriam Webster defines omniscient as "possessed of universal or complete knowledge."[229] Epistemologically human knowledge comes from ideas. Ideas are defined as representational images, concepts, and judgments.[230] God does not have ideas in his mind in the same way humans do. To Aquinas, God's knowledge is an eternal simple gaze. God sees and knows all, all at once.

Humans have a natural knowledge of divine attributes. Humans can know God analogously by God's creative effects. Humans can know God naturally by inference. Humans can, by inference, know the cause by the effects as effects by necessity point to a cause. Humans know God's knowledge analogously by humanity's bent towards a desire for meaning, logic, and reason, but this knowledge is linear and confined. God is the first mover and the cause of all. Humans can know God naturally from potential to actual in the effects of the universal cause. In P1 Q2 A3 Aquinas states,

"After all, to effect movement is just to lead something from potentiality into actuality. But a thing cannot be led from potentiality into actuality except through some being that is in actuality in a relevant respect; for example, something that is hot in actuality- say a fire- makes a piece of wood, which is hot in potentiality, to be hot in actuality, and it thereby moves and altars the piece of wood.... For what is hot in actuality cannot simultaneously be hot in potentiality; rather it is cold in potentiality. Therefore, it is impossible that something should be both mover and moved in the same way and with respect to the same thing, or, in other words, that something should move itself. Therefore, everything that is moved must be moved by another."[231]

To know a cause perfectly through its effects is impossible, according to Aquinas. Aquinas posits that human conceptions cannot know God's essence because human conceptions are trapped within time, within temporality. When humans conceive of omnipotence, it is temporally thought. Humans, having experienced existence within time and therefore conceive of omnipotence within a linear sequence. Limitation necessitated by a temporal experience is just one aspect of how God's knowledge and power differ from humanities. When God is said to be omnipresent, humans being subject to time think of God's presence in the continual present, but time is not a construct for God; God is not subject to time; time is subject to God.

God sees the whole and therefore is not limited by time, space or matter. God is not bound by a myopic micro linear view but sees cognitively in a full 360 degrees. God's knowledge is not limited to experience, the present, or the past. God is not trapped in temporality. Robert Sokolowski states, "temporality is the condition for perceptions, memories, and anticipations and for the self that lives in them."[232]

Given the qualitative difference, humans' lack of knowledge or even the ability to quantify God's knowledge leaves humanity in no position to assert much of anything about God's omniscience. What God would or would not, could or could not do. Stephen Wykstra, in his response to William Rowe, asserts that humans do not have reasonable epistemic access to God's knowledge.[233] Aquinas appears to agree with this premise in chapter LXXI of the *Summa Contra Gentiles* when he argues,

"The good of the whole is of more account than the good of the part. Therefore, it belongs to a prudent governor to overlook a lack of goodness in a part, that there may be an increase of goodness in the whole."[234]

GOD'S OMNIPOTENCE AND HUMAN HAPPINESS

According to *The Cambridge Dictionary of Philosophy*, power is "an ability or capacity to yield some outcome."[235] Humans think of power in terms of relations, acting and being acted upon, active and passive. When God is said to be all-powerful, it is always active, for God is never acted upon; God's power is not passive. The process of events through time has no bearing on his omnipotence. Aquinas states Q25 A1 in his answer that, "Whence it most fittingly belongs to Him to be an active principle, and in no way whatsoever to be passive. On the other hand, the notion of active principle is consistent with active power. For active power is the principle of acting upon something else whereas passive power is the principle of being acted upon by something else, as the Philosopher says (Metaph. v, 17). It remains, therefore, that in God there is active power in the highest degree."

What of pain and evil? What do pain and evil say of God's power, knowledge, and goodness? Eleonore Stump, in her theodicy titled *Aquinas On The Sufferings of Job*, quotes Aquinas as stating, "If all the pain a human being suffers is from God, then he ought to bear it patiently, both because it is from God and because it is ordered toward good; for pains purge sins, bring evildoers to humility, and stimulate good people to love God."[236] In P2 Q3 of the *Summa Theologiae*, Aquinas says, "Final and perfect happiness cannot consist in anything other the vision of the divine essence."[237] In Aquinas, there are two types of happiness: natural happiness, which is achieved by practicing or making a habit of the moral virtues, and supernatural or perfect happiness, which requires practicing or making a habit of the moral virtues but also requires being united to God through the Holy Spirit.

According to Aquinas, happiness is not a feeling or something that passively happens to us. Happiness is a state or activity of living the human life well. By which we attain what is truly good for us. What is truly good requires the opportunity to practice moral virtues and being united to God. These opportunities often manifest in pain and suffering. Humans are most human when making decisions oriented toward a good goal. Humans have disordered passions. Lowly passions within humans rebel against what is higher in humans and thus distort what humans think is truly good. Humans are not very adept at knowing what is truly good. Humans often assert pleasure as the ultimate good and then question God's power, knowledge and goodness if God does not grant the pleasure sought.

Aquinas says, "Now it sometimes happens that God hearkens not to a person's pleas but rather for his advantage. A doctor does not hearken to the pleas of the sick person who requests that the bitter medicine be taken away; instead he hearkens to the patient's advantage, because doing so produces health, which the sick person wants most of all."[238]

Aquinas believes pain and suffering are not an indictment on

God's omnipotence, omniscience, or goodness as perfect happiness is only found in humanity seeking God and that often (if not always) requires refining in the fires of pain and suffering. Aquinas states,

> "If therefore the human intellect, knowing the essence of some created effect, knows no more of God than that he is; the perfection of that intellect does not yet reach the first cause in an absolute way, but there remains in it the natural desire to seek the cause. For the reason it is not yet perfectly happy."[239]

The issue is not whether God's power to remove suffering or grant pleasures says anything quantitatively about God's power but rather qualitatively do humans have an understanding about what it means to be human and perfectly happy in light of God's omnipotence. Are humans even in a position to relate the human understanding of power to that of God so that it would be more like God's omnipotence than unlike it?

The difference between human knowledge and God's knowledge is not simply a quantitative matter (of there potentially being goods we might not know), but the difference is qualitative. In P1 Q13 A2: *Whether any name can be applied to God substantially*, Aquinas points out that God is known in three ways, by the relation between cause and effect, by negation, and by analogy. The first way to name God is by causality. There are goods humans experience and this effect of good points to a cause by analogy. The second is through negation; God's goodness is not univocal or a synonym to human goodness; it is dissimilar. Humans can know God's goodness by what human goodness lacks. Third is God's preeminence; divine goodness is qualitatively different from human goodness.

Aquinas is between two poles. One pole asserts humans understand the divine attributes accurately, and thus the definition as given in the problem of evil arguments is univocal. The other pole says there is no similarity between God's power, knowledge, goodness, and human understanding. Humans cannot know anything of God on this pole, which renders the whole problem of evil moot.

The definition of God as an omnipotent, omniscient, and wholly good God is not inaccurate, but it is incomplete. "It is impossible for something to be predicated univocally of God and creatures. The reason for this is that every effect that is not an adequate result of the power of the efficient cause receives the likeness of the agent, not in its full degree."[240] Aquinas also states, "For these names express God, so far as our intellects know Him...Therefore the aforesaid names signify the divine substance, but in an imperfect manner."[241] It is a mistake to reduce knowledge of God down to two unacceptable positions.

Therefore like Inigo to Vizzini, when the atheologian (atheist) or even the theologian (theist) defines God as an omnipotent, omniscient, and wholly good being and intends that definition to be taken as univocal, It is plausible that God might say something akin to, "You keep using those words. I do not think they mean what you think they mean."[242]

- Analogy- illustrating correspondence between two situations.
- Univocal- having exactly the same or only one possible meaning.
- Equivocal- open to multiple meanings and interpretations. Not necessarily the same at all.
- Qualitative difference- a difference in essence or nature.
- Quantitative- a difference in degree.

Conclusion

In 2006, I deconstructed my blind belief in the attributes of God. I doubted mightily during this time, but I tried to make sure I did not trade a bias towards one worldview for another. I decided to doubt my doubt and give the views of the divine attributes I had been holding the same footing as not keeping them. Here is the conclusion I came to. By 2007, my faith was stronger than ever and I had reconstructed my belief in the divine attributes but with an expanded view on what those attributes meant. In this theodicy, I have argued that contrary to the critics, God could not have created a world of free creatures where evil could not or would not exist. God created the potential for evil when God created beings with free will (angelic and human), but God did not actualize the privation of evil. The actualization of evil (particularly moral evil) is necessitated only by the free choices of beings with free will. It is plausible that evil (pain and suffering) has a beneficial impact on the ultimate good and therefore contrary to the critics, it is both plausible and probable that God has good reasons for allowing evil. Humanity's epistemic situation is such that humans cannot fully comprehend why God would allow suffering but this does not make it implausible nor even improbable that there are no reasons. Humanity's epistemic situation also is such that humans cannot fully comprehend the divine attributes espoused even by the critics in the definition of God in the problem of evil. There is implicit ignorance within the definition even the critics use to define God (should such a being exist). Humans can only comprehend the divine attributes by analogy and therefore cannot judge whether God lives up to the definition. The three arguments above were used to show why evil and an omnipotent, omniscient, and wholly good God is not merely possible but plausible and probable. Working through this reconstruction I was able to recover my belief in an omnipotent, omniscient, and omni-good God despite the existence of suffering and evil. Some of which still makes no sense at all to me, but like Human League put it, "I'm only human, of flesh and blood I'm made." All I can do with suffering is Sing On through it, even when I can't understand it. All I can do is run to my father, even knowing he is allowing the pain. If I believe in the divine attributes, then I also must trust he has a good reason for allowing suffering and evil.

Sing On

CH.
Sing On when trouble comes your way just
Sing On your friends have gone away
Sing On Sing On Sing On
Sing On
Lift your hands
Praise his name and Sing On

V.1
We don't blame the ocean
For its rushing tide
And it don't change its beauty
When ships crash in the night
The waves just ebb and flow
Sometimes high sometimes low so don't you know
When push comes to shove
Just look above and trust His love Sing On

CH.
Sing On When you feel betrayed just
Sing On When one you love is in the grave
Sing On Sing On all you can do is Sing On
Sing On
Lift your hands
Say his name and Sing On

V.2
Like the parent let the scalpel
Of the surgeon's knife
Give their child a scar for
The rest of their lives
Though the child don't know why

It's to fix a hear that ain't right
So trust him in the dark
Like you do in the light
That'll testify, and sing On

CHORUS
Sing On When there's more questions than answers
Sing On Cause the doctor says its cancer
Sing On Sing on Sing On
Sing On
Lift your hands
Say his name and Sing On

CHORUS
Sing On when nothing dries your tears just
Sing On You keep on reeling in the years you
Sing On ain't nothing you can do but
Sing On
Raise your hands
Say his name and Sing On[243]

DISCUSSION QUESTIONS

1. What is the primary difference between the logical problem of evil and the evidential problem of evil?

2. In the What are the critics saying section, which philosophers make a logical argument against the existence of God and which are making an evidential argument against the existence of God?

3. In what way does Dr. Strange in the Possible Worlds section make a Leibnizian argument? Discuss the ideas of potentiality and actuality in light of the dialogue between Strange and Tony Stark?

4. In your own words describe what is meant by a state of affairs obtaining?

5. In your own words describe what is meant by transworld depravity? How does Classic Loki affirm Transworld depravity?

6. How does Plantinga reconcile God's omniscience and God's limitations on what worlds are possible for him to create?

7. How does Bruce Nolan exemplify the concept of virtue development? Bruce was gifted by God with divine attributes. Bruce receives all he could ever want but in the process loses his girlfriend. In the end Bruce finally learns that love is about sacrifice, what you give not what you get. Could Bruce have developed the virtues he did without going through the suffering he did?

8. Does a good parent always want their children to be happy? Explain the difference between love and kindness.

9. Both *Lord Knows* and *Sing On* reference cancer, why do you think this theme reoccurs in the author's work? Is there a difference in tone between the references to cancer? If so why do you think there is a difference?

10. 2 Corinthians 4:17 states, "For our light and momentary troubles are achieving for us an eternal glory that far outweighs them all." Weigh this against the quote from the movie *Eternals*, do they agree with one another? If so in what ways?

11. Describe what is meant by seeability. How does the concept of seeability impact what can be assumed by what appears?

12. What is the difference between the terms univocal, equivocal, and analogous?

13. What is meant by the assertion that God (and his divine attributes) is qualitatively not quantitatively different than humans?

14. What is meant by God being simple?

15. What is the difference between essence and existence?

16. What does Aquinas mean by the good of the whole is better than the good of the part in regard to the divine attributes?

17. How can suffering be ordered toward good? Can even a fawn suffering for days be ordered towards good? The author describe his beloved pet of 12 years dying, justify how this can be ordered toward good?

18. In *Sing on* the first verse references the Simone Weil quotes her book *Waiting for God* when she says, "The sea is not less beautiful in our eyes because we know that ships are sometimes wrecked by it. If it altered the movement of its waves to spare a ship it would be a creature gifted with discernment and choice, and not this fluid perfectly obedient to every external power. It is this obedience which makes the sea's beauty." Why is natures obedience to its laws what makes it beautiful? Would a good God necessarily always interfere with the laws of nature?

19. The second verse of *Sing On* is inspired from the work

of Marilyn McCord Adams who states, "the two-year-old heart patient is convinced of its mother's love, not by her cognitively inaccessible reasons, but by her intimate care and presence through its painful experience." What point do you think Adams is trying to make?

20. Danish Philosopher and father of existentialism Soren Kierkegaard states, "It is the duty of the human understanding to understand that there are things which it cannot understand." Correlate this statement to how the author frames the divine attributes within the Thomistic concept of analogy?

BIBLIOGRAPHY

Adams, Marilyn McCord, and Robert Merrihew Adams. *The Problem of Evil*. Oxford, UK: Oxford University Press, 2009.

Aquinas, Thomas, and Frederick Christian Bauerschmidt. *Holy Teaching: Introducing the Summa Theologiae of St. Thomas Aquinas*. Grand Rapids, MI: Brazos, 2005.

Audi, Robert, ed. *Cambridge Dictionary of Philosophy*. 2nd ed. New York, NY: Cambridge University Press, 1999.

Audi, Robert. "State of Affairs." In *Cambridge Dictionary of Philosophy* 2, 2:876. New York, NY: Cambridge University Press, 1999.

Avengers: Endgame. Film. S.l.: Marvel, 2019.

Back to the Future. USA: Universal Studios, 1985.

Bauerschmidt, Frederick Christian. *Thomas Aquinas: FAITH, Reason, and Following Christ*. Oxford, UK: Oxford University Press, 2015.

Bruce Almighty. United States: Universal Studios, 2003.

Burch, R. "Plantinga and LEIBNIZ'S Lapse." *Analysis* 39, no. 1 (1979): 24–29. https://doi.org/10.1093/analys/39.1.24.

Copan, Paul. *Loving Wisdom a Guide to Philosophy and Christian Faith*. Grand Rapids, MI: William B. Eerdmans Publishing Company, 2020.

Eternals. Walt Disney Studios, 2021.

Foltz, Bruce V., Mohammad Azadpur, David Bradshaw, Peter J. Casarella, and Sarah Pessin. "28/Thomas Aquinas." Essay. In *Medieval Philosophy: A Multicultural Reader*, 293–314. London, UK: Bloomsbury Academic, 2019.

"Good." In *The New Merriam-Webster Dictionary*. Springfield, MA: Merriam-Webster Inc., 1989.

Howard-Snyder, Daniel. *The Evidential Argument from Evil*. Bloomington: Indiana University Press, 1996.

Hume, David. *Dialogues Concerning Natural Religion*. La Vergne, TN: Antiquarius, 2021.

Kvanvig, Jonathan L. "'He Who Lapse Last Lapse Best.'"

Southwest Philosophy Review 10, no. 1 (1994): 137–46. https://doi.org/10.5840/swphilreview199410114.

Leibniz, Gottfried Wilhelm, and Lloyd Strickland. *Leibniz on God and Religion: A Reader.* New York, NY: Bloomsbury Academic, 2016.

Leibniz, Gottfried Wilhelm. *Theodicy.* Whithorn, Newton Steward, Dumfries & Galloway: Anodos Books, 2019.

Lennon, Thomas M., and Michael Hickson. "Pierre Bayle." Stanford Encyclopedia of Philosophy. Stanford University, December 5, 2017. https://plato.stanford.edu/entries/bayle/.

Lewis, C. S. *The Four Loves.* Brantford, ON: W. Ross MacDonald School Resource Services Library, 2017.

Lewis, C. S. *The Problem of Pain.* United States: Valde Books, 2021.

Martinich, Aloysius P. *Early Modern Philosophy: Essential Readings with Commentary.* Oxford, UK: Blackwell Publishing, 2007.

"Molinism." Merriam-Webster. Merriam-Webster. Accessed August 11, 2021. https://www.merriam-webster.com/dictionary/Molinism.

Nieuwenhove, Van Rik, Joseph P. Wawrykow, and David B. Burrell. "Analogy, Creation, and Theological Language." Essay. In *The Theology of Thomas Aquinas*, 77–98. Notre Dame, IN: University of Notre Dame Press, 2010.

Pavelich, Andrew. "The Moral Problem with the Free Will Defense against the Problem of Evil." *The Heythrop Journal* 60, no. 5 (2017): 678–88. https://doi.org/10.1111/heyj.12654.

Pieper, Josef, Richard Winston, and Clara Winston. *Guide to Thomas Aquinas.* San Francisco, CA: Ignatius Press, 1991.

Plantinga, Alvin. *God, Freedom and Evil.* Grand Rapids, Mich: William B. Eerdmans, 2008.

The Princess Bride. United States: Twentieth Century Fox Film Corporation, 1987.

Scheinman, Andrew, and William Goldman. *The Princess Bride.* Santa Monica, CA: MGM Home Entertainment, 2001.

Simpson, Christopher Ben. *Modern Christian Theology*. London, UK: Bloomsbury T&T Clark, 2016.

Simpson, Christopher Ben. *Modern Christian Theology*. London, UK: Bloomsbury T&T Clark, 2020.

Sokolowski, Robert. *Introduction to Phenomenology*. Cambridge, UK: Cambridge University Press, 2008.

Spurgeon, C. H. *Sermons on Great Prayers of the Bible*. Peabody, MA: Hendrickson Publishers, 2015.

Textor, Mark. "States of Affairs." Stanford Encyclopedia of Philosophy. Stanford University, May 12, 2021. https://plato.stanford.edu/entries/states-of-affairs/.

Webster, Noah. "Omniscient." In *Https://Www.merriam-Webster.com/Dictionary/Omniscient*, 2021.

Whole. *Loki*. Atlanta, GA: Disney+, 2021.

Endnotes

163. David Hume, *Dialogues Concerning Natural Religion* (La Vergne, TN: Antiquarius, 2021).

164. Ibid.

165. Gottfried Wilhelm Leibniz and Lloyd Strickland, *Leibniz on God and Religion: A Reader* (New York, NY: Bloomsbury Academic, 2016), 9.

166. Aloysius P. Martinich, *Early Modern Philosophy: Essential Readings with Commentary* (Oxford, UK: Blackwell Publishing, 2007), 233.

167. Christopher Ben Simpson, *Modern Christian Theology* (London, UK: Bloomsbury T&T Clark, 2020), 102.

168. Thomas M. Lennon and Michael Hickson, "Pierre Bayle," *Stanford Encyclopedia of Philosophy* (Stanford University, December 5, 2017), https://plato.stanford.edu/entries/bayle/.

169. C. S. Lewis, *The Four Loves* (Brantford, ON: W. Ross MacDonald School Resource Services Library, 2017), 176.

170. Gottfried Wilhelm Leibniz, *Theodicy* (Whithorn, Newton Steward, Dumfries & Galloway: Anodos Books, 2019), 71.

171. Written by Jason Lee McKinney (Zekers and ZiZi Music (BMI); and Scott Faircloff (Scottfair Music (ASCAP)

172. Marilyn McCord Adams and Robert Merrihew Adams, *The Problem of Evil* (Oxford, UK: Oxford University Press, 2009), 26.

173. Marilyn McCord Adams and Robert Merrihew Adams, *The Problem of Evil* (Oxford, UK: Oxford University Press, 2009), 29.

174. Daniel Howard-Snyder, *The Evidential Argument from Evil* (Bloomington: Indiana University Press, 1996), 2.

175. Marilyn McCord Adams and Robert Merrihew Adams, *The Problem of Evil* (Oxford, UK: Oxford University Press, 2009), 129–130.

176. Daniel Howard-Snyder, *The Evidential Argument from Evil*

(Bloomington: Indiana University Press, 1996), 3.

177. Daniel Howard-Snyder, *The Evidential Argument from Evil* (Bloomington: Indiana University Press, 1996), 14.

178. Daniel Howard-Snyder, *The Evidential Argument from Evil* (Bloomington: Indiana University Press, 1996), 14.

179. Daniel Howard-Snyder, *The Evidential Argument from Evil* (Bloomington: Indiana University Press, 1996), 23–24.

180. Andrew Pavelich, "The Moral Problem with the Free Will Defense against the Problem of Evil," *The Heythrop Journal* 60, no. 5 (August 2017): pp. 678–688, https://doi.org/10.1111/heyj.12654, 679.

181. Daniel Howard-Snyder, *The Evidential Argument from Evil* (Bloomington: Indiana University Press, 1996), 193.

182. Daniel Howard-Snyder, *The Evidential Argument from Evil* (Bloomington: Indiana University Press, 1996), 204.

183. *Avengers: Endgame* (Marvel, 2019).

184. Robert Audi, "State of Affairs," in *Cambridge Dictionary of Philosophy* (New York, NY: Cambridge University Press, 1999), p. 876.

185. Alvin Plantinga, *God, Freedom and Evil* (Grand Rapids, MI: William B. Eerdmans, 2008), 35.

186. Mark Textor, "States of Affairs," *Stanford Encyclopedia of Philosophy* (Stanford University, May 12, 2021), https://plato.stanford.edu/entries/states-of-affairs/.

187. Alvin Plantinga, *God, Freedom and Evil* (Grand Rapids, MI: William B. Eerdmans, 2008), 36,37.

188. Marilyn McCord Adams and Robert Merrihew Adams, *The Problem of Evil* (Oxford, UK: Oxford University Press, 2009), 178.

189. Alvin Plantinga, *God, Freedom and Evil* (Grand Rapids, MI: William B. Eerdmans, 2008), 40.

190. Gottfried Wilhelm Leibniz, *Theodicy* (Whithorn, Newton Steward, Dumfries & Galloway: Anodos Books, 2019), 39.

191. Jonathan L. Kvanvig, "'He Who Lapse Last Lapse Best,'"

Southwest Philosophy Review 10, no. 1 (1994): pp. 137–146, https://doi.org/10.5840/swphilreview199410114, 138.

192. Alvin Plantinga, *God, Freedom and Evil* (Grand Rapids, MI: William B. Eerdmans, 2008),43.

193. *Avengers: Endgame* (Marvel, 2019).

194. Loki (Atlanta, GA: Disney+, 2021).

195. C. S. Lewis, *The Problem of Pain* (United States: Value Books, 2021), 57.

196. Alvin Plantinga, *God, Freedom and Evil* (Grand Rapids, MI: William B. Eerdmans, 2008), 51.

197. C. S. Lewis, *The Problem of Pain* (United States: Value Books, 2021), 18.

198. Alvin Plantinga, *God, Freedom and Evil* (Grand Rapids, MI: William B. Eerdmans, 2008), 51.

199. Alvin Plantinga, *God, Freedom and Evil* (Grand Rapids, MI: William B. Eerdmans, 2008), 53.

200. *Bruce Almighty* (Universal Studios, 2003).

201. *Eternals* (Walt Disney Studios, 2021).

202. Daniel Howard-Snyder, *The Evidential Argument from Evil* (Bloomington: Indiana University Press, 1996), 103–115.

203. C. H. Spurgeon, *Sermons on Great Prayers of the Bible* (Peabody, MA: Hendrickson Publishers, 2015).

204. C. S. Lewis, *The Problem of Pain* (United States: Value Books, 2021), 32.

205. C. S. Lewis, *The Problem of Pain* (United States: Value Books, 2021), 34.

206. Daniel Howard-Snyder, *The Evidential Argument from Evil* (Bloomington: Indiana University Press, 1996), 35–45.

207. Marilyn McCord Adams and Robert Merrihew Adams, *The Problem of Evil* (Oxford, UK: Oxford University Press, 2009), 169–170.

208. Marilyn McCord Adams and Robert Merrihew Adams, *The Problem of Evil* (Oxford, UK: Oxford University Press, 2009), 217.

209. Marilyn McCord Adams and Robert Merrihew Adams, *The Problem of Evil* (Oxford, UK: Oxford University Press, 2009), 45.

210. Marilyn McCord Adams and Robert Merrihew Adams, *The Problem of Evil* (Oxford, UK: Oxford University Press, 2009), 201.

211. Marilyn McCord Adams and Robert Merrihew Adams, *The Problem of Evil* (Oxford, UK: Oxford University Press, 2009), 203.

212. *Back to the Future* (Universal Studios, 1985).

213. Marilyn McCord Adams and Robert Merrihew Adams, *The Problem of Evil* (Oxford, UK: Oxford University Press, 2009),87–88.

214. Daniel Howard-Snyder, *The Evidential Argument from Evil* (Bloomington: Indiana University Press, 1996), 151–157.

215. Daniel Howard-Snyder, *The Evidential Argument from Evil* (Bloomington: Indiana University Press, 1996), 129.

216. Daniel Howard-Snyder, *The Evidential Argument from Evil* (Bloomington: Indiana University Press, 1996), 317.

217. Daniel Howard-Snyder, *The Evidential Argument from Evil* (Bloomington: Indiana University Press, 1996), 318–325.

218. Daniel Howard-Snyder, *The Evidential Argument from Evil* (Bloomington: Indiana University Press, 1996), 100.

219. *The Princess Bride* (Twentieth Century Fox Film Corporation, 1987).

220. Thomas Aquinas and Frederick Christian Bauerschmidt, *Holy Teaching: Introducing the Summa Theologiae of St. Thomas Aquinas* (Grand Rapids, MI: Brazos, 2005), 69.

221. Thomas Aquinas and Frederick Christian Bauerschmidt, *Holy Teaching: Introducing the Summa Theologiae of St. Thomas Aquinas* (Grand Rapids, MI: Brazos, 2005), 66.

222. Van Rik Nieuwenhove, Joseph P. Wawrykow, and David B. Burrell, "Analogy, Creation, and Theological Language," in *The Theology of Thomas Aquinas* (Notre Dame, IN: University

of Notre Dame Press, 2010), pp. 77–98, 78.

223. Thomas Aquinas and Frederick Christian Bauerschmidt, *Holy Teaching: Introducing the Summa Theologiae of St. Thomas Aquinas* (Grand Rapids, MI: Brazos, 2005), 69.

224. Thomas Aquinas and Frederick Christian Bauerschmidt, *Holy Teaching: Introducing the Summa Theologiae of St. Thomas Aquinas* (Grand Rapids, MI: Brazos, 2005), 70.

225. Christopher Ben Simpson, *Modern Christian Theology* (London, UK: Bloomsbury T&T Clark, 2016), 13–14.

226. Van Rik Nieuwenhove, Joseph P. Wawrykow, and David B. Burrell, "Analogy, Creation, and Theological Language," in *The Theology of Thomas Aquinas* (Notre Dame, IN: University of Notre Dame Press, 2010), pp. 77–98, 82.

227. "Good," in *The New Merriam-Webster Dictionary* (Springfield, MA: Merriam-Webster Inc., 1989).

228. Robert Sokolowski, *Introduction to Phenomenology (Cambridge*, UK: Cambridge University Press, 2008), 6.

229. Noah Webster, "Omniscient," in Https://Www.merriam-Webster.com/Dictionary/Omniscient, 2021.

230. Robert Audi, ed., *Cambridge Dictionary of Philosophy, 2nd ed.* (New York, NY: Cambridge University Press, 1999), 411.

231. Bruce V. Foltz et al., "28/Thomas Aquinas," in *Medieval Philosophy: A Multicultural Reader* (London, UK: Bloomsbury Academic, 2019), pp. 293–314, 305.

232. Robert Sokolowski, *Introduction to Phenomenology* (Cambridge, UK: Cambridge University Press, 2008), 6.

233. Daniel Howard-Snyder, *The Evidential Argument from Evil* (Bloomington: Indiana University Press, 1996), 126.

234. Marilyn McCord Adams and Robert Merrihew Adams, *The Problem of Evil* (Oxford, UK: Oxford University Press, 2009), 45.

235. Robert Audi, ed., *Cambridge Dictionary of Philosophy, 2nd ed.* (New York, NY: Cambridge University Press, 1999), 727.

236. Daniel Howard-Snyder, *The Evidential Argument from Evil*

(Bloomington: Indiana University Press, 1996), 55.

237. Thomas Aquinas and Frederick Christian Bauerschmidt, *Holy Teaching: Introducing the Summa Theologiae of St. Thomas Aquinas* (Grand Rapids, MI: Brazos, 2005), 110.

238. Daniel Howard-Snyder, *The Evidential Argument from Evil* (Bloomington: Indiana University Press, 1996), 55.

239. Thomas Aquinas and Frederick Christian Bauerschmidt, *Holy Teaching: Introducing the Summa Theologiae of St. Thomas Aquinas* (Grand Rapids, MI: Brazos, 2005), 110–111.

240. Thomas Aquinas and Frederick Christian Bauerschmidt, *Holy Teaching: Introducing the Summa Theologiae of St. Thomas Aquinas* (Grand Rapids, MI: Brazos, 2005), 70.

241. Thomas Aquinas and Frederick Christian Bauerschmidt, *Holy Teaching: Introducing the Summa Theologiae of St. Thomas Aquinas* (Grand Rapids, MI: Brazos, 2005), 71.

242. *The Princess Bride* (Twentieth Century Fox Film Corporation, 1987).

243. Written by Jason Lee McKinney (Zekers and ZiZi Music (BMI)

Part 4

Which God and In What Language?
A Defense of Christian Exclusivism and the Uniqueness of Jesus Against Plurality and Inclusivism.

INTRODUCTION

Ted Lasso is an Emmy-winning TV show about an American football coach who accepts the head coaching job for the English professional soccer club, the Richmond Greyhounds. In episode one of season two, the opening scene finds the team in the final minute of stoppage time, and a penalty occurs, giving a player a direct penalty kick. The following dialogue transpires between Coach Lasso and his assistant coaches.

NATE
Is it OK if I pray?
TED
Yeah, of course. But to which god and in what language, you know?
COACH BEARD
You could cross your fingers and make a wish.[244]

Later in season two, the following discussion happens between the coaches and the marketing director Keeley when the team owner's father passes away.

[Int. Coaches' office]

KEELEY

So, where do you think her father is right now?

ROY

In the drawer of a funeral home.

KEELEY

No. I mean, like, spiritually.

ROY

In the drawer of a funeral home.

TED

You know, growing up, I used to believe that if you did good things, you went to heaven. You did bad things; you went to hell. Nowadays, I know we all just do both. So, wherever he is, I hope he's happy.

HIGGINS

I like to imagine a heaven where animals are in charge, and humans are the pets. I'd like to spend eternity curled up in front of a fire at Cindy Clawford's feet.

TED

Yeah.

NATHAN

I'd like to be reincarnated as a tiger ... and then ravage anyone who looked at me wrong.

COACH BEARD

You know, if you weigh a person's body right after death, it's 21.3 grams lighter, and some say that's the weight of the soul.

KEELEY

Wow.

ROY

Whoever figured that out clearly weighed someone, murdered them, then weighed them again. You live, you die, you're done. Good night.[245]

These scenes in general and Ted's dialogue within them illustrate the next step in the serious seeker's or doubter's dilemma. Once the serious seeker has crossed into a belief that there is something rather than nothing because of a necessarily existing first causal agent and concludes it plausible, perhaps probable, that the causal agent is omnipotent, omniscient, wholly good and evil exists the question becomes, did this causal agent reveal themselves to humanity or not? If so, how did they reveal themselves, and is humanity accountable to respond?

I had never heard the word Muslim until my freshman year of college where I had a young Egyptian lady as an English composition teacher. What I remember about her is just a few bullet point things:

1. She spoke English very poorly and could not conjugate a verb to save her life
2. She was very sweet and tried very hard
3. She made killer baklava and
4. She seemed very sincere and devout not only in her devotion to Muhammad but also, she believed in Jesus.[246]

Wait what? Muslims believed in Jesus? My mind was blown. I mean Jesus was an American white guy, right? How in the world had an Egyptian lady even heard about Jesus, with his pale skin and blue eyes? What did this mean for my faith? I was taught that not only were atheists, Jews, new agers, and Catholics going to hell but most likely those charismatics too because they didn't really believe in the real Jesus like good Baptists did. That being said I did not grow up in a legalistic household at all. Other than my paternal grandparents that I mentioned in the earlier parts of the book, I did not have any truly religious people in my life (other than the super Pentecostals who lived up the street). My dad is best described as an agnostic. He believed there was something bigger than us out there but he didn't believe it could be known what that something was and so humans weren't accountable to it. My mom had a deep spiritual interest, but it was not that impactful on her life. She was searching. I remember she even got into new age crystals for a while. I am happy to say my mom's faith has grown and solidified over the years. If you are counting I grew up with four views of God. My grandparents loving and wise Father; My grandparents church's angry God who demanded I not fail, or he would send me straight to hell along with all the other people who couldn't measure up; my Dad's minimal deism, his *there must be something but who knows what it is*; and my mom's endless search for exactly what and who God was. The result is that I grew up with only two fundamental religious truths, you had to believe in Jesus, and you had to be a good person to escape hell. *Bam!* End of story—you were saved. The way I grew up you didn't need to read the Bible or go to church or really even know what it meant to "believe" in Jesus. The crazy thing for me is that this Muslim lady knew way more about Jesus than I did. For instance, Jesus was not white! He was a middle eastern man.

I began to question if what I knew about religion was correct. How did I know the image of Jesus I grew up with was the correct one? How did I know that the Christian Jesus was the real Jesus and not the Muslim Isa? If the main criteria were being a good person and believing in Jesus, this young Muslim professor had me beat by a mile. Could it be that Christians and Muslims both go to heaven? If Jesus is God maybe the main thing is to believe in God and be a good person which would mean that people from any religion could go to heaven. Finally, if Jesus died for everyone then maybe everyone goes to heaven. I personally would like that a lot better. I would prefer everyone go to heaven if it were up to me. I was deconstructing what it means to be a Christian and what it meant for people to obtain eternal life. It took me some time, but I was able to answer most of these questions and reconstruct my belief that Jesus was indeed the only way to heaven.

This part of the book is a reconstructive defense of Christian exclusivism and the uniqueness of Jesus against plurality and syncretism. I am walking you through my thought process in how I reconstruct my faith in Jesus being the only way to God.

Reconstruction is not a one-time thing; I find myself having to redo reconstruction from time to time even today. The evidence, philosophy, propositions and arguments that convince me remain relatively the same as the first time I deconstructed from my view of Christianity in college. When I went through this Jason Sudeikis was still playing AAU basketball not playing the role of Ted Lasso. I found and still find it pretty clear and never really doubted that the three major monotheistic religions of the world all make exclusive claims. I did have to reconstruct how these claims are incompatible with a pluralistic and inclusive view of religions. I was also able to reconstruct a strong belief that Christianity makes more coherent and plausible claims than the other major monotheistic religions. This part of the book will argue that it is plausible and much more probable to infer that the creator wants to be an active parent. Just because I am arguing this now, this does not mean I did not go through a deconstruction process and a lot of doubts about the exclusive claims of Jesus. A lot of my doubts came from the fact that I did not want it to be this way. I did not want the claims of Jesus to be exclusive. I would welcome a universalist view of salvation and I tried to find ways to justify that view, but I just could not reconcile it intellectually. The three major monotheistic religions make claims that are mutually exclusive. Contemporary society, myself included, really struggles with holding the tension of paradox. Paradox is almost like malware in our operating systems, it just does not compute. Yet there is much about existence that is a paradox. Soren Kierkegaard said of paradox, "One must not think slightingly of the paradoxical ... for the paradox is the source of the thinker's passion, and the thinker without a paradox is like a lover without feeling: a paltry mediocrity." If God the causal agent of existence did give divine revelation and there are claims of divine revelation that are mutually exclusive then those claims cannot be syncretized, one must be true, and the others must be false.

A little reminder that this book is called *Deconstructing a Disciple's Doubt*. It is not called *Deconstructing ALL Disciples EVERY*

Doubt. This section of the book is going to leave some things out simply because they are not things I have struggled with and given that fact I am not in a position to honestly address them from the standpoint of a doubter. I am not going to compare Christianity to any specific polytheistic or pantheistic belief system. I have just never doubted that if there is a God, there is only one God. To me if there were more than one God then that God does not have the divine characteristics of God and therefore is something less than God. A demigod is no God at all. I am not saying doubting whether there is more than one God or whether the universe is God are inferior doubts or not something that legitimately does not need to be worked through, it just is not something I have struggled with. I have for sure had my doubts about whether God existed (see Part 1) but never doubted that if there is a God, there is only one of them. I am also not going to address whether or not Jesus (the man) existed historically. I have never had a doubt that the man actually existed. I have doubted Jesus being God for sure but never that the guy existed. While his existence cannot be proved historically there is at least as much evidence of his existence as there is of any other historical figure. In fact Bart Ehrman an atheist New Testament scholar says in his book *Did Jesus Exist?*, "The idea that Jesus did not exist is a modern notion. It has no ancient precedents. It was made up in the eighteenth century. One might as well call it a modern myth, the myth of the mythical Jesus."[247] Ehrman goes on to say, "Despite the enormous range of opinion, there are several points on which virtually all scholars of antiquity agree. Jesus was a Jewish man, known to be a preacher and teacher, who was crucified (a Roman form of execution) in Jerusalem during the reign of the Roman emperor Tiberius, when Pontius Pilate was the governor of Judea."[248] I am not going to spend any time arguing or trying to build a case of Jesus existing as pretty much anyone who has studied the history agrees the guy existed. Finally, I am not going to address any of the miracles of Jesus other than his resurrection. In my mind if the guy raised himself from the dead then any of the other miracles are fair game. If I can get myself to be convinced of the resurrection, the inference to the best explanation is that the other miracles are entirely possible.

In her book *Confronting Christianity,* Rebecca McLaughlin retells a story from a Hindu text that illustrates the idea of religious pluralism. The traditional parable recounts how, phenomenologically, the revelation of the elephant's nature appears different to a group of blind men. The blind men hold varying epistemic positions, and each has access to a different part of the elephant (one the tail, another the trunk). Each of the blind men thinks they grasp the total objective truth of the elephant's nature. The parable's point is that to the blind man holding the tail, the elephant appears like a rope which is the truth from his position. It is not the total truth. McLaughlin states, "This story paints a vivid picture of our individual limitations."[249] The problem is that only the narrator is in the epistemic situation to see the whole elephant. Thus, the contradictions are genuine to the blind men. This analogy breaks down because there is no narrator for humanity who is in the position of knowing the entire situation. This does not however mean that there is no elephant. The elephant is there and is objectively real. The only way humans can know this is by divine revelation. Each person sees in part and knows in part, but this does not make the totality of the truth relative. The whole truth excludes any of the blind men's perspective being complete or being truly correct. Only a divine causal agent could have the total perspective. What if the elephant could speak to the blind men and reveal the totality of itself to them?

If the necessarily existing causal agent (God) did not give special revelation other than the general revelation of creating and setting the universe in motion, it would seem the order of the universe and existence itself are the only revelations (ala natural theology). If the necessarily existing causal agent is indifferent to humans, then it follows that humans are minimally accountable to respond or seek a relationship with the causal agent. This is what my dad believed. Suppose the causal agent did not give special revelation to humanity other than by creating the universe. Why would humans be expected to seek to know or understand the causal agent's character or motives for having created? I would assert that this form of belief is a sort of minimal deism. If this is the case, the serious seeker or doubter can end the journey here and go no further, but what if this causal agent (this Creator) did intend to give special revelation to humanity? What if the creator has used existence and nature to give special revelation to humanity but did not stop there? What if that creator expects humans to respond in some form or fashion to the creator for having created? What if the creator not only sets things in motion and allows all that happens to happen passively but is active within creation? What if the creator has stepped into humanity itself and wants to have a relationship with humans? Further what if the creator wants to have a personal relationship with humans. Further still what if no amount of religious ascetic fervor could ever earn a human's way into relationship with the Creator but the Creator makes a way for a relationship with humans out of nothing but pure love.

Even if the doubting disciple has established that there is a causal agent, which is evidentially good, what is more likely: the Creator sets things in motion and then only observes or the Creator is active within the universe and actively desiring a response from that creation? Is the Creator an absentee father who made the baby and then steps away, or is the Creator a dad who wants to teach, provide for, and play catch with his creation (even if at times that means letting his creation learn some painful lessons)?

This part of the book will argue that it is plausible and much more probable to infer that the Creator wants to be an active parent. If the Creator is an active parent desiring a response from humanity, humans have a much greater responsibility to respond actively. This is theism. Further classical theism is the belief in one God who is omnipotent, omniscient, and omni-good.

If the doubting disciple has reached the epistemic attitude of classical theism, the final question becomes, as Ted Lasso stated, "Which God?" Do all religions just take different paths to the same mountain top? Do all religions worship the same God? Or did the Creator reveal themselves in a particular way, and is the Creator's expectation that humans are accountable to that revelation? The rest of this part of the book will access these questions. I will outline the differences between polytheism, pantheism, monotheism, and pluralism; the exclusive claims of the three major monotheistic religions; if the exclusive claims can be reconciled; why and where Christianity differs from Islam and Judaism; the uniqueness and exclusivity of the resurrection of Christ, if belief in Jesus can coincide and intermingle with other paths to God, and finally if the Bible is still trustworthy and culturally relevant.

- Pluralism- the belief that all religions are equally valid and have equal access as a path to God(s). The belief that many or all religions lead to God. Many or all religions lead to salvation.
- Inclusivism- the belief that many or all religions have a partially valid claim and access to God.
- Syncretism- the blending of different religious faiths. Creating a homogenized belief system in order to reconcile differences between faiths.
- Exclusivism- the belief that only one religion has access to God. The belief that there is only one way to God.
- Particularism- the belief that there is a particular path/belief for salvation. Particularism and exclusivism are very closely related.
- Universalism- The belief that all humans will be saved by God no matter what religious beliefs or behaviors the individual person may exhibit.

The world has over 4,000 world religions ranging from Hinduism, Buddhism, Taoism to Jedism (worshiping the force).[250] Comparing all all 4,000 goes beyond the scope of the intent here. To narrow the scope, I will address the different overarching systems of belief and then focus on the religions within one of those systems (monotheism).

It is appropriate here to give some definitions. The world religions mostly fall into three systems of belief, pantheism, polytheism, and monotheism. Pantheism equates God with the forces and laws of the universe.[251] In pantheism, God is not the creator of the universe but the universe itself. Pantheistic religions include Buddhism and Confucianism.[252] Polytheism is the belief in or worship of more than one god.[253] Polytheistic religions include Hinduism and Taoism. Finally, as a reminder from Part 2 of the book, monotheism is the doctrine or belief that there is but one God.[254] Monotheistic religions include Islam, Judaism, and Christianity. The three largest religions in the world make particular and exclusive claims. There are forms of universalism. There is monotheistic syncretism where exclusive claims of one of the monotheistic religions is homogenized with another religion's exclusive claims. There is monotheistic inclusivism is the belief that salvation comes through one religion's path ultimately faithful followers of all monotheistic religions are grafted into that path by their faithfulness to their religion. Monotheistic Pluralism is the belief that all monotheistic religions lead to God and salvation. Monotheistic Exclusivism/Particularism is the belief that salvation comes only through the exclusive claims of one of the monotheistic religions. The distinctions between these are at times subtle but vitally important because all of the three major monotheistic religions are making exclusive and particularistic claims.

DO ISLAM, JUDAISM, AND CHRISTIANITY ALL CLAIM TO BE THE TRUTH?

Christianity and Islam are the two largest religions in the world.

Both are Abrahamic religions along with Judaism. They have historically had and presently maintain the most prominent influence upon humanity. All three religions are orthodoxically exclusivist and view pluralism in essence as evil or heresy. Rebecca McLaughlin says, "Monotheism is at its heart exclusive and universal."[255] McCoy, Corduan, and Stoker assert, "An exclusivist is diagnosed by interfaith scholars as those who insist on dividing people."[256] Exclusivism is indicted as having too particular a path to God, too particular of an ethical creed, too particular a salvation. In this regard, Islam, Judaism, and Christianity are all guilty. However, just because they are guilty of being exclusivist religions does not make them wrong.

ISLAM'S CLAIMS

Islam traces its origin back to the prophet Mohammed. Mohammed never claimed to be God.[257] Islam contends that one God (Allah) is not a trinity (Quran, 112:1). The Christian doctrine of the Trinity is heresy according to the teachings of the Quran.[258] In Quran 5:73–75 it states,

"Indeed, they disbelieve who say: 'God is the third of three (in a trinity),' when there is no god but one God. If they desist not from what they say, truly, a painful punishment will befall the disbelievers among them. Would they not rather repent to God and ask His forgiveness? For God is Oft-Forgiving, Most Merciful. The Messiah (Isa), son of Mary, was no more than a messenger."

God the Son and the Holy Spirit are seen as other Gods and thus heretical as God is exclusively one in Islam.[259] The Quran, as revealed to the prophet Mohammed over about 20 years, is the final revelation given by Allah to humankind and Mohammed is the last and ultimate prophet.[260] Islam teaches that Jesus (Isa) was a prophet, sent by Allah and born of the Virgin Mary, but he was not divine nor the Messiah nor a redeemer (Quran 5:17). Islam teaches that Jesus was not crucified (Quran 4:157) but was raised to Heaven by

Allah (4:158). According to Jacob S. Dharmaraj and Glory E. Dharmaraj, "Islam demands religious action not theological analysis."[261] Soteriologically speaking salvation is a matter of ascetic ascent and never certain.[262] God gave the law through the Quran. Humanity's primary objective is to obey and observe the law not to have a personal relationship with God.[263] Islam is based upon a concept of fairness and reward unlike Christianity's grace. Grace is thought to remove any motivation for leading a moral life.[264] God is both good and evil which is in direct contradiction with Christianity and Judaism's teachings that God is good. Islam has five pillars of faith.

THE FIVE PILLARS ARE THE CORE BELIEFS AND PRACTICES OF ISLAM:

1. Profession of Faith (shahada). The belief that "There is no god but God, and Muhammad is the Messenger of God" is central to Islam.
2. Prayer (salat). Muslims pray facing Mecca five times a day: at dawn, noon, mid-afternoon, sunset, and after dark. Prayer includes a recitation of the opening chapter (sura) of the Quran and is sometimes performed on a small rug or mat used expressly for this purpose.
3. Alms (zakat). In accordance with Islamic law, Muslims donate a fixed portion of their income to community members in need.
4. Fasting (sawm). During the daylight hours of Ramadan, the ninth month of the Islamic calendar, all healthy adult Muslims are required to abstain from food and drink.
5. Pilgrimage (hajj). Every Muslim whose health and finances permit it must make at least one visit to the holy city of Mecca, in present-day Saudi Arabia.[265]

JUDAISM'S CLAIMS

Judaism traces its origins back to the Hebrew leader Abraham founded Judaism around 2000 B.C. Judaism is the oldest of the monotheistic faiths. Judaism contends belief in one God (Yahweh). "Hear Israel, the Lord is our God, the Lord is one" (Deuteronomy 6:4). The Hebrew *Tanakh* comprised of the Torah (Law), Nevi'im (Prophets), and Ketuvim (Writings) is the only Holy and inspired word of God. Judaism is a nationalistic religion in that salvation is found in both the practice of living in adherence to the law but also identifying as a member of God's chosen people (whether by ethnicity, national citizenship, or being a Judaist). In the book *Religion and the Creation of Race and Ethnicity*, author Jacob Neusner states,

> "Judaism is a religion, with normative beliefs and practices. Jews who practice Judaism always belong to the ethnic group, the Jews. But matters are not so simple. Thus, by converting to Judaism, the religion, a gentile becomes not only a Judaist—one who practices Judaism—but a Jew. Such a one is then part of the Jewish community as much as of the community of Judaism."[266]

Judaism believes Jesus was an ordinary Jew, not the Messiah. Jesus has no relevance to Judaism. Judaism is still waiting for the Messiah or more common a Messianic age.[267] Judaism believes Jesus was crucified for his claim to be divine but remained dead. Judaism teaches that salvation is achieved through good works, prayers, and the justice of God but rejects the Christian teaching that salvation is by grace alone.[268] Like Islam Judaism rejects the Christian doctrine of the Trinity and asserts the oneness of God.[269]

The thirteen creedal articles of faith as articulated by Moses Maimonides:

1. Belief in the existence of the Creator, who is perfect in every manner of existence and is the Primary Cause of all that exists.
2. The belief in God's absolute and unparalleled unity.
3. The belief in God's non-corporeality, nor that He will be affected by any physical occurrences, such as movement, or rest, or dwelling.

225

4. The belief in God's eternity.
5. The imperative to worship God exclusively and no foreign false gods.
6. The belief that God communicates with man through prophecy.
7. The belief in the primacy of the prophecy of Moses our teacher.
8. The belief in the divine origin of the Torah.
9. The belief in the immutability of the Torah.
10. The belief in God's omniscience and providence.
11. The belief in divine reward and retribution.
12. The belief in the arrival of the Messiah and the messianic era.
13. The belief in the resurrection of the dead.[270]

CHRISTIANITY'S CLAIMS

Christianity was founded by Jesus of Nazareth, who was crucified around A.D. 30 in Jerusalem. Christianity contends for one God, who exists in three distinct persons (Trinity): Father, Son, and Holy Spirit (Matthew 28:19). The belief in the Trinity directly contradicts the teachings of both Islam and Judaism. Christianity asserts the Bible as the holy text given by God to man. Traditionally Christians believed God inspired the authors of the books in the Bible in their writings. Thus, Christians refer to the Bible as the Word of God (2 Timothy 3:16). The doctrine written in the canon of scripture directly contradicts the assertions of Judaism (the Torah) and Islam (the Quran) as the ultimate Holy books. Christians believe Jesus is the Messiah, the second person of the Trinity and born of the Virgin Mary (Mark 1:1; Mathew 1:23; Luke 1:33–34). The belief of Jesus as Messiah contradicts that of Judaism and of Islam. Christians believe Jesus to be divine and co-equal to God the Father. John 1:1–2 states, "In the beginning was the Word, and the Word was with God, and the Word was God. He was in the beginning with God." Christians believe Jesus was put to death by crucifixion. The Christian belief that Jesus was crucified directly contradicts that of Islam. Christianity teaches that Jesus rose from the dead. "The angel said to the women, "Do not be afraid, for I know that you are looking for Jesus, who was crucified. He is not here; he has risen, just as he said. Come and see the place where he lay" (Mathew 28:5–6). The belief that Jesus rose again contradicts that of Judaism. Christianity teaches that God's grace achieves salvation through faith in Jesus Christ alone.[271] "For by grace you have been saved through faith, and that not of yourselves; it is the gift of God, not of works, lest anyone should boast" (Ephesians 2:8–9). Salvation by grace alone through Jesus' sacrifice on a cross directly contradicts the teachings of both Judaism and Islam.

A commonly used Christian statement of faith across denomination lines is the Apostles Creed. The statement is as follows:

"We believe in God the Father Almighty, Maker of heaven and earth. And in Jesus Christ, His only Son, our Lord. Who was conceived by the Holy Spirit; Born of the Virgin Mary, Suffered under Pontius Pilate; Was crucified, dead and buried. He descended into Hell; The third day He rose again from the dead, He ascended into heaven; And sits on the right hand of God the Father Almighty, From thence He shall come to judge the living and the dead.

"We believe in the Holy Spirit, The Holy catholic Church, the Communion of Saints, The Forgiveness of sins; The Resurrection of the body; And the life everlasting. Amen."[272]

- Soteriology- The doctrine of how a human obtains salvation.

CAN THESE CLAIMS BE RECONCILED (SYNCRETISM)?

Can the three major Abrahamic faiths who all trace their origins back to the same man and all share at least some fundamental beliefs be traveling the same mountain of faith headed to the same destination. Are they all as children of Abraham included in the same ascension to God? Or are the differences in the three major monotheistic religions substantial and contradictory enough in their essence to preclude that?[273] The above outline of each of the faiths major beliefs and teachings show Islam, Judaism and Christianity are fundamentally and significantly different enough that the followers of each must believe the followers of the other two are mistaken at a minimum.[274] Alvin Plantinga puts forth, "He (follower of exclusive religions) must therefore see himself as privileged with respect to those others. There is something of great value, he must think, that he has and they lack."[275] In the article titled "Christians, Muslims, Jews, and Their Religions," author Jacques Waardenburg states, "From the outset of their encounters, these communities stressed the originality of their own religions and their own religious identity in contrast to each other. In present-day terms, no syncretism was officially allowed."[276] Tim Keller emphasizes how profound the differences between the three religions are by illuminating a statement constructed at a conference where all three faiths were represented. The statement agreed to is, "If Christians are right about Jesus being God, then Muslims and Jews fail in a serious way to love God as God really is, but if Muslims and Jews are right that Jesus is not God but rather a teacher or prophet, then Christians fail in a serious way to love God as God really is."[277] The significant tenets, teachings, and scriptures of Islam, Judaism, and Christianity all avow one singular path to God. Each of the three maintains and professes that their religion is the only path to God, and all others are false. To support the claim that all three religions are all basically the same is to ignore their exclusive claims and to reject each religion at its core. The Islamic confession of faith (Shahadah) states, "There is no God but God and Muhammad is the messenger of God."[278] Additionally, Islam claims that all prophets and messengers are human and not divine. Conversely, Christianity claims that Jesus was God and is the only way into a relationship with God (John 14:6). Logically speaking this proposition cannot be syncretized with any other religion. John 14:6 states, "I am the way, and the truth, and the life. No one comes to the Father except through me." Stated as a logical proposition is as follows:

P1: If anyone comes to the Father, then one comes through Jesus.
P2: One does not come through Jesus.
So, one does not come to the Father. [valid by modus tollens]
P2: One comes to the Father.
So, one comes through Jesus. [valid by modus ponens]
　　Note: here I received some great guidance and help from Richard Knopp, Ph.D.

- Modus Ponens-the rule of logic stating that if a conditional statement (if *p* then *q*) is accepted, and the antecedent (*p*) holds, then the consequent (*q*) may be inferred.
- Modus Tollens- the rule of logic stating that if a conditional statement ("if *p* then *q*) is accepted, and the consequent does not hold (*not-q*), then the negation of the antecedent (*not-p*) can be inferred.

Luke writes in Acts 4:12, "And there is salvation in no one else; for there is no other name under heaven that has been given among men by which we must be saved." In 1 John 5:12 reads, "He who has the Son has the life; he who does not have the Son of God does not have the life." These scriptures indicate that from Jesus own words and those of his closest followers, Christianity does not allow for multiple paths to God. Edward P. Meador's enlightens, "Being one with God, Jesus exclusively has the power to give life. As the word who was with God and was God and who brought everything into existence that has come into existence (Jn. 1:1–4), Jesus alone had and has the creative power to heal, rebirth, recreate, and resurrect.[279] In her book *Faith and Fratricide*, Rosemary Ruether posits that Christianity has been unable to accept the validity of non-Christian religions. The first Christians held exclusive views of salvation or a "realized eschatology." For salvation, Jesus had to be accepted as the Messiah, not a messiah, for a person to become a Christian.[280] Tim Keller in *Making Sense of God* undergirds this qualitative difference by comparing the claims of Jesus to other major religious leaders, "Buddha emphatically said he was not god, and Muhammad, or course, would never, ever have claimed to be Allah, nor did Confucius identify himself with heaven."[281] C. S. Lewis, in his work *God in the Dock*, advances, "If Christianity is untrue, then no honest man will want to believe it, however helpful it might be: if it is true, every honest man will want to believe it, even if it gives him no help at all."[282] Pluralism goes beyond respecting other religions' tenets and other cultures' beliefs. Religious pluralism has what Michael Hakmin Lee describes as a willingness to "grant legitimacy to religious beliefs and, in some way, their correspondences to reality."[283] Jesus eliminates any notion of syncretism, inclusivism or pluralism with those who do not accept him as savior. Jesus demands all or nothing. He is either the son of God or he is not, there is no other way to assess his exclusive claims.

1 John 5:11–13, "And this is the testimony: God has given us eternal life, and this life is in his Son. Whoever has the Son has life; whoever does not have the Son of God does not have life. I write these things to you who believe in the name of the Son of God so that you may know that you have eternal life."

Mathew 7:13–14 states, "Enter through the narrow gate. For wide is the gate and broad is the road that leads to destruction, and many enter through it. But small is the gate and narrow the road that leads to life, and only a few find it." Christianity teaches that any individual can accept Jesus as savior and become a part of God's family, while Judaism asserts that God has a unique and exclusive covenant with Jews. In Christianity, salvation cannot be earned but is a gift from God, but in both Islam and Judaism, salvation at least partially depends on the work and diligence of the follower. These beliefs are incompatible as a gift is either free or it is not. It is not a gift if a friend wants to take me to dinner as a birthday present but wants me to pay for the dessert. Christianity's assertion that Jesus is God is irreconcilable with Judaism's assertion that he was only a man (and a heretic). While both Christianity and Islam incorporate Jewish scriptures into their canons, the additions are outright rejected by Judaism. While both Judaism and Christianity affirm Jesus was crucified, one claims he remained dead, and the other claims he rose from the dead. These are mutually exclusive claims. Both claims cannot be true. Either Jesus was raised from the dead, or he was not. Finally, while both Islam and Christianity affirm Jesus' virgin birth, Islam rejects Jesus as divine while Christianity asserts that Jesus is God in the flesh. Islam, Judaism, and Christianity's core beliefs do not in any way allow for a pluralistic view. Either they are all wrong, or one alone is correct. While Islam, Judaism and Christianity all share some truths, each religions exclusive claims do not allow for them to share the ultimate and transcendent truth.

In her book *Confronting Christianity*, Rebecca McLaughlin posits, "To our modern (used to mean contemporary not from modernity) ears, the idea of one religion claiming to be the truth is anathema."[284] Even in pantheism and polytheism where in the former the universe itself is God and the latter where there are any number of Gods, their claims exclude the truth claims of Christianity, Islam, and Judaism. Therefore, the claim that all paths lead to God necessitates that claims of there being one path to God are false (even if the belief is held that exclusive beliefs are among the many paths to God). In more simple terms, a polytheist rejects Islam's claims exclusivity as false even though the polytheist accepts that Muslims will achieve the optimal outcome in the afterlife.

- Didache- Second century teaching on Christian ethics and church practice.

Unity is NOT Syncretism

One of the challenges is mistaking religious inclusivism and syncretism with unity of the universal Christian church (not universalism, simmer down). A unified body is at the heart of what Jesus wants. John 13:35 says, "by this everyone will know that you are my disciples, if you love one another." The Apostle Paul says in 1 Corinthians 1:10, "I appeal to you, brothers and sisters, in the name of our Lord Jesus Christ, that all of you agree with one another in what you say and that there be no divisions among you, but that you be perfectly united in mind and thought." Paul again in his letter to the Galatians 3:28 reaffirms, "There is neither Jew nor Gentile, neither slave nor free, nor is there male and female, for you are all one in Christ Jesus." The Apostle Peter says in 1 Peter 3:8, "Finally, all of you, be like-minded, be sympathetic, love one another, be compassionate and humble." Apostolic Father Ignatius in 110 C.E. in his letter to the Ephesians states, "It is fitting that you should glorify Jesus Christ, who has glorified you, in every way, so that by a unanimous obedience you may be perfectly joined together in the same mind and in the same judgment and may all speak the same thing concerning the same thing, and so that, as you are subject to the bishop and the elders, you may be made holy in every way." In chapter 4 of the Didache it is stated, "You shall not long for division, but shall bring those who contend to peace." John Calvin once said in a letter to Cardinal Sadolet, "The only true bond of Church unity is Christ the Lord, who has reconciled us to God the Father, and will gather us out of our present dispersion into the fellowship of His body, that so, through His one Word and Spirit, we may grow together into one heart and one soul." Finally, Jesus says in John 17:21–23, "As you, Father, are in me and I am in you, may they also be in us, so that the world may believe that you have sent me. The glory that you have given me I have given them, so that they may be one, as we are one, I in them and you in me, that they may become completely one, so that the world may know that you have sent me and have loved them even as you have loved me."

I give these quotes to show just how important it is that out of fear of inclusivism and syncretism the church does not forgo the unity God so deeply desires and commands of his followers. Christians cannot and should not divide over every doctrinal jot and tittle in the name of Jesus. It does not honor him. There are fundamental and foundational doctrines that cannot be compromised (deity of Christ, authority of scripture, salvation by grace, bodily resurrection) but when it gets into the minutia details of whether you put your right hand in or your right hand out and whether you shake it all about in baptism we should leave copious amounts of grace for other believers theology and hold to heaps of humility in our own theology. Francis Chan states in his book *Until Unity,* "Too often, we have made doctrine the crux of our evaluations of other believers over and above the presence of the Holy Spirit. I know I have. If you are willing to let the presence of the Spirit take precedence over exact theological alignment in secondary issues, I believe you will find a much more diverse, beautiful family of believers because it is the family that God has made, not the one you have chosen."[285] There have been times that my doubts and deconstructions have had nothing to do with doctrine or the Bible or the nature of truth nor the meaning of existence but simply by how little unity there is amongst those who claim to love Jesus and follow him. Francis Chan goes on to say in *Until Unity,* "Jesus suffered and died to unite us with the Father and with each other. To disregard unity is to disparage the cross."[286] So where is the line? Does that mean everyone who claims the name of Jesus is on the same team? Unfortunately, no, but that does not mean that

233

any differences in doctrine make someone a part of some other team either. The early church fathers spent a great deal of time and energy outlining what the core tenets of the Christian faith are, they outlined them in the creeds. I listed the Apostles Creed before and below I am listing the Nicene Creed (from the first Nicene Council). The creeds themselves cannot be given the same weight as scripture yet they are immensely important in defining what is orthodox in Christianity and what is not. If we can lock in agreement to these creeds, you are a brother or sister of mine as far as I am concerned regardless of your denominational affiliation.

THE NICENE CREED

We believe in one God, the Father almighty, maker of heaven and earth, of all things visible and invisible. And in one Lord Jesus Christ, the only Son of God, begotten from the Father before all ages, God from God, Light from Light, true God from true God, begotten, not made: of the same essence as the Father. Through him all things were made. For us and for our salvation he came down from heaven; he became incarnate by the Holy Spirit and the virgin Mary and was made human. He was crucified for us under Pontius Pilate; he suffered and was buried. The third day he rose again, according to the Scriptures. He ascended to heaven and is seated at the right hand of the Father. He will come again with glory to judge the living and the dead. His kingdom will never end. And we believe in the Holy Spirit, the Lord, the giver of life. He proceeds from the Father, and with the Father and the Son is worshiped and glorified. He spoke through the prophets. We believe in one holy catholic and apostolic church. We affirm one baptism for the forgiveness of sins. We look forward to the resurrection of the dead, and to life in the world to come. Amen.

Unified

Intro:
One God One Way
One Church One Faith

Vs. 1
We believe in the Father
We believe in the Son
We believe in the Spirit
Blessed 3 in 1
We believe He created
The whole universe
Seen and Unseen
Heaven and Earth
Let the Church say amen

Ch.
One God One way One Creed One Faith Together
One sacrifice to give us life forever
Unified under Christ Unified under Christ
Let the church say Amen

V.2
We believe in one Lord
Jesus Christ
The only begotten
Light from Light
Conceived by the spirit
Through a virgin girl
Fully God fully man
To redeem the world
Let the Church say Amen[287]

V. 3
We believe that he suffered
He was crucified
And on the 3rd day
He came back to life
He ascended to heaven
Sits at the right hand
To judge to the quick and dead
And His kingdom will never end
Let the Church say Amen

Why is Christianity Different?

When Ted Lasso asks which God, he is asking an epistemological question but when Ted states, "I used to believe that if you did good things, you went to heaven. You did bad things; you went to hell. Nowadays, I know we all just do both. So, wherever he is, I hope he's happy," he is asking a soteriological question.[288] Ted is stating a soteriological understanding that is based upon works; a salvation based upon earning salvation. In Judaism and Islam Ted's understanding of salvation is orthodox, however Ted's understanding of salvation is in direct contradiction to the soteriology of Christianity. In Christianity salvation is by grace through faith. In Christianity Jesus is the only path to God but that path is made available to all and cannot be earned. Ephesians 2:8–9 states, "For it is by grace you have been saved, through faith—and this is not from yourselves, it is the gift of God—not by works, so that no one can boast." I would assert to Ted that he is correct, we all do both good and bad, but that is not the point. The point is that Jesus claimed to be God, asserting himself as the only true religion and lived the most beautiful qualitatively different life that makes that claim one not of judgment but love.[289]

How is the teaching of Christianity different from Judaism and Islam? First as Timothy Keller states in *The Reason for God: Belief in an Age of Skepticism*, "the Christian Gospel is that I am so flawed that Jesus had to die for me, yet I am so loved and valued that Jesus was glad to die for me. This leads to deep humility and deep confidence at the same time. It undermines both swaggering and sniveling. I cannot feel superior to anyone, and yet I have nothing to prove to anyone. I do not think more of myself nor less of myself. Instead, I think of myself less."[290]

Keller goes on to say, "In the Christian understanding, Jesus does not tell us how to live so that we can merit salvation. Rather, he comes to forgive and save us through his life and death in our place. God's grace does not come to people who morally outperform others, but to those who admit their failure to perform and who acknowledge their need for a savior."[291] Christianity is a religion not for the pious but for the downtrodden. It is for ragamuffins; it is for the chosen who were not chosen by the world. Paraphrasing *The Ragamuffin Gospel*, Brennan Manning outlines in his description of a ragamuffin exactly who Christianity is for; Christianity is a religion for the bedraggled, beaten-up, and burnt-out. It is for the heavy, burdened, weak-kneed, who do not have it all together, those looking for a hand-out of grace. It is for the inconsistent, sinful, limited, faulty, bent, and bruised who fear they are a constant disappointment to God and others. Christianity is for "smart people who know they are stupid and honest disciples who know they are scalawags."[292] In *Making Sense of God*, Tim Keller makes the following statement, "Jesus astonished everyone by being willing to eat with tax collectors, collaborators with the occupying Roman imperial forces … Jesus deliberately and tenderly touched lepers (Luke 5:13), people who were considered physically and ceremonially contaminated but who were desperate for human contact. Yet he also ate repeatedly with Pharisees, showing that he was not bigoted toward the bigoted."[293] Salvation in Judaism is about living a pious life of following the law and rabbinic interpretations of that law. Salvation in Islam is about God's mercy but about God's mercy once the follower has tipped the scales of living a righteous life. Salvation in Christianity cannot be earned. In fact, in Romans 3:10–12 it is stated, "As it is written: "There is no one righteous, not even one; there is no one who understands; there is no one who seeks God. All have turned away, they have together become worthless; there is no one who does good, not even one." Salvation in Christianity cannot be earned, it is a gift.

THE EXCLUSIVITY OF THE RESURRECTION

Jesus of Nazareth was crucified. This fact is not disputed by atheists, Christian, Jewish, or otherwise historians, theologians, or philosophers. Bart Ehrman, professor of religion at the University of North Carolina states, "One of the most certain of history is that Jesus was crucified on orders of the Roman prefect of Judea, Pilate."[294] Further John Dominic Crossan, co-founder of the Jesus Seminar says, "That he [Jesus] was crucified is as certain as anything historical ever can be."[295] Jesus existed and was crucified. Islam rejects that Jesus was crucified. The fact of the crucifixion is mutually exclusive, he either was crucified, or he was not. The dispute for all others comes regarding the resurrection.

Some claim that maybe the Romans thought Jesus had died but that he in fact was still alive. To this I would argue that the Romans were experts at killing and probably had a pretty good idea of how to diagnose if someone were dead or not. The swoon theory as it is called does not seem very plausible. The apostles claimed he appeared to them and most all of them died for that claim. I don't know many people who would die for a conspiracy or a lie. Paul states he appeared to 500 people (I will get to why this is so significant in the next section). Even skeptics admit the disciples believed Jesus appeared to them. Gerd Lüdemann, an atheist historian states, "It may be taken as that Peter and the disciples had experiences after Jesus' death in which Jesus appeared to them as the risen Christ."[296] Bart Ehrman, again weighs in "Why, then, did some of the disciples claim to see Jesus alive after his crucifixion? I don't doubt that some of the disciples claimed this ... Paul, writing about 25 years later, indicates that this is what they claimed, and I don't think he is making it up. And he knew at least a couple of them, whom he met just three years after the event."[297] The evidence is pretty clear the disciples believed he rose from the dead. There are some that claim the resurrection was a group hallucination. The problem with this is that Jesus appeared to those who were not looking for him such as Paul and James.

Paul is a particularly interesting case. Paul had status. Paul had no good reason to give up his life. In *The Case for Christ's Resurrection* by Gary R. Habermas. Habermas delineates the transformation of Saul into Paul and that of the other disciples. While the other apostles had known Jesus in his lifetime and had already conceded what minor status in the community they may have had, Paul did not know Jesus prior to the resurrection. Paul was a staunch opponent of Jesus during Jesus' lifetime. Unlike the other apostles, Paul had significant status in both the Roman and Jewish communities. Paul was a Roman citizen (Acts 22:27) and a well-educated Pharisee (Phil 3:4–6). It could be argued that Peter, John, and James (as well as the others) may have suffered from either confirmation bias or ulterior motives for proclaiming the resurrection of Jesus because of their prior commitment to the Rabbi, Paul did not have this prior commitment. I would seriously doubt the Apostles would stick with ulterior motives to the point of death. I also doubt confirmation bias would have made them so delusional that the Apostles could not tell Jesus was dead or not. Paul had much more to lose and nothing to gain from converting to Christianity. Habermas asserts, "Paul's reason is very clear: he was persuaded that he had seen the risen Lord."[298] Paul believed he had an experience with the risen Christ. Paul's situation is significant because neither confirmation bias nor ulterior motives can be reasonably or even plausibly claimed to be a factor in Paul's conversion and subsequent life. Paul believed in Jesus and the experience he had with Jesus. Furthermore, Paul being an educated man makes it difficult to categorize him as gullible or naïve. Paul was a well-educated dual citizen (so to speak) with high moral character and significant status, which gave it all up to make tents, preach a message to gentiles, and spend numerous stints in prison. Paul's only motivation could be that he was convinced the message of Jesus and his resurrection happened. Paul himself states in 1 Cor. 15:17, "And if Christ has not been raised, your faith is futile; you are still in your sins." Jesus claimed to be God and his followers claimed he rose from the dead. These two claims are the very foundation of Christianity, and they are both exclusive. A person cannot be a Christian if they do not believe these two claims.

Neither Abraham nor Mohammed claimed to be God, nor did

they claim to raise from the dead. Tim Keller, in his book *Reason for God*, states, "If Jesus rose from the dead, then you have to accept all that he said; if he didn't rise from the dead, then why worry about any of what he said? The issue on which everything hangs is not whether or not you like his teaching but whether or not he rose from the dead."[299] Christians themselves concede that if the resurrection did not occur, their faith is false, not partially true, false. Jesus claimed to be God and was raised from the dead, so the C. S. Lewis' trilemma applies (with the addition of the possibility of Jesus just being a legend).[300] Lewis in his book *Mere Christianity* states,

"A man who was merely a man and said the sort of things Jesus said would not be a great moral teacher. He would either be a lunatic—on a level with the man who says he is a poached egg—or else he would be the Devil of Hell. You must make your choice. Either this man was, and is, the Son of God: or else a madman or something worse."[301]

Stated as a chain of disjunctive syllogisms (either/or):

P1 Jesus is liar or Lord.
P2 Jesus is not liar.
Therefore, Jesus is Lord.
P2 Jesus is a liar.
Therefore, Jesus is not Lord.
P1 Jesus is lunatic or Lord.
P2 Jesus is not a lunatic.
Therefore, Jesus is Lord.
P2 Jesus is a lunatic.
Therefore, Jesus is not Lord.
P1 Jesus is legend or Lord.
P2 Jesus is not a legend.
Therefore, Jesus is Lord.
P2 Jesus is a legend.
Therefore, Jesus is not Lord.

    Note: here I received some great guidance and help from Richard Knopp, Ph.D.

**Note: I know it is a stretch to chain together several valid disjunctive syllogisms in order to reach for sound logic but in this particular case because there are really only four options, I think it works.

Jesus was either David Koresh, Charles Manson, a complete mythological character (see the beginning of this part of the book) or he was God. He did not leave any room to be a good teacher. The resurrection is the most particular and exclusive claim in history. C. S. Lewis is his book *Miracles* testifies, "The miracle of the resurrection, and the theology of that miracle, comes first."[302] Finally, on this point, evidentially, the inference to the most logical conclusion is that the tomb was empty, and Jesus was indeed raised from the dead. The reasons are the transformed lives of the apostles, the fact that the tomb was in Jerusalem so the site could be checked, and the expertise of Roman soldiers in killing.[303]

- Syllogism- an instance of a form of reasoning in which a conclusion is drawn (valid or not) from two assumed propositions, each of which shares a term with the conclusion, and shares a common or middle term does not present in the conclusion (e.g., all dogs are animals; all animals have four legs; therefore, all dogs have four legs).
- Disjunctive syllogism- A syllogism of only two possibilities. If one of them is ruled out, then the other must take place. Either/or proposition.

Views of Scripture and its Reliability

I was raised to believe that every single word in the Bible was exactly as if God had written it ... in English ... old English, but to Americans. I was raised with the assumption that God took the hand of ancient middle eastern men and physically wrote the

King James version of the Bible through them, which would have been amazing considering English was not even a language yet. That would have made perfect sense for God to do. I was raised to believe that every word of the Bible was written to be taken literally and applied exactly to our modern culture just as it did when it was written, I mean after all it was written to Americans right? I was taught to ask myself what scripture was saying to me. I was taught to eisegete scripture and not exegete.

- Eisegete- placing meaning into a text which was not the original intent of the author or as originally understood by its audience. Placing meaning into the text that is not inherently present in the text itself.
- Eisegesis- interpreting to scripture from the readers cultural context, personal application, and within the readers personal assumptions.
- Exegete- placing meaning of a text upon the intended original intend of the as originally understood by its audience. Allowing the inherent context and message of the text to dictate its meaning.
- Exegesis- interpreting from scripture the framework of literary form, author intention and the intended audience cultural contextualization.

Eventually I began to realize there were problems with seeing the Bible as primarily written for modern audiences. This is not to say the transcendent truth of the Bible is antiquated or outdated. Transcendent truth is eternal and unchanging. It is simply to keep in mind that the Bible primarily communicates divine revelation indirectly through intersubjectivity. It might be a good idea to refer to the graph in Part 2 of the book on the nature of truth again.

An example is the Apostle Paul's letter to the church in Rome or his letter to Timothy. Paul was writing divinely revealed transcendent truths through his singular subjective self (personality, perceptions, and experience) to a particular singular subjective Timothy who was alive during that time and in a mentor/mentee relationship with Paul. Paul was not writing to Timothy McCarty who grew up down the street from me in the mid '80s in rural Indiana. In Paul's letter to the church in Rome, Paul was communicating through his singular subjective self (personality, perception, experience) a divinely revealed message to the church in Rome in 57 C.E. The church in Rome in that time was filled with a group of singular subjective selves that were collectively intersubjectively dealing with problems, questions and issues that were particular to their time and place in history. Paul's intent was communicating to that church in that time. When we read the Bible, we should not be primarily looking for what it says to us individually but rather exegete what the author of that book intends on communicating to the original audience. We must exegete as best we can what the text communicated to them and how would they have understood it in their time. We should not be looking for what the text says to us but rather what the text says. This is not to say that the Holy Spirit can never use scripture to directly speak to an individual. That can and assuredly will happen. However, we can be sure that God would not divinely reveal to any of us a message from a passage of text that runs counter to what the originally intended message to the originally audience was. The Bible communicates God's revelation to us indirectly through intersubjectivity. Going back to the letter Paul wrote to the church in Rome. Paul received God's divine message directly to his soul. Paul communicated that direct revelation through his subjective self and all that means to other subjective selves (the church in Rome). We now read that indirect intersubjective communication about God's divine revelation through our own subjective contemporary selves (personalities, experiences, perceptions) and intersubjectively through our contemporary communities of faith. The divine revelation is unchanging. God's transcendent truth is just as true today as it was yesterday and will be in the future but our contemporary cultural lenses through which we filter that revelation is different today than the culture in which it was written. Who we are as individuals is an additional lens through which we each see scripture. If we are believers in Christ, we all have the same Holy Spirit within us, but the aforementioned lenses often effect and can cloud how we see scripture. Especially if we do not do our best to remove the contemporary biases and put ourselves in the shoes of the author's original intent as well as into the shoes of how the original intended audience would have interpreted and understood the authors words. All this might seem trivial and circular, but it really becomes important when you realize there are very real discrepancies between singular subjective selves perspectives on certain events in the Bible.

Reading the Bible eisegetically became very problematic for me as I became more aware of the very real discrepancies in the Gospels' account of the empty tomb. If God literally and supernaturally took Matthew's pen and Mark's pen (or Peter's mouth to Mark's pen … however that happened) and wrote out his message then why does Mark record both Marys' by name at the tomb while Matthew just says the other Mary? Further why no mention of Joanna like Luke does? Luke's account has the women arriving very early in the morning which seems to agree with Matthew and Mark's account that have the empty tomb being discovered at dawn. John has the empty tomb being discovered while it was still dark. Objectively (objective truth/natural law) either the sun was up, or it was not. Matthew has one angel at the tomb while John has two angels. Mark and Luke don't say they are angels at all but rather humans, though they both have them in fancy clothes (well Mark has a singular young man). Matthew and Luke have the women running and telling the disciples the good news, but Mark says that they say nothing. If God literally by a sort of divine possession took the

245

pen and wrote the accounts for the men, then logically there should be no discrepancies; but there are discrepancies. Did God use the subjective perspectives of the men who wrote the Gospels by allowing their interpretations, perceptions, and personalities to report on the empty tomb? If so, the discrepancies move from evidence against the authority of the Bible to evidence for the Bible. But if eyewitness accounts differ this actually bolsters the authenticity and authority of scripture while removing even the possibility for inerrancy (a concept I was taught was essential). Objectively not all the accounts of the empty tomb could be without error, but like detectives who dismiss when eyewitness testimony is too similar, the errors could substantiate the reports not weaken them. These are just a few examples of what lead me to wrestle with the Bible all together. I did not even get into issues with the genealogies or the age of the earth or how some manuscripts differ in Goliath's height or how certain passages (such as John 8:1–11) placement moves around within or even between books in the New Testament depending on the manuscript.

Today there are challenges to the historicity of the texts or whether the Bible is still culturally relevant regarding issues such as slavery, women's rights and equality, and human sexuality. There are for sure issues that caused me doubt what I assumed and to deconstruct what I believed about the Bible. What I did not know is whether this meant the Bible was unreliable or just my understanding of what the criterion for reliability was. I set out to first see if I could reconstruct my trust in scripture by unpacking what it meant for it to be reliable, trustworthy, and the disseminator of ultimate reality.

There are five main ways in which to view the Bible. Those views are the Bible is inerrant, infallible, authoritative, mythical, or manipulation. Not all of these views are mutually exclusive. A person may hold several of the views at once. For example, someone could view the Bible as both infallible as well as inerrant. A person may see the Bible as a myth and a manipulation. However, a person could not reasonably hold that the Bible as a whole is myth and infallible or authoritative and manipulation. You may hold any one, a combination of any two or all three of the first three views (inerrant, infallible, authoritative) listed. You may even hold that parts of the Bible are myth and still hold that it is inerrant, infallible, and authoritative. If the intent of that part of the Bible was written as a novella for instance (see the book of Judith in the Septuagint or how some interpret the book of Job) or as a vision (parts of Daniel and Ezekiel) or even as illustration for teaching (Jesus' parables) it could be both myth AND inerrant and infallible.

- Inerrancy- there are no errors whatsoever in the Bible, no errors of fact, no errors of contradiction and no errors of words. God took the pen of the authors and wrote directly through them. A strong inerrant position conceives of the Bible as very literal which leaves little room for narrative style.
- Infallibility- the Bible is trustworthy. There is no error of meaning or principle. The Bible is not capable of making an error in meaning or principle.
- Authoritative- The Bible is the word of God, preeminent in guiding Christians in both knowledge of, communion with God as well as practice of Christianity. Does not necessitate that there are not errors of translation or perspective but does affirm there are no errors of intent. Example: Differences in the genealogies or narratives around the tomb. Also does not necessitate a literal translation where the author did not intend on being taken literally.
- Myth- The Bible is simple written down traditional stories, early history the Jewish people and their place in the world. A myth has correspondence to actual events but is exaggerated in order to embellish meaning and significance.

- Manipulation-intentional deception in order to control people.

Many, if not most, people misunderstand what the Bible is. The Bible is not a book, it is a collection of books. A collection of books written in a number of styles, with different intentions, and to different audiences and cultures, with multiple purposes. Because of these differences in audiences' cultures and author's intentions, not all of the Bible can be interpreted the same way. You will hear people say they take the Bible literally when in fact they do not. I am not saying that there aren't passages, sections or even whole books of the Bible that should not be taken literally, I am saying the intent of the author should dictate whether what is written should be taken literally. When someone asks me if I take the Bible literally, I answer sometimes depending on if the author of that part of the Bible is trying to convey history or are they trying to convey transcendent truth allegorically or even through poetry. Sometimes parts of the Bible should be taken literally AND figuratively. The same passage or book can have very real historical literal meaning as well as convey deep allegorical and figurative truth. Discerning if a passage is to be taken literally or figuratively is not always easy as we are thousands of years removed from the cultures and audiences that were the original readers. For example, is the creation story meant to be taken literally or not? Many great, sincere, and truth-seeking Christians disagree with each other on this issue. The point I will make is that I don't think it would have mattered as much to the original audience whether it was a literal six days or a figurative six days. Ancient Jews would have had no problem believing God could do anything he wanted to do including creating the world in a literal six days. They also were not a culture that was bound to see truth as reduced to the objective so they would not have had to reconcile the creation story to science. Lastly, Ancient Jews were used to paradox and allegory, they would not have felt the need to even filter the story of creation in the same way we automatically do in our contemporary culture. I believe (this is speculative I know) that ancient Jews would not see what all the fuss is about and most likely think us modern Christians are missing the bigger point all together. Even early on Christians often fell into the ditches of either taking the Bible too literally (ala the school of Antioch) or too figuratively (ala the school of Alexandria). Faithful hermeneutics dictates exegesis of a passage based upon the context and intent of the passage being interpreted and not eisegesis based upon assumptions and presuppositions of the interpreter. As stated earlier this is difficult as we are all subjective individuals with assumptions of our worldview which includes our presuppositions about scripture. It is imperative that we seek a multitude of voices as checks and balances. The school of Alexandria was correct in that we often think of God as far too anthropomorphic (he does not have the whole world in his physical hands) but also when the Bible says that Mary gave birth to Jesus that is to be taken literally. When church father Origen questions how there were "days" in the creation story when there was no sun or moon yet, his call to not take that passage too literally should be heeded but at the same time the overemphasis of Christ's divinity reduces his very literal nature of being human asserted in 1 Timothy 2:5 as either nominal at best or perhaps completely false. It is not either figurative or literal but both/and/and depends.

The Bible has history, entertaining stories, poetry, philosophy, research, and personal letters. Unlike the Quran it was written by many different authors and written in many ways. The Old Testament was written over a long period of time while the New Testament was written in a very compact time. It claims to be the direct revelation of God through prophets, teachers, and leaders. It is the Christian holy scripture. A short side bar, there is a movement among some Christians that asserts the Christian faith should leave the Old Testament behind and only consider the New Testament authoritative. I won't spend a lot of time on this, but I will say that Jesus took the Old Testament as authoritative, and he quoted it. Relegating the Old Testament to the archaic is a non-sequitur if we are to take Jesus as authoritative. Scripture means a body of writings considered sacred or authoritative. Lots of religions have scripture, but the Bible is the Christian scripture. The Bible has many purposes but if there is a single purpose of the Bible, it would be to reveal the transcendent truth of God to humanity in ways that objective truth (the natural world) could never do. The Bible without a doubt (see what I did there) has been the most influential work in western culture. Psychologist and philosopher Jordan Peterson says the Bible is the fundamental presupposition for all which other western thought and linguistic production comes from. Peterson says, "it isn't that the Bible is true. It's that the Bible is the precondition for the manifestation of truth. Which makes it way more true than just true."[304] Saint Augustine says, "The Holy Scriptures are our letters from home." The Bible is transcendent truth revealing God who holds and is ultimate reality (the whole truth). It is because of this fact that Christians assert it is the key to being truly human and fully who we are; that reading, knowing and living out the precepts, principles, ethics, and loving relationship with God as spoken of in the Bible changes humans not away from their true identity but into their true identity. D.L. Moody says, "The Bible was not given for our information but for our transformation."

For all the Bible claims it is, it is not God. The Bible claims to be the truth about God, but it does not claim to be God. It should not be the object of Christians worship, but rather the primary tool for knowing God. The Bible is not a complete, exact, or always clear revelation of God but orthodox Christianity teaches that it is sufficient, necessary, and authoritative. The Bible does not tell humans everything about everything. The Bible does contain errors, many errors in fact. This is not disputed amongst Bible scholars. It is widely acknowledged and accepted. Craig L. Blomberg in his book *Can We Still Believe the Bible?*, discusses the nature of the 400,000 variants found between manuscripts of the Bible. Blomberg articulates several factors that make this initially shocking number more understandable. The first being there are over 25,000 manuscripts of the Greek New Testament and 10,000 manuscripts of the Latin and an average of just 16 variants in these manuscripts. Furthermore, most variants cluster on specific passages, meaning the external evidence in the majority of passages in the manuscripts agree. Additionally, the variants are due to different names for Jesus, a misspelled word "heer," or a letter that has been "lef" off. While minor accidental mistakes are most certainly still mistakes, they do not change the passage's meaning nor significantly inhibit translators' ability to ascertain the original doctrinal assertions. Is the reader of the statement two sentences ago not able to ascertain the meaning of the sentence even with the mistakes in spelling and a letter being left off of a word? Blomberg posits, "No orthodox doctrine or ethical practice of Christianity depends solely on any disputed wording."[305] The doctrinal consistency of manuscripts despite errors is substantial evidence for the authority of scripture, not against it. Blomberg states that while scripture has not been inerrantly conserved, it is a "remarkably close approximation of God's inerrant autographs and can guide us theologically and ethically in every walk of life."[306] The errors don't change much as far as meaning nor cloud what the intended meaning is. Bart Ehrman states, "The vast majority of these hundreds of thousands of differences are completely and utterly unimportant and insignificant and don't matter at all."[307]

These errors however are still a big problem for those who hold a strict inerrant view like I was taught. The errors may not change any of the intended meaning, but they are errors. Now many who hold a strict inerrant view would say that if we had the original manuscripts these errors would not appear. I totally agree as far as grammatical errors or letters left out but not when it comes to discrepancies. Biblical literalists often assert a view of biblical inerrancy that is untenable. The narrow literalist view of inerrancy is that the Bible was handed down from God to the writers' word for word, almost as if the Holy Spirit possessed their personhood and God only wrote through them. Blomberg posits a broader view of inerrancy. Blomberg quotes Paul Feinberg, who offers the following definition, "Inerrancy means that when all facts are known, the Scriptures in their original autographs and properly interpreted will be shown to be wholly true in everything that they affirm, whether that has to do with doctrine or morality or with social, physical, or life sciences."[308] While this definition is broader than the strictest of definitions of inerrancy it still almost has a God of the gaps implicit in the phrase "when all facts are known." The emphasis on facts reveals a very modern worldview. The issue of facts is blurry when not first seen through the lens of intent. What is the author's intent, and to whom were they trying to communicate this intent is far more critical to the authority of scripture than the facts, even if those facts have to do with doctrine. Blomberg additionally posits that the definition of error is far more important than the definition of inerrancy.[309] Suppose the author's intended message is not to communicate facts but rather a theological point. In that case, historical inaccuracies such as Nebuchadnezzar never being the king of the Assyrians in the book of Judith are not an error. The intent of the book of Judith is a Novella, just a short story to illustrate a truth of principle. The marrying of Nebuchadnezzar (king of Babylon) and the Assyrians is an excellent representation of Israel's oppressors in general. The Jewish audience would have understood this as the intent. It is an error only for contemporary readers who focus on the error of fact as a violation of inerrancy and not the intent. Blomberg posits that the theology of a book in the Bible can be without error even if the historicity is not. Furthermore, Blomberg posits, "Once we determine, as best we can, what a passage affirms, according to the conventions of its style, form, and genre, a commitment to inerrancy implies acceptance of the truth of those affirmations. Nevertheless, commitment to inerrancy does not exclude a priori any given literary style, form, or genre that is not inherently deceptive."[310] For example a midrash is a reimagining or embellishment to enhance the theology of a text. This technique was a part of Jewish culture. The intention would have been understood by the original audience. Blomberg addresses midrash in the New Testament, particularly in the book of Matthew. The original readers of the text were Jewish and would have been aware of the technique and the reason for the literary style. Blomberg states, "They would have recognized the potentially unhistorical elaboration that Matthew added and would not have viewed the redactional parts of Matthew's Gospel the same way they did the traditional parts."[311] Modern readers must not take their modern assumptions of literary styles into reading ancient texts. The same can be said of pseudonymous works. Everyone who reads philosophy knows Dionysius the Areopagite was not the actual person. This is not considered intentionally deceptive but rather a tribute to the person. Blomberg summarizes this point by pinpointing that it is anachronistic to "insert a later culture's standard into a world that had not yet developed such a standard."[312]

- School of Antioch- Christian theological institution in Syria, traditionally founded in about AD 200, that stressed the literal interpretation of the Bible and the completeness of Christ's humanity, in opposition to the School of Alexandria (see Alexandria, School of), which emphasized the allegorical interpretation of the Bible and stressed Christ's divinity. Flourishing in the 4th–6th century, the School of Antioch produced several significant theologians, including Diodore of Tarsus, Theodore of Mopsuestia, St. John Chrysostom, and Theodoret of Cyrrhus.
- School of Alexandria- According to Britannica, "the first Christian institution of higher learning, founded in the mid-2nd century AD in Alexandria, Egypt. Under

its earliest known leaders (Pantaenus, Clement, and Origen), it became a leading center of the allegorical method of biblical interpretation, emphasized the full divinity of Christ and the personal unity of his divine and human natures," emphasized the full humanity of Christ and the distinction between his divine and human natures.

- Hermeneutics-a method of Biblical interpretation.
- Midrash- According to myjewishlearning.com, a midrash is "an interpretive act, seeking the answers to religious questions (both practical and theological) by plumbing the meaning of the words of the Torah. Midrash is used to mean inquiring into any matter, including occasionally to seek out God's word.) Midrash responds to contemporary problems and crafts new stories, making connections between new Jewish realities and the unchanging biblical text."

$\sim$

DISCREPANCIES IN THE GOSPELS

J. Warner Wallace in his book *Cold-Case Christianity: A Homicide Detective Investigates the Claims of the Gospels* states, "The traditional definition of biblical inerrancy maintains that the Bible is accurate and completely free of error. Inerrancy does not require, however, that the biblical texts be free of any personal perspective or idiosyncrasies. In fact, the existence of these distinctive features only helps us recognize the accounts as true eye-witness statements written by real people who revealed their human gifts (and limitations) along the way. These characteristics can help us have confidence in both the accuracy and the reliability of the accounts."[313] The four Gospels—Matthew, Mark, Luke and John were accepted as the four Gospels very early on. Irenaeus (Eye-run-A-us) insisted on these four being the only Gospels. In his book *Against Heresies* written around 180 he states, 'it is not possible that there can be either more or fewer than four." This is significant as Irenaeus was taught by Polycarp who was taught by the Apostle John. If we play six degrees of Kevin Bacon that is only three degrees from Jesus himself. The Gospels of Matthew and John are direct eyewitness accounts. The Gospel of Mark considered to be the firsthand account of Peter transcribed by Mark. The Gospel of Luke is thought to be compiled research from the account of Jesus' mother Mary, the Apostle Peter's account (as transcribed by Mark), as well as potentially a lost source often called Q, and by Luke's own words other eyewitnesses. Luke is using multiple sources as any good researcher would.

It is true that none of the original manuscripts of the Gospels have been found. Proving the versions we have are exactly identical as the original is impossible. However, if the original text is the requirement, then much of accepted history cannot meet the requirement either. Dr. Richard Knopp created this graphic demonstration to illustrate this point.

GREEK N.T. MANUSCRIPTS & OTHER ANCIENT WRITINGS

AUTHOR	BOOK	DATE WRITTEN	EARLIEST COPIES	TIME GAP	# of COPIES
Homer	Iliad	900 BC	415 BC	485 yrs.	1,900
Livy	History	25 BC	4th Cent. AD	325 + yrs.	475
Josephus	Antiquities of the Jews	93 AD	> 800 AD	700 + yrs.	20
	New Testament	AD 48-95	c. 114 fragment c. 200 books c. 250 most of NT c. 325 complete NT	+50 yrs 100 yrs 150 yrs 225 yrs	5,800
	(However, 5,046 manuscripts are 10th century or later.)				

**Chart by Richard A. Knopp, Ph.D.

Josephus' account of Jewish and Roman history is pretty widely accepted even though we only have 20 copies, and those copies are 700 years after the events. We have fragments of the New Testament that are only 50 years removed and 200 copies of whole books only 100 years removed. If we are going to keep the same level of scrutiny, then the Gospels pass the test. The ECREE made popular by Carl Sagan, "Extraordinary claims require extraordinary evidence" is often used to assert the Bible should be held to a higher standard. What makes a claim extraordinary? Would it not be overwhelming evidence of the exact opposite? It seems the only fair measure is normal historical evidence criterion and the number of copies and the close proximity of the events of those copies. Based on this measurement the New Testament meets that criterion extraordinarily. J. Warner Wallace states, "If skeptics were willing to give the Gospels the same 'benefit of the doubt' they are willing to give other ancient documents, the Gospels would easily pass the test of authorship."[314] From this I am going to operate under the assumption that the Gospels were written by the people who are commonly believed to write them and there is no error of intent. John 8:1–11 is a passage not found in many of the early manuscripts. The early manuscripts were John 8:1–11 is found it is not always in the same spot in John and can even be found in Luke. It in some ways was a passage searching for a home. Principally the content of the passage is in line with Jesus' character and the doctrine of the rest of scripture but it is a passage that is on a little shakier ground than most of the rest of the Gospels. The other often mentioned problematic passage is found in Mark 16. The two oldest manuscripts we have that date back to the 300s conclude with verse 8. Other than these two passages the manuscripts of the Gospels are remarkably consistent, intact, and free of error of intent.

I am at this point going refer back to the nature of truth. Objective truth dictates that there could not both be two angels and only one angel at the tomb. Objective truth also dictates either there were three Mary's at the tomb, or it was just Mary Magdalene. Objective truth makes the two options mutually exclusive. It also makes it impossible that God supernaturally possessed the authors and took their pens and wrote the accounts of the empty tomb, unless God does not possess the divine attributes addressed in Part 3 of the book. If God does possess the divine attributes and there are mutually exclusive discrepancies in the objective truth of the events, then that must therefore mean that either the writers of the Gospels intentionally lied about some details or there is some subjective truth to them. Let me give an example. My oldest son (Zeke- lead singer and songwriter for Tooth & Nail recording artist Idle Threat) and I went to see Gary Clark Jr. in concert a few summers ago. When we got back from the show and were telling my wife about it we had different recollections on the order of the set list. We both noted that GCJ opened with his song "Bright Lights," but we differed on when he played his cover of the Beatles song "Come Together." We were both telling the subjective truth. Neither of us were lying nor were we delusional. We were telling the absolute truth as it were true to us, but we both could not be objectively correct. Either one or perhaps both of us were incorrect when it came to objective truth. This is the same with the discrepancies in the Gospels. Each Gospel reports the subjective truth of the perspective of the eyewitnesses, but they cannot all be correct when it comes to the objective truth. This is not a mark against the reliability of the Gospels but for it. The fact that my son and I remember things slightly different is good evidence that we are both telling the truth. If our perspectives lined up perfectly it would be reasonable to think either one of us was not there at all and was just borrowing the others true perspective or that we got together before hand and determined what the story was going to be. Just because an account is incorrect as far as objective truth does not mean the account is untrue or not reliable. Again, I will let J. Warner Wallace detective and apologist weigh in:

"There are times when an eyewitness gets something wrong. In fact, I've seen this repeatedly over the course of my career. Witnesses are people and people make mistakes. But the fact that a witness might be wrong about a particular detail or element of the crime does not necessarily disqualify them or render their testimony unreliable. If that were the case, we would never be able to prosecute anyone for anything. When examining the reliability of an eyewitness and encountering some factual error, I've got to determine (1) if the errant aspect of the statement is relevant to the larger issues in the case, and (2) the reason why the witness got the detail wrong in the first place. If a victim of a robbery misidentifies the kind of shirt the suspect wore at the time of the robbery, I have to ask myself this misidentification makes the victim an unreliable witness."[315]

The question becomes, do the discrepancies in the empty tomb accounts change the primary narrative or do they corroborate the truth of the primary narrative? The primary narrative of the empty tomb is that Jesus rose from the dead, there was some sentient being(s) there telling women (or woman) that Jesus was not there. Jesus then first appeared to a woman or women. All that seems to line up and the differences between the accounts only substantiate that the writers did not collude beforehand.

There are a number of other issues like the empty tomb in the Bible that require wrestling through. To cover all of them is beyond the scope of this book. I would however highly recommend reading Craig L. Blomberg's *Can We Still Believe the Bible?* and *Is the New Testament Reliable?* by Paul Barnett to answer and wrestle through those with you. I used the empty tomb as an example to illustrate how I have wrestled through some of my own deconstruction and doubt with the Bible. What I have wrote here is by no means exhaustive.

THE NEW TESTAMENT CANON

"Canon" is a Greek word meaning "rule" or "measuring stick." It is often posited that Emperor Constantine decided what books would be in the Bible. This is false. So how was it decided what books to include and which not to include in the Bible? Christian church leaders worldwide gathered to answer major questions, including which books should be regarded as "Scripture." These gatherings included the Council of Nicea in C.E. 325 and the First Council of Constantinople in C.E. 381. In 382 Pope Damasus commissioned Jerome, the leading biblical scholar of his day, to produce an acceptable Latin version of the Bible (called the Latin Vulgate) from the various translations then being used. His revised translation of the Gospels appeared about 383. The exact 27 books were not finally agreed and formally ratified in C.E. 393 at the Council of Hippo and in C.E. 397 by the Council of Carthage. However, Irenaeus listed 20 of the 27 books as far back as C.E. 180, and Origen's canon included all 27 New Testament books as far back as C.E. 250, so most of the New Testament canon was settled only three degrees from Kevin Bacon (or Jesus in our case) and all of the New Testament was settled within 4 generations. Even as far back as the end of the first century C.E., most of the church had agreed on which books should be considered scripture. The earliest church members took guidance from the writings of Peter, Paul, Matthew, John, and others. The later councils and debates were largely useful in weeding out inferior books that claimed the same authority. Below are graphs by Dr. Richard Knopp detailing the canonization of the Bible and when the books that were canonized were written.

The New Testament itself was written in the first century C.E. Jesus was crucified between 30–33 C.E. The Apostle Paul converted to Christianity from 33–36 C.E. and the book of Galatians was written in 48–50 C.E. This means that the first book of the New Testament was written not more than 20 years after Jesus was crucified. All of Paul's epistles were written within 30 years of Jesus' crucifixion. This means doctrines of Jesus' deity, death and resurrection were all present in the very beginnings of the Christian church. It is important to note as Tim Keller states in

The Reason for God, "It is not only Christ's supporters who were still alive. Also still alive were many bystanders, officials, and opponents who had actually heard him teach, seen his actions, and watched him die. They would have been especially ready to challenge any accounts that were fabricated."[316] The New Testament was simply written too close to Jesus' life for fabrication to have not been called out.

Having established that the early church agreed upon the 27 books in the New Testament, next I want to address how they came to agreement. What was the criteria? Why were some books included and others not included? There are books that almost made the canon such as the *Didache*, 1 *Clement*, *The Letter of Barnabas*, *The Shepherd of Hermas*, *The Apocalypse of Peter* but ultimately did not make the cut. I would highly recommend you read all of these books even though they are not canonized. They are still quite helpful in understanding biblical doctrine and church history. So how did the counsels decide if a book should be included in the Bible. Below are the criteria used for whether a book was ultimately canonized:

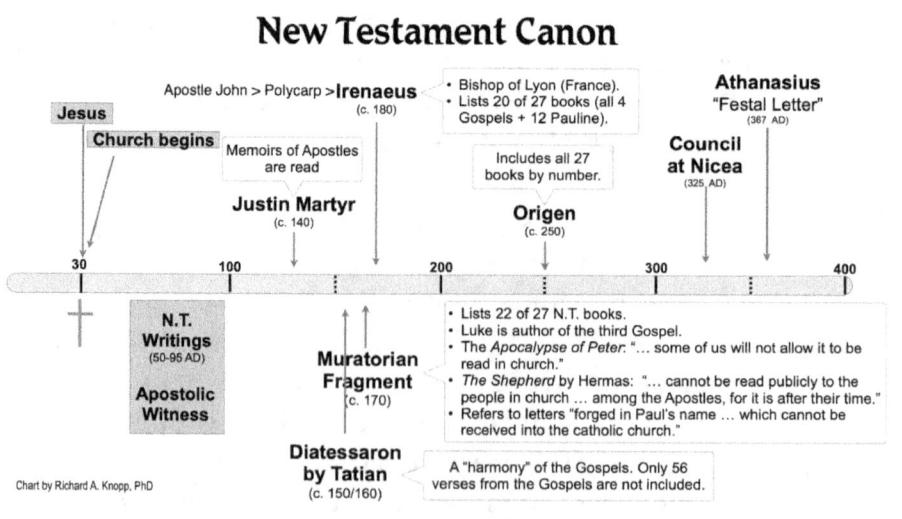

Chart by Richard A. Knopp, Ph.D.

260

1. Was it written by one of Jesus' disciples, someone who was a witness to Jesus' ministry, such as Peter, or someone who interviewed witnesses, such as Luke?
2. Was it written in the first century C.E., meaning that books written long after the events of Jesus' life and the first decades of the church weren't included?
3. Was the content (message, principles, etc.) consistent with other portions of the Bible known to be valid, meaning the book couldn't contradict a trusted element of Scripture?
4. Was it widely used and by local churches and universally accepted within the broader Church?

CULTURAL DIFFERENCES BETWEEN NOW AND THEN (EXAMPLE THE BIBLE AND WOMEN)

It is asserted often that the Bible is misogynistic and endorses the subjugation of women. If you eisegete how the Bible treats women and filter it through our contemporary culture the criticism is fair. However, as we talked about before, reading an ancient text

Earliest New Testament Books & Events

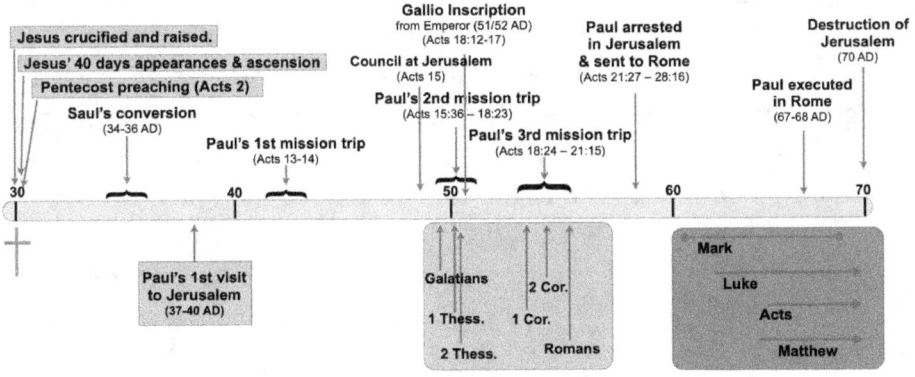

Chart by Richard A. Knopp, PhD
NOTE: While disagreements exist even among conservative biblical scholars especially on the dates for the Gospel accounts, a strong case exists for the earlier dates of Mark, Luke, and Matthew displayed here. Dates displayed are generally adopted from the NIV Study Bible.

**Chart by Richard A. Knopp, Ph.D.

through contemporary cultural criticism is a contemptible mistake. For the cultures the Bible was written in, contextually the Bible affirms women and raises them to a status that runs counter to the cultures they existed in. Tim Keller says in *The Reason for God*,

> "We think of the Anglo-Saxons as primitive, but someday others will think of us and our culture's dominant views as primitive. How can we use our time's standard of 'progressive' as the plumb line by which we decide which parts of the Bible are valid and which are not? Many of the beliefs of our grandparents and great-grandparents now seem silly and even embarrassing to us. This process is not going to stop now."[317]

In *Confronting Christianity* McLaughlin focuses on the fact that females were often portrayed in the Bible in a positive light in the parables. Eve is described as a helper. On the surface this seems to confirm the denigration of women but in the original Hebrew the word used for helper is a word that God uses as a self-description. In fact, Eve being described as a helper implies that Adam was someone who needed help. The fact that Jesus first appeared and was first recognized by women at the empty tomb ran completely counter to the culture at the time. Women were not even allowed to testify in court, yet Jesus chose to appear to women first. Another example would be that Jesus performed his first miracle at the behest of his mother (John 2:1–11), and one of Jesus' final earthly concerns on the cross was that John takes care of his mother (John 19:25–27). Women were a part of his ministry from beginning to end. Women traveled with him throughout his ministry along with the 12 disciples (Luke 8:1–3) Jesus repeatedly showed how deeply he cared for and valued women, he rescued them form stonings, equated them as co-heirs to the promise of Abraham (Luke 13:16–17), He protected them from divorce (Mathew 19).

I am particularly fond of a story found in the Greek (Septuagint) version of the book of Daniel, the story of Susanna. In this story, the beautiful woman Susanna is falsely accused and convicted of adultery by Hebrew judges. These judges were the same two men who tried to bully Susanna into having an illicit sexual encounter with the two of them. It was, in fact, Susanna's rejection that motivated the men to make the accusation. As Susanna was being taken to be stoned, she prayed to God, and He heard her prayer. God impressed upon Daniel to investigate further. Daniel did the old Law and Order separate the witnesses' trick and discovered Susanna to be blameless. I love this story because it shows that God was always concerned with women's rights and was never okay with men bullying their way with women.

Some passages of the Bible are hard to read and not insert our contemporary subjective selves. Christians don't always agree on which of these passages are hermeneutically sealed theologically speaking and which ones are more cultural. Passages such as 1 Timothy 2:12; Ecclesiastes 7:28; 1 Corinthians 14:34–35; and Ephesians 5:22 can cause women grief and distress. Some of these passages have been used by men in the church as a bludgeoning tool, others have simply been misunderstood or misapplied, and yet others are just difficult to accept even when exegeted correctly. As far as the Bible and equality for women, the church should be leading the way to defend equality for women. This does not give right morally for women to demand their rights. In Christianity men should give up their rights as well. Jesus came as a servant, and the Bible asserts the expectation that Jesus' follows serve one another not demand their own rights. The giving up of rights for a group of people who have been marginalized and subjugated for thousands of years gives rise to tension and potentially resistance from that group of people. I won't begin to pretend like I understand what a command to give up your rights feels like to a group of people that have been subjugated yet it is clear that Jesus, who gave up all his rights to himself completely, asks all his followers to do the same. Yet he also asks his followers to look out for and defend the rights of others. Men have done very poorly in defending the honor and treating women in the church as Daughters of

Abraham. The juxtaposition of how Christians have executed what Jesus expects is tragic, deserves sincere repentance and must be rectified. Rebecca McLaughlin posits on the theology of roles in marriage the bigger truth as, "In the drama of marriage, the wife's needs come first, and the husband's drive to prioritize himself is cut down with the brutal axe of the Gospel."[318]

The tension or difficulty created by history does not mean we can ignore or throw whole passages out. It does not mean we can just claim they have no application today. This would be a mistake. If the Bible is authoritative that means even the passages that are figurative or need to be contextualized to a culture still have transcendent truth to teach us. If the Bible is scripture, then none of it can be thrown out or ignored ever. However, this does not mean the application of some of these verses should not change as culture changes. Christians have a wide array of views on where to draw that line and I am not going to try and solve exactly where good doctrine in modern times falls on each point in the complementarian verse egalitarian debate here. What I will say is even if it is hard to get passed some of the more difficult passages this does not make Christianity false. Tim Keller says, "To stay away from Christianity because part of the Bible's teaching is offensive to you assumes that if there is a God, he wouldn't have any views that upset you."[319]

- Complementarian- the theological view that men and women have different but complementary roles and responsibilities in marriage, family life, and religious leadership.
- Egalitarian- the theological view that are equal in all respects to responsibilities in marriage, family life, and religious leadership.

CONCLUSION

I have given examples of how I have worked through apologetically and hermeneutically the discrepancies of the Gospel accounts of the empty tomb as well as the apologetics of the Bible's views on women. These are not exhaustive in any way. I know there are other questions and other doubts regarding the Bible that I have not addressed. I only picked these two because they are ones that have caused me to doubt and given me pause. I have had to deconstruct through and reconstruct to quite a few other issues with my world-view, my doubts, and interpretations of scripture. Each time though as with these examples I came to be convinced and am still convinced when I have my days of thinking "is all this really true?" of Biblical authority, infallibility, and inerrancy *of intent*. The inference to the most plausible and probable conclusion is that there is a divine text with authority given to man by God and that text is the Bible. I do not personally use the word inerrant often because of how it can be misinterpreted and confusing given the 400,000 technical errors in the manuscripts that we have of the Bible. On a theological level though when it comes to inerrancy of intent, I agree there is no error in the Bible. I believe the Bible is the word of God, preeminent in guiding Christians in both knowledge of and communion with God as well as in the practice of Christianity. This does not necessitate a denial of any errors of translation or perspective but does affirm there are no errors of intent. Example: Differences in the genealogies or narratives around the tomb. Also, it does not necessitate a literal translation where the author did not intend on being taken literally. I do sometimes wonder if some of my own "confusion" with the Bible is only due to my unwillingness to stay in the tension of its paradox. Soren Kierkegaard echoes the sentiment when he says,

> "The Bible is very easy to understand. But we Christians are a bunch of scheming swindlers. We pretend to be unable to understand it because we know very well that the minute we understand, we are obliged to act accordingly."[320]

When Ted Lasso says, "Yeah, of course. But to which god and in what language, you know?" he brings up a very poignant issue of which religion (if any) has the message revealed by the creator? Are the world's religions genuinely making competing claims, or do they each hold an aspect of ultimate reality? Are all religions just differing parts of an elephant? I think the answer to Ted's question of which God carries what Rebecca McLaughlin calls "life or death" consequences.[321] To answer Ted's second question, "You know, growing up, I used to believe that if you did good things, you went to heaven. You did bad things; you went to hell. Nowadays, I know we all just do both. So, wherever he is, I hope he's happy." Ted has a misunderstanding of the message of Christianity. Christianity is exclusive, but exclusively a religion where the founder consistently said not to be afraid to be people who were used to being afraid. Christianity is a religion exclusively where a middle eastern first-century man claimed to be God yet did not seek power or gain. Christianity is a religion where the founder is the only leader to both claim to be God and yet inspire a movement that would transform the world and become the most prominent religion within that transformed world.

DISCUSSION QUESTIONS

1. What type of religious perspective is Ted asserting in his question of which God?
2. What type of religious view did you grow up with?
3. Tim Keller says all religions hold narrow views, explain how even religious pluralism and inclusivism are narrow in their religious views?
4. While Judaism and Christianity come from many authors and many sources, Islam comes primarily from one single source. Do you see this as a strength or weakness for Islam? Why?
5. Explain the soteriological differences between the three major monotheistic religions?
6. Which of the three monotheistic religions has the narrowest view of salvation? Explain why.
7. Define the difference between syncretism and unity? Why do Christians have such a hard time discerning between the two?
8. If all three of the major monotheistic religions legitimately trace their foundations back to God's promise to Abraham why can't there be unity within them?
9. Are all young Jewish girls, Muslim girls, and Christian girls daughters of Abraham? Why or why not?
10. Why do you think to contemporary ears the value of religious exclusivism seems so offensive?
11. Do you agree with the author about the creeds being a doctrinal litmus test for unity?
12. Did the early church fathers see the creeds as a litmus tests?
13. Do the messages in *Liturgy* and *Paperback Novels* contradict one another? Why or why not?
14. Do you trust modern theologians or teachers more in matters of Christian unity or the early Church fathers? Why?
15. In your own words describe what a ragamuffin is? In Christianity is salvation only for ragamuffins?

16. Why is Jesus' bodily resurrection so important to Christianity? Why can it not just be a spiritual resurrection?

17. In the trilemma plus one outlined by the author, if Jesus is not Lord which of the other three (lunatic, liar, or legend) is the most likely to be true? Why?

18. Growing up what was your view of scripture?

19. What is you view of scripture now?

20. Did this chapter challenge or change your view of inerrancy? How and why?

21. If you read the Bible, do you tend to try and exegete or eisegete from the text?

22. Is trying to find what scripture is saying to you eisegeting or exegeting? Is it a mistake to read scripture that way? Why or why not?

23. How do we try as a subjective self to get into the mindset of the original readers of books of the Bible? Can we ever completely accomplish this? Is it worth the effort to try and put ourselves in their position? Why?

24. If someone asks, "How can you take the Bible literally?" how would you answer?

25. If someone says the Bible contains no errors or mistakes what would you say to them?

26. Does the book of Judith contain an error when it says that Nebuchadnezzar was the king of the Assyrians? Why or why not?

27. Do you tend to view scripture through a school of Antioch lens or school of Alexandria lens? Why? What is the danger in this tendency?

28. Why do the discrepancies in the Gospel accounts of the empty tomb actually help substantiate the claims?

29. How do you discern when the Bible is instructing within a cultural context and when it is instructing values for all times and everywhere? What is the criteria for these decisions?

30. Religiously explain why the elephant in the room is the

tension between religious exclusive claims and subjective perception?

31. The Kierkegaard quote in the conclusion, do you agree with him or disagree? Why or why not?

BIBLIOGRAPHY

Meadors, Edward P. "Why Jesus Is The Only Way." *Journal for Baptist Theology and Ministry* 2, no. 2 (2004): 99–112.

Adams, Marilyn McCord. "The Primacy of Christ ." *Sewanee Theological Review* 47, no. 2 (2004).

Al-Maududi, Arsyil A'la. *Towards Understanding Islam*. Kuala Lumpur: Place of publication not identified, n.d.

Anderson, Tawa J., W. Michael Clark, and David Naugle. *An Introduction to Christian Worldview: Pursuing God's Perspective in a Pluralistic World*. Downers Grove, IL: IVP Academic, an imprint of InterVarsity Press, 2017.

"Apostles' Creed." Encyclopædia Britannica. Encyclopædia Britannica, inc. Accessed November 27, 2021. https://www.britannica.com/topic/Apostles-Creed.

Baghramian, Maria, and J. Adam Carter. "Relativism." Stanford Encyclopedia of Philosophy. Stanford University, September 15, 2020. https://plato.stanford.edu/entries/relativism/#HidParDef.

Becker, Jane. "Ted Lasso." Episode. 2, no. 10: No Weddings and A Funeral, 2021.

Beckwith, Francis J., William Lane Craig, J P Moreland, and Gary R. Hamermas. *To Everyone an Answer: A Case for the Christian Worldview*. Grand Rapids, MI: IVP Academic, 2014.

Beckwith, Francis J., William Lane Craig, and Gary R. Habermas. "Chapter 11. The Case For Christ's Resurrection." Essay. In *To Everyone an Answer: A Case for the Christian Worldview*, edited by J. P. Moreland, 180–98. Downers Grove, IL: IVP Academic, 2014.

Beilby, James K., and Paul R. Eddy. *The Historical Jesus: Five Views*. Seoul, Korea: Holy Wave Plus, 2014.

Blomberg, Craig L. *Can We Still Believe the Bible?: An Evangelical Engagement with Contemporary Questions*. Grand Rapids, MI: Brazos Press, 2014.

Boyd, Gregory A., and Paul R. Eddy. *Lord or Legend?: Wrestling with the Jesus Dilemma*. Eugene, OR: Wipf & Stock, 2010.

Brazier, P. H. "'God … or a Bad, or Mad, Man': C.S. Lewis's Argument for Christ - a Systematic Theological, Historical and Philosophical Analysis Ofaut Deus Aut Malus Homo." *The Heythrop Journal* 55, no. 1 (2010): 1–30. https://doi.org/10.1111/j.1468-2265.2010.00625.x.

Burkle, Howard R. " JESUS CHRIST AND RELIGIOUS PLURALISM." *Journal of Ecumenical Studies* 16, no. 3 (1979): 457–71.

Burnett, Chris. "HOW WOULD PAUL ENGAGE TODAY'S SECULARIZING SOCIETY?: AN EXEGETICAL REVISITING OF ACTS 17." *The Masters Seminary Journal* 30, no. 1 (2019): 147–67.

Carson, D. A. T*he Gagging of God: Christianity Confronts Pluralism*. Grand Rapids, MI: Zondervan, 2011.

Casiday, Augustine. "Sin and Salvation: Experiences and Reflections." *The Cambridge History of Christianity*, 2007, 501–30. https://doi.org/10.1017/chol9780521812443.022.

Chan, Francis. *Until Unity*. Elgin, IL: David C. Cook, 2021.

"The Changing Global Religious Landscape." Pew Research Center's Religion & Public Life Project, July 27, 2020. https://www.pewforum.org/2017/04/05/the-changing-global-religious-landscape/.

Childers, Alisa. *Another Gospel?: A Lifelong Christian Seeks Truth in Response to Progressive Christianity*. Carol Stream, IL: Tyndale Momentum, the Tyndale nonfiction imprint, 2020.

Clendenin, Daniel B. Many Gods, *Many Lords: Christianity Encounters World Religions*. Grand Rapids, MI: Baker Books, 1996.

Copan, Paul. *Loving Wisdom: Christian Philosophy of Religion*. Grand Rapids , MI: Chalice Press, 2012.

Corduan, Winfried. *In the Beginning God a Fresh Look at the Case for Original Monotheism*. Nashville, TN: B&H Publishing Group, 2014.

Crossan, John Dominic. *Jesus: A Revolutionary Biography*. San Francisco, CA: Harper, 1994.

"Deism." Accessed November 4, 2021. https://languages.oup.com/google-dictionary-en/.

Dharmaraj , Jacob D., and Glory E. Dharmaraj . "Sin and Salvation: Christianity and Islam." Bangalore Theological Forum, 2016, 46–67.

Ehrman, Bart D. *Did Jesus Exist?: The Historical Argument for Jesus of Nazareth*. New York, NY: HarperOne, an imprint of HarperCollinsPublishers, 2013.

Ehrman, Bart D. *The New Testament a Historical Introduction to the Early Christian Writings*. New York, NY: Oxford University Press, 2020.

Elnes, Eric. "Can You Hear Me Now? 5G Faith in a Pluralistic World.'" *International Congregational Journal* 17, no. 1 (2018): 103–18.

Emberson, Iain A. Comparison table between Christianity, Islam and Judaism. Accessed November 8, 2021. http://christianityinview.com/xncomparison.html.

Geffre, Claude. "Christian Faith and Religious Pluralism." *Theology Digest* 38, no. 1 (1991): 15–18.

Geisler, Norman L., and Patrick Zukeran. *The Apologetics of Jesus: A Caring Approach to Dealing with Doubters*. Grand Rapids, MI: BakerBooks, 2009.

Geivett, R. Douglas, Gary R. Habermas, and Geivett, Assistant Professor of Philosophy R. Douglas. *In Defense of Miracles a Comprehensive Case for God's Action in History*. Downers Grove, IL: InterVarsity Press, 2014.

Groothuis, Douglas. *Truth Decay: Defending Christianity against the Challenges of Postmodernism*. Downers Grove, IL, IL: IVP, InterVarsity Press, 2000.

Grudem, Wayne. *Christian Beliefs: 20 Basics Every Christian Should Know*. Grand Rapids , MI: Inter-Varsity Press, 2010.

Habermas, Gary R., and Mike Licona. *The Case for the Resurrection of Jesus*. Grand Rapids, MI, MI: Kregel Publications, 2004.

Habets, Myk. "On Getting First Things First:ï¿1/2assessing

Claims for the Primacy of Christ." *New Blackfriars* 90, no. 1027 (2009): 343–64. https://doi.org/10.1111/j.1741-2005.2008.00240.x.

Hunt, Brendan. *Ted Lasso*. Episode. 2, no. 1: Goodbye Earl, 2021.

"Jordan Peterson's Realization about the Bible." YouTube, January 25, 2022. https://youtu.be/Vt9K6kmpx44?t=225.

Keller, Timothy. *Making Sense of God: An Invitation to the Sceptical*. London, UK: Hodder & Stoughton Ltd, 2018.

Keller, Timothy. *The Reason for God: Belief in an Age of Skepticism*. New York, NY: Penguin Books, 2018.

Kennedy, D. James. *Why I Believe*. Waco, TX: Word Books, 1980.

Kierkegaard, Søren, Howard Vincent Hong, and Edna Hatlestad Hong. *The Essential Kierkegaard*. Princeton, NJ: Princeton University Press, 2000.

Lee, Michael Hakmin. "Faith, Reason, and Christian Witness in a Pluralistic World: Interdisciplinary Reflections on the Epistemology of Religious Disagreement." *Missiology: An International Review* 40, no. 1 (2012): 63–75. https://doi.org/10.1177/009182 961204000107.

Lewis, C. S. *Surprised by Joy*. New York, NY: CreateSpace, 2016.

Lewis, C. S. *The Abolition of Man*. New York, NY: Exciting Classics, 2013.

Lewis, C. S., and Walter Hooper. *God in the Dock: Essays on Theology and Ethics*. Grand Rapids, MI: Wm. B. Eerdmans Publishing Co., 2014.

Lewis, Clive Staples. *Miracles: A Preliminary Study*. New York, NY: Collier Books, 1978.

Lewis, Clive Staples. *Mere Christianity*. New York, NY: Simon and Schuster, 1996.

Licona, Mike. *The Resurrection of Jesus: A New Historiographical Approach*. Nottingham, UK: Apollos, 2018.

Lüdemann Gerd, and Özen Alf. *What Really Happened to Jesus: A Historical Approach to the Resurrection*. Louisville, KY: Westminster John Knox Press, 1996.

Manning, Brennan. *The Ragamuffin Gospel*. Colorado Springs,

CO: Multnomah Books, 2015.

McCoy, Daniel J., Winfried Corduan, and Henk Stoker. "Christian and Buddhist Approach to Religious Exclusivity. Do Interfaith Scholars Have It Right?" *HTS Teologiese Studies* / Theological Studies 72, no. 3 (2016). https://doi.org/10.4102/hts.v72i3.3266.

McDowell, Josh, and Don Douglas Stewart. *Handbook of Today's Religions.* Nashville, TN: T. Nelson, 1992.

McGrath, Alister E. *The Landscape of Faith: An Explorer's Guide to the Christian Creeds.* London, UK: Society for Promoting Christian Knowledge, 2018.

McGrath, Alister E., Ravi Zacharias, Alister E. McGrath, and Alister E. McGrath. *Doubting: Growing through the Uncertainties of Faith.* Downers Grove, IL: IVP Books, an imprint of InterVarsity Press, 2006.

McLaughlin, Rebecca. *Confronting Christianity.* Wheaton, IL: Crossway, 2019.

Meadors, Edward P. "Why Jesus Is the Only Way." *Journal for Baptist Theology and Ministry* 2, no. 2 (2004): 99–112.

Merleau-Ponty, Maurice, and Colin Smith. *Phenomenology of Perception.* Las Vegas, NV: Franklin Classics, 2018.

"Monotheism." Merriam-Webster. Merriam-Webster. Accessed November 4, 2021. https://www.merriam-webster.com/dictionary/monotheism.

Neely, Brent. "The Gospel in a Plural World: Interrogating the Relationship between Proclamation and Compassion." *Evangelical Missions* Quarterly 53, no. 4 (2017): 40–45.

"Pantheism." Merriam-Webster. Merriam-Webster. Accessed November 4, 2021. https://www.merriam-webster.com/dictionary/pantheism.

Perkins, Pheme. "Christianity and World Religions." *Interpretation: A Journal of Bible and Theology* 40, no. 4 (1986): 367–78. https://doi.org/10.1177/002096438604000404.

Pieper, Josef, Richard Winston, and Clara Winston. *Guide to Thomas Aquinas.* San Francisco, CA: Ignatius Press, 1991.

Plantinga, Alvin. *The Analytic Theist*. Grand Rapids, MI: Eerdmans, 2003.

"Polytheism." Merriam-Webster. Merriam-Webster. Accessed November 4, 2021. https://www.merriam-webster.com/dictionary/polytheism.

Poplin, Mary S. I*s Reality Secular?: Testing the Assumptions of Four Global Worldviews*. Downers Grove, IL: Intervarsity Press, 2014.

Prentiss, Craig R., and Jacob Nuesner. "Chapter 5. Jew and Judaist, Ethnic and Religious." Essay. In *Religion and the Creation of Race and Ethnicity: An Introduction*, 85–100. New York, NY: New York University Press, 2003.

"Relativism." Merriam-Webster. Merriam-Webster. Accessed November 4, 2021. https://www.merriam-webster.com/dictionary/relativism.

Ruether, Rosemary Radford. *Faith and Fratricide*. New York, NY: Seabury Press , 1975.

Shamash, Yoav. Shahadah. *Israel: Agam*, 2012.

Sharp, Mary Jo. *Why I Still Believe: A Former Atheist's Reckoning with the Bad Reputation Christians Give a Good God*. Grand Rapids, MI: Zondervan, 2019.

Strobel, Lee, and Jane Vogel. *The Case for Christ: A Journalist's Personal Investigation of the Evidence for Jesus*. Grand Rapids, MI: Zondervan, 2017.

"Subjective Definition & Meaning." Dictionary.com. Dictionary.com. Accessed November 7, 2021. https://www.dictionary.com/browse/subjective.

Tennent, Timothy C. "Postmodernity, the Paradigm and the Pre-Eminence of Christ." *Evangelical Quarterly* 86, no. 4 (2014): 291–302. https://doi.org/10.1163/27725472-08604001.

Tennent, Timothy C. "Postmodernity, the Paradigm and the Pre-Eminence of Christ." *Evangelical Quarterly* 86, no. 4 (2014): 291–302. https://doi.org/10.1163/27725472-08604001.

Thangaraj, M. Thomas. "Jesus the Christ—the Only Way to God and to Human Flourishing." *Journal of Ecumenical Studies*

52, no. 1 (2017): 44–49. https://doi.org/10.1353/ecu.2017.0010.

Thangaraj, M. Thomas. "Jesus the Christ—the Only Way to God and to Human Flourishing." *Journal of Ecumenical Studies* 52, no. 1 (2017): 44–49. https://doi.org/10.1353/ecu.2017.0010.

"Theism." Our Dictionaries | Oxford Languages. Accessed November 4, 2021. https://languages.oup.com/dictionaries/#oed.

Waardenburg, Jacques. "Christians, Muslims, Jews, and Their Religions." *Islam and Christian–Muslim Relations* 15, no. 1 (January 2004): 13–33.

Wallace, J. Warner. *Cold-Case Christianity: A Homicide Detective Investigates the Claims of the Gospels*. Colorado Springs, CO: David C Cook, 2013.

Wallace, J. Warner. "Why We Should Expect Witnesses to Disagree." *Cold Case Christianity*, March 25, 2019. https://coldcasechristianity.com/writings/why-we-should-expect-witnesses-to-disagree/.

www.whyislam.org. *Concept of God in Islam*. Piscataway, NJ: Why Islam, 2008.

Yancey, Philip. *The Jesus I Never Knew*. Grand Rapids, MI: Zondervan Publishing, 2006.

ENDNOTES

244. "Ted Lasso," Season 2, no. 1: Goodbye Earl 2021.

245. "Ted Lasso" Season 2, no. 10: No Weddings and A Funeral, 2021.

246. Arsyil A'la Al-Maududi, *Towards Understanding Islam* (Kuala Lumpur: Place of publication not identified, n.d.), 76.

247. Bart D. Ehrman, *Did Jesus Exist?: The Historical Argument for Jesus of Nazareth* (New York, NY: HarperOne, an imprint of HarperCollinsPublishers, 2013), 96.

248. Ibid., 12.

249. Rebecca McLaughlin, *Confronting Christianity* (Wheaton, IL: Crossway, 2019), 49.

250. "The Changing Global Religious Landscape," Pew Research Center's Religion & Public Life Project, July 27, 2020, https://www.pewforum.org/2017/04/05/the-changing-global-religious-landscape/.

251. "Pantheism," Merriam-Webster (Merriam-Webster), accessed November 4, 2021, https://www.merriam-webster.com/dictionary/pantheism.

252. Mary S. Poplin, *Is Reality Secular?: Testing the Assumptions of Four Global Worldviews* (Downers Grove, IL: Intervarsity Press, 2014), 173.

253. "Polytheism," Merriam-Webster (Merriam-Webster), accessed November 4, 2021, https://www.merriam-webster.com/dictionary/polytheism.

254. "Monotheism," Merriam-Webster (Merriam-Webster), accessed November 4, 2021, https://www.merriam-webster.com/dictionary/monotheism.

255. Rebecca McLaughlin, *Confronting Christianity* (Wheaton, IL: Crossway, 2019), 58.

256. Daniel J. McCoy, Winfried Corduan, and Henk Stoker, "Christian and Buddhist Approach to Religious Exclusivity. Do Interfaith Scholars Have It Right?," *HTS Teologiese*

Studies / Theological Studies 72, no. 3 (August 2016), https://doi.org/10.4102/hts.v72i3.3266, 2.

257. Jacob D. Dharmaraj and Glory E. Dharmaraj, "Sin and Salvation: Christianity and Islam," *Bangalore Theological Forum*, 2016, 47.

258. Josh McDowell and Don Douglas Stewart, *Handbook of Today's Religions* (Nashville, TN: T. Nelson, 1992), 389.

259. Arsyil A'la Al-Maududi, *Towards Understanding Islam* (Kuala Lumpur: Place of publication not identified, n.d.), 76.

260. Ibid.,391.

261. Jacob D. Dharmaraj and Glory E. Dharmaraj, "Sin and Salvation: Christianity and Islam," *Bangalore Theological Forum,* 2016, 46.

262. Josh McDowell and Don Douglas Stewart, *Handbook of Today's Religions* (Nashville, TN: T. Nelson, 1992), 396.

263. Jacob D. Dharmaraj and Glory E. Dharmaraj, "Sin and Salvation: Christianity and Islam," *Bangalore Theological Forum*, 2016,46.

264. "Concept of God in Islam," *Concept of God in Islam* (Piscataway, NJ: Why Islam, 2008).

265. Josh McDowell and Don Douglas Stewart, *Handbook of Today's Religions* (Nashville, TN: T. Nelson, 1992), 389–390.

266. Craig R. Prentiss and Jacob Nuesner, "Chapter 5. Jew and Judaist, Ethnic and Religious.," in *Religion and the Creation of Race and Ethnicity: An Introduction* (New York, NY: New York University Press, 2003), pp. 85–100, 85.

267. Josh McDowell and Don Douglas Stewart, *Handbook of Today's Religions* (Nashville, TN: T. Nelson, 1992), 372.

268. Ibid., 373.

269. Ibid., 373.

270. Ibid., 367.

271. Iain A. Emberson, "Comparison table between Christianity, Islam, and Judaism," accessed November 8, 2021, http://christianityinview.com/xncomparison.html.

272. "Apostles' Creed," *Encyclopædia Britannica* (Encyclopædia Britannica, inc.), accessed November 27, 2021, https://www.britannica.com/topic/Apostles-Creed.

273. Timothy Keller, *The Reason for God: Belief in an Age of Skepticism* (New York, NY: Penguin Books, 2018), 4.

274. Alvin Plantinga, *The Analytic Theist* (Grand Rapids, MI: Eerdmans, 2003), 192.

275. Ibid.,192.

276. Jacques Waardenburg, "Christians, Muslims, Jews, and Their Religions," *Islam and Christian–Muslim Relations* 15, no. 1 (January 2004), 16.

277. Ibid., 5.

278. Yoav Shamash, Shahadah (Israel: Agam, 2012).

279. Edward P. Meadors, "Why Jesus Is The Only Way," *Journal for Baptist Theology and Ministry* 2, no. 2 (2004): pp. 99–112, 103.

280. Rosemary Radford Ruether, *Faith and Fratricide* (New York, NY: Seabury Press, 1975), 180, 246.

281. Tim Keller, *Making Sense of God* (New York, NY: Penguin Books, 2016), 237.

282. C. S. Lewis and Walter Hooper, *God in the Dock: Essays on Theology and Ethics* (Grand Rapids, MI: Wm. B. Eerdmans Publishing Co., 2014), 108–109.

283. Michael Hakmin Lee, "Faith, Reason, and Christian Witness in a Pluralistic World: Interdisciplinary Reflections on the Epistemology of Religious Disagreement," *Missiology: An International Review* 40, no. 1 (2012): pp. 63–75, https://doi.org/10.1177/009182961204000107, 66.

284. Rebecca McLaughlin, *Confronting Christianity* (Wheaton, IL: Crossway, 2019), 48.

285. Francis Chan, *Until Unity* (Elgin, IL: David C. Cook, 2021), 156.

286. Ibid.,44.

287. Written by Jason Lee McKinney (Zekers and ZiZi Music

(BMI); and Greg Williams (Greg A. Williams Music (BMI)

288. "Ted Lasso" Season 2, no. 10: No Weddings and A Funeral, 2021.

289. Tim Keller, *Making Sense of God* (New York, NY: Penguin Books, 2016), 237.

290. Timothy Keller, *The Reason for God: Belief in an Age of Skepticism* (New York, NY: Penguin Books, 2018),18.

291. Ibid., 20.

292. Brennan Manning, *The Ragamuffin Gospel* (New York, NY: WaterBrook Multnorah, 2005), 14.

293. Tim Keller, *Making Sense of God* (New York, NY: Penguin Books, 2016), 233.

294. Bart D. Ehrman, *The New Testament: A Historical Introduction to the Early Christian Writings* (New York, NY: Oxford University Press, 2016), 261–262.

295. John Dominic Crossan, *Jesus: A Revolutionary Biography* (San Francisco, CA: Harper, 1994), 145.

296. Lüdemann Gerd and Özen Alf, *What Really Happened to Jesus: A Historical Approach to the Resurrection* (Louisville, KY: Westminster John Knox Press, 1996), 80.

297. Bart D. Ehrman, T*he New Testament a Historical Introduction to the Early Christian Writings* (New York, NY: Oxford University Press, 2020), 282.

298. Gary R. Habermas and Mike Licona, *The Case for the Resurrection of Jesus* (Grand Rapids, MI, MI: Kregel Publications, 2004), 182.

299. Timothy Keller, *The Reason for God: Belief in an Age of Skepticism* (New York, NY: Penguin Books, 2018), 210.

300. Rebecca McLaughlin, *Confronting Christianity* (Wheaton, IL: Crossway, 2019), 58.

301. Clive Staples Lewis, *Mere Christianity* (New York, NY: Simon and Schuster, 1996), 56.

302. Clive Staples Lewis, *Miracles: A Preliminary Study* (New York, NY: Collier Books, 1978), 143–144.

303. Francis J. Beckwith et al. and Gary R. Habermas. "Chapter 11. The Case For Christ's Resurrection." *To Everyone an Answer: A Case for the Christian Worldview* (Grand Rapids, MI: IVP Academic, 2014), 189.

304. "Jordan Peterson's Realization about the Bible," YouTube, January 25, 2022, https://youtu.be/Vt9K6kmpx44?t=225.

305. Craig L. Blomberg, *Can We Still Believe the Bible?: An Evangelical Engagement with Contemporary Questions* (Grand Rapids, MI: Brazos Press, 2014), 27.

306. Ibid., 41.

307. Alisa Childers, *Another Gospel?: A Lifelong Christian Seeks Truth in Response to Progressive Christianity* (Carol Stream, IL: Tyndale Momentum, the Tyndale nonfiction imprint, 2020), 133–134.

308. Craig L. Blomberg, *Can We Still Believe the Bible?: An Evangelical Engagement with Contemporary Questions* (Grand Rapids, MI: Brazos Press, 2014), 123.

309. Ibid., 126.

310. Ibid., 164

311. Ibid., 166.

312. Ibid., 171.

313. J. Warner Wallace, *Cold-Case Christianity: A Homicide Detective Investigates the Claims of the Gospels* (Colorado Springs, CO: David C Cook, 2013).

314. J. Warner Wallace, "Why We Should Expect Witnesses to Disagree," *Cold Case Christianity*, March 25, 2019, https://coldcasechristianity.com/writings/why-we-should-expect-witnesses-to-disagree/.

315. J. Warner Wallace, "Why We Should Expect Witnesses to Disagree," *Cold Case Christianity*, March 25, 2019, https://coldcasechristianity.com/writings/why-we-should-expect-witnesses-to-disagree/.

316. Timothy Keller, *The Reason for God: Belief in an Age of Skepticism* (New York, NY: Penguin Books, 2018), 105.

317. Timothy Keller, *The Reason for God: Belief in an Age of Skepticism* (New York, NY: Penguin Books, 2018), 116.

318. Rebecca McLaughlin, *Confronting Christianity* (Wheaton, IL: Crossway, 2019), 143.

319. Timothy Keller, *The Reason for God: Belief in an Age of Skepticism* (New York, NY: Penguin Books, 2018), 116.

320. Søren Kierkegaard, Howard Vincent Hong, and Edna Hatlestad Hong, *The Essential Kierkegaard* (Princeton, NJ: Princeton University Press, 2000).

321. Rebecca McLaughlin, *Confronting Christianity* (Wheaton, IL: Crossway, 2019), 48.

Part 5

Personal Experience

We can't overlook the role personal experience plays in our faith, and our doubt, in our deconstructions and reconstructions. Most of the time intellectual questioning is tied to painful personal experience. We are singular subjective selves. We can't help but be affected by what happens to us and around us. Our perspective is more than natural, more than normal, it is unavoidable. Rainer Maria Rilke, in his work *Letters to a Young Poet*, says the following of experience, "Have patience with everything that remains unsolved in your heart. Try to love the questions themselves, like locked rooms and like books written in a foreign language. Do not now look for the answers. They cannot now be given to you because you could not live with them. It is a question of experiencing everything. At present you need to live the question. Perhaps you will gradually, without even noticing it, find yourself experiencing the answer, some distant day."[322] Our lived world is lived through our eyes, through our perception of our own experience. I know in my own life my doubts have come from not just intellectual questions about existence, truth, suffering and religion but from my own experiences. The inverse is true as well. The times I have had great faith and experienced the joy of security of belief even if only temporary is because of my experience as well. I think it is a mistake to dismiss personal experience. As I spoke about in Part 2 of the book it is impossible. I can't ever really disconnect myself from myself. This is not to say that the only thing I can be connected to is myself but that I am always experiencing, God, the world, and others through my personal experience. If you take the issue of suffering and the role it plays in deconstruction, it is not the fact that suffering exists that affects me deeply but my encounter with it either from own suffering, the suffering of someone close to me, or even the impact the suffering of those distant from me has on my own emotions.

We do not and are utterly incapable of encountering the world objectively. I do not, you do not, Billy Graham did not, C.S. Lewis did not, Thomas Aquinas did not, Stephen Hawking did not, Richard Dawkins does not, no human ever has been able to rid themselves of personal experience and the absolute tole and role it plays upon our worldviews. In a sense we are indoctrinated by our personal experience. This deeply affects our doubts and our faith. Soren Kierkegaard says, "If I am capable of grasping God objectively, I do not believe, but precisely because I cannot do this I must believe."[323] Faith requires an element of doubt. At the end of the day if I am honest and I believe I can extrapolate this to all humanity, it is not my intellectual questions or cognitive doubts that are the prime motivators for my many deconstructions but the pain of personal experience with disappointments, disasters, death, depression, and disruptions. I don't think this voids my intellectual questions at all, I just don't think they are at the root of my doubts and deconstructions. I also don't think the intellectual philosophical reconstructions of my beliefs are at the root of my maintaining and returning to faith repeatedly. I think it is my experience of faith with God that makes redemption possible. Paraphrasing Oswald Chambers, experience is not what makes redemption real, but experiences produced by redemption prove themselves by leading me beyond myself. In this the final Part of the book I am going to be much less academic and philosophical. The reason is that I have tried to funnel down from the biggest of and most general questions starting in Part 1 and work my way to more specific questions in Part 4. Now it is down to experience. Philosophy will play a part for sure. Again, philosophy did not give me my faith, but it has talked me back into it many times. The focus will be on my personal experiences as illustration for how all of our personal experiences are at the core of our doubts and our faith, our deconstructions and reconstructions. It is the lived experience of doubts and faith that make them real and the living through them that give them meaning. I will share three stories here of personal experience that have shaped my life in profound ways. I will be telling them out of chronological order.

SECLUSION

The time in my life when I doubted my beliefs the most by far and had the biggest deconstruction near demolition of my faith was my sophomore year of college. My first wife and I had just spent a year going to school six hours away from home. During that year we were destitute financially, we had car issue after car issue. While we made a few great friends at school, we were mostly lonely and isolated. On top of that she became pregnant halfway through the year. We were 19 years old at the time and not in any way ready to be parents. When she went for the first ultrasound I could not attend as I had a class during that time. When I picked her up from work that night she got in the car and showed me the ultrasound picture. She asked a question I will never forget, "how many babies do you see?" At first, I was sure I heard her wrong, and then my heart sank. I saw baby A and baby B next to two little black oval shapes with little white dots in them. At 19 years old I was going to a father to twins.

Given that we were having twins, we were suffering financially, and that we weren't really enjoying the college we were attending, we decided to move closer to home. We knew we would need the community we had come to depend on so that summer we moved to go to school a little less than an hour from home. Early that fall the twins were born (that is a whole epic story in itself, remind me to tell you that some other time) and we were settling into school. To backtrack a little, my senior year of high school (1992) and my ex-wife's freshman year of college while we were dating, we joined a Bible study at the church I had been attending for a few years. We were the youngest in the group by several years, but we felt we made real connections there. One of my best friends (James—I'm not using real names in these stories) was in the group and my ex made a close connection with one of the other women in the group (Angel). These people were our friend group, several of them played music at our wedding. So when we moved back, we were especially looking forward to reconnecting with them. Once we moved closer to home, we began to spend the weekends back in our hometown staying with family and attending this Bible study. We were still destitute financially and exhausted from taking care of twins, but life was far better in that the University we were attending was much more supportive of us and we were back with our friends in the Bible study.

That is until we encountered a couple we were acquainted with (fellow scene kids if you will) at the local mall who also knew one of the young couples in the Bible study group. The couple we were acquainted with proceeded to tell a sordid tale of character assassination of the female of the couple in the Bible study group. Even to the point of claiming the couple's young daughter was not the husbands. My wife (at the time) and I were not sure how to handle this so she decided she would disclose the gossip to Angel her closest friend in the Bible study to get advice before we took it to the couple the gossip was about. As innocent as our motivation, it was a misguided approach, and proved to be a fatal mistake. The message that ended up getting back to the entire Bible study was that my ex and I were the culprits of the gossip. We did not know we were being blamed for the gossip until we pulled into the parking lot the Sunday evening following the incident at the mall. We were looking forward to fellowship and community, but we were met in the parking lot by the leader of the group (Clive). Clive informed us that the couple whom the gossip was about did not want to be in a Bible study group with us any longer nor did they want to discuss the situation. The group also asked that we no longer attend the same church as them. We were then informed that the Bible study group felt the right thing to do was back up the couple the gossip was about and as us to leave immediately.

We spent the next year without any fellowship with other Christians. We were teenagers with twins, on our own with no friends to speak of. This was the group that encouraged us to get married so young so we would not "burn with lust" and then abandoned us over a misunderstanding. It hurt. We were lonely, felt abandoned and I began to question the goodness of God and even more so the goodness of his people. At that time, the words of the following Brennan Manning quote haunted and challenged me, "The greatest single cause of atheism in the world today is Christians who acknowledge Jesus with their lips and walk out the door and deny Him by their lifestyle. That is what an unbelieving world simply finds unbelievable."[324] At first, I filtered this quote as an indictment on those people. I thought God commanded us to love one another, be patient with one another, forgive one another. We received none of that in this situation. I can honestly say my ex and I were trying to do the right thing. These were people who were older than us (although looking back now they were just kids too) and we looked up to them, we were counting on them to show the love of Jesus to us, and they failed.

I had a long period of being bitter towards Christians. I doubted not so much God's existence at this time, but I did doubt his goodness and I completely deconstructed from thinking God had anything to do with church or Christians. Ironically, we did keep going to church. We kept going to the same church. We found out which service the Bible study group attended, and we would go to the other service. We would wait for the service to start, slip to the balcony, sit in the corner with low lighting and then slip out before the last song to make sure we did not make anyone feel uncomfortable with our presence there.

I did have some Christians reach out during this time but for about a year I became like a beat dog being offered a friendly hand. I did not trust that I would not be beat down more. My faith was damaged. I was not just doubting, but my openness to the world of faith closed. The only things that did not keep it from closing all together were: 1) I was introduced to *The Ragamuffin Gospel* from Brennan Manning, and 2) I was introduced to the book *What's So Amazing About Grace* by Phillip Yancey.

It is not an exaggeration to say that Brennan Manning's work over the years has been medicine to my soul. In this alcoholic Franciscan Priest spoke God to my heart. Brennan spoke of Jesus and reassured me that Jesus was madly and completely in love with me. He did not and would not reject me… ever for any reason. Jesus was more disappointed with the actions of those in the Bible study than I was. Jesus rejected my excommunication. Manning states, "The story goes that a public sinner was excommunicated and forbidden entry to the church. He took his woes to God. 'They won't let me in, Lord, because I am a sinner. 'What are you complaining about?' said God. 'They won't let Me in either.'"[325] In a time where I had no friends, no fellowship, Jesus became my friend. I encountered a Jesus who was always on my side, not a Jesus of my own creation but the Jesus who always really was, and is, and is to come. As I began to see Jesus for who he really was I also began to see myself as the ragamuffin I truly was, broken, bedraggled, and dragged down by my own pride and selfishness. Slowly I began to see the other people in the Bible study group the same way. After a while I read this quote, "Christians who acknowledge Jesus with their lips and walk out the door and deny Him by their lifestyle" not as those people but as me. What gave me the right to be bitter when I had done so much wrong myself? What gave me the right to play the victim? Who was I to accept Jesus' forgiveness for myself and yet not forgive others? The people in that Bible study group were victims too. We are all victims of being human. They were flawed, and frail ragamuffins like me. Once I could see them that way, which is who they always were, and not as the mentors

I expected them to be I began to forgive them. Phillip Yancey put it this way, "All of us in the church need "grace-healed eyes" to see the potential in others for the same grace that God has so lavishly bestowed on us."[326] I came to realize I was as much villain as victim in this story, but Jesus loved me anyway… and he loved each one of them just as much as he loved me. When my children were small and wronged one of their siblings, I comforted the one who had been wronged and I made sure there were consequences for the one who perpetrated the wrong, but I never once abandoned or disowned either of them. I never stopped wanting the best for both. If the one who was wronged in this situation had held on to the offense and disowned, disavowed, or distanced themselves from their sibling I would have been disappointed with them. My problem in this situation ultimately was not about what "those people" did to me. It was about two things.

1. Did I believe Jesus loved me as much as he said he did?
2. Because of that love, was I going to choose to see "those people" the way he did?

While I was learning to love myself as Jesus did and love others the same God was leading some of the people in the Bible study to seek my ex and I out and ask our forgiveness. There is power in the words I am sorry if you aren't too bitter to let them sink in. Sorry does not deny the pain or perception and the experience of what happened but it can dramatically reframe your perspective and experiences in the future. This event was incredibly painful, and I almost fully and permanently deconstructed out of church, but healing did occur. Within two years of this experience, I was a full-time employee of that very church and most of the relationships between myself and those in the Bible study had been fully repaired. Clive, the leader of that Bible study is a pastor now and is a dear friend. Clive has been there for me repeatedly since that time. He has shown up with care and wisdom, prayer, and willingness as a true and loyal brother in Christ. I am thankful for Clive. Some years later I received a phone call from Brennan Manning himself.

I got to speak to him and thank him for the powerful impact his work had on my life. Not all painful experiences come full circle and end with a redemptive ending but this one does for the most part. But even this story is not without its lasting impact. To this day the couple whom the gossip was about has not spoken to me since and as far as I know they still believe the gossip originated with me and my ex. I know this is not true and there has been about 90% restoration from the experience and from my perspective that is pretty good. It is through these breakdowns that often the greatest breakthroughs happen.

Breakdowns and Breakthroughs

V.1
Little Faith has lost all hope
She can't find a way to cope
Harsh words screamed another fight
Baby girl she left home tonight
Daddy doesn't know who she's become
Shorts skirts and the ring in her tongue
It's too much in the atmosphere of untrust

Pr.
All alone on a bus to Detroit
She's free to find her own voice

Ch.
Breakdowns and breakthroughs
She's got nothing else to lose and even less to prove
Breakdowns and Breakthroughs
As long as it gets her through
into the arms of truth

V.2
Freedom's dreams are just a lie
Now she gets paid for what men like
But the pills and thrills can't fill her solitude
So she dials the first number she ever knew
Familiar voice on the machine
Hesitation and a nervous plea
"Daddy can I come home it's me."

Pr.
Cause whatever it takes to find some grace
To catch a ray of sun in this place

CHORUS

Bridge.
Her hands quiver and shake
Is it too little, too late
Does rejection wait at the bus gate
Does her father's heart still hold a place
She steps off the bus into the station
To see her family and friends in a welcome home celebration
Her Daddy runs to meet and before she makes a sound
He says' "my baby, you were lost but now your found."[327]

Salvation

In the 2021 movie *Spider-Man: No Way Home*, Peter Parker's true identity has been revealed to the world. Peter asks Dr. Strange to cast a spell for everyone to forget who he is but then interrupts the spell by asking that those closest to him remember him. This opens gateways to other universes and allows several super villains in to cause havoc. To prevent further catastrophe and at Parker's request, Dr. Strange fixes the spell, sending the alternate Spider-Men and their villains back to their respective universes, while making everyone forget Parker's existence. Even those closest to him.

Peter

What's happening?

Dr. Strange

They are starting to come through and I can't stop them.

Peter

There's got to be something we can do? Can't you just cast the spell again but the original way before I screwed it up?

Dr. Strange

We're too late for that they're here. They're here because of you!

Peter

What if everyone forgot who I was?

Dr. Strange

What?!

Peter

They're coming here because of me, right? Because I'm Peter Parker. So cast a new spell, but this time make everyone forget who Peter Parker is. Make everyone forget … me.

Dr. Strange

No.

Peter

But it would work right?

DR. STRANGE

Yeah it would work. You got to understand that would mean that everyone who knows and loves you ... we ... we'd have no memory of you. It would be as though you never existed.

PETER

I know. Do it.[328]

Peter Parker's sacrifice of his own existence (at least in the perception of others) shows a lowering of himself. It is a giving up of oneself for the good of those he loves. Peter allows all connection with those he loves to be severed so that he could fix what was wrong in the world. There is something messianic in that. Jesus, who was God, lowered himself to become a man. He lived a sinless life and died a brutal death on a cross to reconcile humanity to God. Jesus gave himself up to heal the divide between God and his beloved. Death entered the world through the free will of man, but death could not be conquered through the will of man, that required the sacrifice of God. The story of Jesus is one of sacrifice and reconciliation. Jesus' whole mission was to bring humanity back into a right relationship with God, to restore what had been lost and broken. Like Peter Parker, Jesus made this sacrifice out of his great love for humanity. This was his purpose this was his mission. Being a Christian is not about ascending to a cogent doctrine or prescribed moral code. It is believing that Jesus was God, had the mission of reconciliation, and achieved that through death on the cross and his resurrection from the dead. Christianity is also believing that you cannot be a good person because none exist. All humanity needs a doctor, the great physician. Jesus is the only doctor qualified to cure the disease humans have. That disease being sin. Brennan Manning in his book *The Furious Longing of God* says,

> "The gospel is absurd, and the life of Jesus is meaningless unless we believe that He lived, died, and rose again with but one purpose in mind: to make brand-new creation. Not to make people with better morals but to create a community

of prophets and professional lovers, men and women who would surrender to the mystery of the fire of the Spirit that burns within, who would live in ever greater fidelity to the omnipresent Word of God, who would enter into the center of it all, the very heart and mystery of Christ, into the center of the flame that consumes, purifies, and sets everything aglow with peace, joy, boldness, and extravagant, furious love. This, my friend, is what it really means to be a Christian."[329]

In 1991, I was 16—wild, rebellious, promiscuous. I was the drummer in a pretty popular band around my hometown. I drove a souped-up street racing car with five-on-the-floor (always under the speed limit mom, Scout's honor). I had long beautiful blonde hair (if I do say so myself) down to the middle of my back. I was thinly built but cut (not hard to do as a teen), despite being shy I could smooth talk my way into and out of most situations. Good grades came easy, teachers liked me despite all the above. Girls came easy. I had the world by the tail, and I was also completely full of myself. Simultaneously I was incredibly insecure and often depressed. I was not close to my family at the time, which is not completely uncommon for teenagers. But for me there were extenuating circumstances. As I discussed earlier in the book, by this time, I had not spent any significant time with my dad in years. I was my mom's first child, and she came from an incredibly abusive home (verbally, physically, and sexually) with a massive amount of trauma in her childhood. She did her best to end that cycle and did to a great degree but some of it spilled over into her parenting of me. Additionally, my mom and my stepdad's marriage was falling apart at this time and she was busy raising my little sister who was 2 and my little brother who was an infant at the time. As a replacement I put a very high value on friendship during this period of my life I considered my friends to be the ones I could count on and believed they could count on me. This assumption like Simon Peter with Jesus proved to be false, my friends could not count on me (also check out the song *Simon* from Idle Threat, it is a brilliant song).

I mentioned I was quite successful with girls (as a dad now I would have hated me) but the nameless body count did not fill my void, so I decided to look for a real relationship. I decided to clean up my act and find a good girl. I found one at the high school I attended. She was cute, got good grades, was polite and a little shy. She did not care about being popular at all. She was also a Christian. I thought I remembered what that was about, believe in Jesus (like that he existed) and be a good person. I set out to win this girl's affection by being a good person. I had a large ditch to dig out of as I and my best friend at the time had quite the negative reputation.

Running concurrent to me trying to win this girl over, I replaced all the wild behavior for thrill seeking. I traded the adrenaline rush of girls and alcohol with doing dangerous and stupid stuff as well as stuff that would scare me. My best friend at the time (Bill** not using their real names), his older sister (Lydia), and her boyfriend (James) and I would spend the weekends doing stuff like climbing on the roof of our high school's football stadium which was probably 100 feet from the ground and hanging each other off the edge with only the grip of a hand on a shirt to keep us from falling. We would also explore burned down houses or break into an abandon tuberculosis hospital. We began conducting seances and playing around with Ouija boards. This may all seem comical now but at this time society was just past the satanic panic of the '80s. American culture was still in the middle of blaming the occult for every murder that happened. This stuff was scary at the time, especially doing it in abandoned houses. I will say looking back all this paranormal stuff with this group of people was just silly psycho-reactionary thinking based on anticipation or cognitive bias. However, the fact that while I was trying to impress this Christian girl, I was also playing around with the paranormal did bring to the forefront of my mind a very real encounter I had a few years earlier.

I will need to jump back further in time for background in order to get us back to 1991 with the needed information to complete this story. In 1983 I was in 3rd grade. I was molested by some teenagers in my neighborhood. It was awful. I just wanted them to like me, for them to be my friend (I was a lonely kid). I was excited when these two guys who could drive invited me over for a camp out. I had no idea the nightmare I was about to encounter. I kept the events of that night a secret for many months as I was instructed to do. One of the perpetrators confessed to his parents about the night but painted himself as innocent and that it was my idea. He portrayed the event as if I, at nine, was the one who pushed myself on a 16-year-old and a 17-year-old. There was a big meeting between the families on how this was to be handled. The eventual conclusion was that it was to be swept under the rug and never to be spoken about again. I know my parents really felt this was the best solution at the time (and I don't blame them for it) but what it did was tell me that it was my fault, I was to blame. My perception of the decision for it never to be spoken of again made me question my worth, my sexuality, whether I could feel anything but shame again. I did not broadcast this event to people. I did however tell my very best friend at the time (Jeremy) who lived across the street. I hoped I would find acceptance and kindness there but instead Jeremy told his parents who then forbid him from playing with me again for fear I might try something sexual with him. My experience of this rejection let me know that I could not tell anyone ever again about what happened because it was my fault (I know this is not the case now but at the time I was 100% convinced it was my fault). My vow of silence did not mean my former best friend kept silent about it. Jeremy told another kid (Evan) who was his friend about it. Evan, who was five years older than me, began to tease me relentlessly. The teasing become so bad it reached the point where I did not go outside for the last two years we lived in that house (in 5th grade we moved to another neighborhood, and I found great friends there and acceptance. I am still friends with several of the people in that neighborhood today). I was a shut in at nine years old for two years.

In the fall of 1988, I had just started 8th grade and was invited to a party. At this party a few of the girls who came from a different feeder school started to play with the Ouija board. In the previous spring of 1988, Evan had committed suicide. These girls called up Evan on Ouija board before I got into the room. When I did arrive in the room the Ouija board started moving fast (just like the movies, so I was pretty skeptical) and the girls asked the board why it was agitated, and the board said because I was in the room and then began to describe the sex acts that were forced upon me when I was nine. Now I know you might be thinking that this information was passed around from Jeremy to Evan on to others, but the Ouija board described things in detail that I had never told anyone, not Jeremy, not my parents, no one. Unless the perpetrators themselves went around bragging about what they made me do (which I highly doubt), this Ouija board was telling incredibly damaging and embarrassing details about my life. Details that the two girls who were on the board had no clue about. Something metaphysical and beyond the material world was communicating through that Ouija board. I am a skeptic but that was a real experience that I cannot discount or dismiss.

Back to 1991, I was testing limits with my friends and trying to impress this Christian girl. Every day I was trying to pour on the charm. We were chatting on the phone. I was calling her dad Sir (he still hated me). I was putting on the full court press, flowers, poetry, all of it. At the same time James had discovered that Lydia had been cheating on him with several guys. This devastated James. So much so that he eventually went off to Florida for a couple of weeks with another friend of his to clear his head. The same time James was off in Florida I finally got the word that the Christian girl was not interested in me in any way shape or form. No way no how never gonna happen. I decided there was no use trying to be a good person I might as well let loose with some friends that night. As long as I kept my one moral more' to be a loyal friend, everything else was fair game. Bill and I along with several other friends and their significant others went to someone's house to party. The alcohol was a plenty and I partook … a lot. So much so that I had a vague memory of kissing someone but not sure who until I woke up the next morning and lying next to me naked was Bill's longtime girlfriend. I knew right then, I was not a good person, I was selfish and prideful. I had let down someone very important to me. I didn't violate some religious moral code handed down to me by my grandparents or society. I had violated my own moral code. I was the villain. I was a terminally ill patient with no means for a cure. I confessed to Bill which ended the friendship for several years (we are friends again and have been for a long time now). I began to despair and contemplate whether life was worth living at all. There was so many painful experiences that had happened, some wounds like this one were self-inflicted and others like being molested were not, but it all seemed too much. My family was a mess, my dad didn't want me, my mom was distracted and now I had let my friend down. Why go on?

James at the same time was in Florida going through some of the same things. While he was in Florida his friend began to tell James about belief in Jesus. James at first dismissed it because he was a good Catholic boy, he already knew about Jesus. But the more his friend spoke the more James discovered that he had never actually met Jesus, he had never heard what it truly meant to believe in Jesus, to trust him as savior. James became a Christian in Florida. When he came back, he called me up not really knowing what had transpired between Bill and me. I began to tell James about my betrayal. I told James there was no reason for me to try and be a good person, I just could not do it. There was no reason for me to try and have a good life as life was just going to keep screwing me over like it had been. I told him I was tired of being beaten up and I didn't need religion to give the final knock out punch. I got it already, I am awful.

James read Matthew 11:28 to me over the phone, He said Jesus doesn't want to keep you down Jesus says, "Come to me, all you who are weary and burdened, and I will give you rest." He read Mark 2:17 "Jesus said to them, "It is not the healthy who need a doctor, but the sick. I have not come to call the righteous, but sinners." I protested that if there is anything I know is that I can't get it together. I can't even live up to my own moral code much less the moral code of someone else. James said you don't need to live up to any moral code, the fact that you can't is why you need Jesus. James quoted Romans 5:8 "But God demonstrates His own love toward us, in that while we were still sinners, Christ died for us." James said "it is just about believing in faith and this thing called grace that I don't even fully understand. Jesus wants to know us and for us to know him. Why not give it a shot?" I knew experientially that the metaphysical (supernatural) existed because of what happened in '88 with the Ouija board. If I was convinced of life beyond the material, why could there not be a God. I knew though that I was like a real deal sinner. I didn't mess around with those little white sins so to speak. James just reassured that it didn't matter. Later on, I encountered the words of Brennan Manning who wrote it like this in *The Ragamuffin Gospel*, "The sinners to whom Jesus directed His messianic ministry were not those who skipped morning devotions or Sunday church. His ministry was to those whom society considered real sinners. They had done nothing to merit salvation. Yet they opened themselves to the gift that was offered them. On the other hand, the self-righteous placed their trust in the works of the Law and closed their hearts to the message of grace." (38)

I remembered the Jesus my grandmother read me about and he seemed like he was what I would want in a savior, and it sure seemed like I needed one. So that day I began a journey and a relationship with Jesus. I said a prayer sure, but I don't believe it was about that prayer, it was about the relationship that started that day. I didn't understand much but I did think it was worth a shot. I sure wanted to be loved the way James told me Jesus already loved me. I opened a Bible I found lying around the house that day and came upon the verse Hebrews 13:5 where the writer declares, "he has said, 'I will never leave you nor forsake you.' It was not that day but it wasn't long until I came across Romans 8:38–39 where the Apostle Paul says, "for I am convinced that neither death nor life, neither angels nor demons, neither the present nor the future, nor any powers, neither height nor depth, nor anything else in all creation, will be able to separate us from the love of God that is in Christ Jesus our Lord." For a kid that had gone through what I had; having my foundation and rocks, my grandparents pass away, my parents divorce, and my dad having severed a relationship with me. I myself having betrayed and lost a friend, and my mom being unpredictable because of all that was going on in her life—for a kid who had been trying to fill his life with sex and success, thrills and alcohol, to hear that someone loved me and would never, no matter what, leave me or abandon me and that someone was God. To hear that someone promised to stick with me to the end and help me become the man I had stopped believing I could be was a message I was unable to pass up. That day God provided the grace, my feeble and frail faith received the gift.

I have fallen and failed repeatedly but I continually fall into the arms of Jesus who says, "I've got you. Let's dress those wounds, get you some food and some rest and try again. I am so proud of you for trying." This is not a Jesus who demands nothing of me. This is not a Jesus of my own creation but Jesus who demands all of me, who loves me too much to leave me alone to my own device. I don't follow a Jesus that I create but the Jesus that in whom I am a new creation. 2 Corinthians 5:17–19 says, "Therefore, if anyone is in Christ, he is a new creation; old things have passed away; behold, all things have become new. Now all things are of God, who has reconciled us to Himself through Jesus Christ, and has given us the ministry of reconciliation, that is, that God was in Christ reconciling the world to Himself, not imputing their trespasses to them, and has committed to us the word of reconciliation." I don't want to do it on my own, that is a disaster for everyone involved.

It is my faith that justifies me but, in my desire, to be like him I am called to be holy. I want to become a human being filled up with the divine presence. We imitate our hero's, and I was called that day and convinced to make Jesus my hero. Romans 5:1–3 says "Therefore, having been justified by faith, we have peace with God through our Lord Jesus Christ, through whom also we have access by faith into this grace in which we stand, and rejoice in hope of the glory of God." Ephesians 2:8 says, "For by grace you have been saved through faith, and that not of yourselves; it is the gift of God." No matter how good I get at imitating my hero I can never live up to him. I can't be good enough and that is okay, in fact it is the point. Gal 2:16–17, 19–20 says, "Knowing that a man is not justified by works of the Law, but through faith in Jesus Christ, even we have believed in Christ Jesus, in order to be justified by faith in Christ, and not by works of the Law, because by works of the Law shall no one be justified . . . For through the Law, I have died to the Law, that I might live to God. I have been crucified with Christ; it is no longer I who live, but Christ who lives in me; and the life I now live in the flesh I live by faith in the Son of God, who loved me and gave himself for me."

This is my testimony. A testimony is the subjective truth experience of transcendent truth brought about through divine revelation. No two testimonies are the same. No two salvation experiences are the same and, in that sense, what was true for me, what was true for my story may not be true for you or your story. But the intersubjective truth of testimonies should corroborate the absoluteness of the divine revelation. The transcendent truth is that God reached into the very essence of my self, my "I" and called me home to him. The great "I am" that is beyond space, time, matter and all human comprehension through Jesus reached into space and matter and entered time so that by grace and grace alone I might be able to receive the free gift of salvation through faith. Believing that the ultimate reality of things is that Jesus is the son of God, lived a sinless life, and died and rose again so that I might be reconciled to God for all eternity. My "I" was drawn home by the great "I am."

Fr. Stephen Freeman writes, "Sin is not a legal problem because God is not a lawyer. Sin is a death problem. It's far more like a disease than anything else."[330] My salvation, my testimony is my restoration story, my story of being spiritually healed. My life is in post op. The surgery is complete, and the terminal disease removed. I have a new identity for the rest of time. My identity is spiritual death survivor (Romans 6:23; Ephesians 2:1; Colossians 2:13). The rest of my life is recovery. The rest of my life is spiritual therapy, teaching my soul to live and function in the reality of being free from disease. The terminal disease of spiritual death is terminally gone. I am cured, spiritual death isn't in permanent remission, it is eradicated. I was cured by the surgeon's love, his careful hand, his wisdom and ultimately his sacrifice. See in this surgery the surgeon himself had to not just remove the disease from me but had to take it on himself. Now nothing can separate me from the surgeon who himself is the cure. I am convinced that nothing in all creation, will be able to separate us from the love of the surgeon that is in Christ Jesus our Lord. The symptoms of spiritual death (pride, greed, lust, envy, gluttony, wrath, laziness) may still linger in presentation, but the symptoms are phantom. Any spiritual limps, aches or pain I have now are bodily muscle memory of the flesh that has not yet learned the reality that I don't need to walk with a limp anymore. If I follow doctor's orders the lingering phantom symptoms will get smaller and less noticeable over time. The more I exercise and remain disciplined in the spiritual therapy I have been prescribed the less obvious the presentation of the phantom symptoms will be. The great physician has performed a successful surgery, my identity has changed from a person riddled with disease to one who is disease free. I just must learn to live in the reality of that. The soul is fully healed even if the flesh (the body; the senses, the brain) doesn't know it and isn't fully capable of living it yet. Salvation in Christ is not primarily a legal matter. It is not about transferring a name from the guilty side of the ledger to the innocent side of the ledger. Jesus is far more the great physician than the great lawyer. He will for sure act as judge, but his primary role and desire is that of healer.

In my subjective truth experience when I have had times of deconstruction and doubt, I can come back to this time as a marker of something I experienced as a paradigm in my life. My life changed on that day. My perception of what could be possible and what was my true identity was forever shifted. We can make all the intellectual arguments for God we can (and we should) but the most powerful evidence there will ever be for God is a changed life. I pray this testimony helps some of you. May it be a beacon for the fleet.

Beacon for the Fleet

V.1
Been through the roughest water
Thrown miles off course by want to wander
Been thought too far gone
Mist in my eyes salt on my tongue

CH.
Like a west wind a northern star
Lost ship with his share of battle scars
Love's light brought me back from the deep
Let this testimony be a beacon for the fleet

V.2
Left the rest lost my bearings
Stained and cracked and worn past caring
Should be a wreck on the ocean floor
But your love broke through washed me up on the shore[331]

I was reconciled to God that day and have continued to be reconciled to him everyday since. Reconciled indicates a returning, a restoration. I say I was reconciled to God that day because it is in a very real sense a returning (not in a Greek philosophical sense of the soul pre-existing the body way). I had been searching for home, the place where my soul fit. The place where there was no possibility of rejection. A relationship where I could not be let down, where I would always be loved no matter how I failed. I wanted to know the God who compared his love to the shepherd in the parable of the lost sheep in Matthew 18:12–13, "If a man has a hundred sheep and one of them wanders away, what will he do? Won't he leave the 99 others on the hills and go out to search for the one that is lost? And if he finds it, I tell you the truth, he will rejoice over it more than over the 99 that didn't wander away!" That day was not so much an event as a beginning of a relationship, Jesus like the Little Prince and his Rose in the children's book written by Antoine de Saint-Exupéry, was taking time to transform and tame me. Jesus was taking responsibility for me like the Little Prince did for his rose. Jesus had made me his for all of eternity. The Little Prince says of his rose:

> "You are beautiful, but you are empty," he went on. "One could not die for you. To be sure, an ordinary passerby would think that my rose looked just like you—the rose that belongs to me. But in herself alone she is more important than all the hundreds of you other roses: because it is she that I have watered; because it is she that I have put under the glass globe; because it is she that I have sheltered behind the screen; because it is for her that I have killed the caterpillars (except the two or three that we saved to become butterflies); because it is she that I have listened to, when she grumbled, or boasted, or ever sometimes when she said nothing. Because she is my rose."[332]

Jesus likewise says of me and of you, "To be sure, an ordinary passerby would think that Jason looked just like any other human—Jason that belongs to me. But in himself alone he is more important than all the hundreds of other humans: because it is he that I have watered; because it is Jason that I have put under the glass globe; because it is Jason that I have sheltered behind the screen; because it is for Jason that I have killed the caterpillars (except the two or three that we saved to become butterflies); because it is Jason that I have listened to, when he grumbled, or boasted, or ever sometimes when Jason said nothing. Because He is my rose." The only difference between The Little Prince's love for his rose and Jesus' love is that to Jesus every one of us is his rose. All we have to do is let Jesus be our Little Prince.

New Strings on An Old Guitar

V.1

I've been down the lonely road
It was broken and cold
It was dark I was alone
I held a secret I couldn't keep it
Cause it's only with the heart one can rightly see
That you were always calling me
To be abandoned honestly
You're like

Ch.

New Strings on an old guitar
You take this worn and wasted heart
You make it new
Strings that were rusted out
Are bright and clear and ringing loud
You made it new, oh you're making me like you

V.2

I only sang an empty song
It had no substance of the heart
You could only hum along
For the prince it's more than a wish
Times not wasted on his rose
You were bleeding for my soul
You left the 99
Just to pull me to your side
Now I am yours and you are mine

Bridge
I've slowly can see the star light
Through the shadows of the darkest night
Illuminating your design
you're like new strings[333]

- Testimony- a public recounting of a religious conversion or experience. The public profession about your experience of coming to saving faith in Jesus.
- Faith- Hebrews 11:1, "the assurance of things hoped for, the conviction of things not seen."
- Grace- According to Merriam Webster is, "Unmerited divine assistance granted to humans for their regeneration or sanctification."
    i. Theologian John Stott called grace, "Grace is love that cares and stoops and rescues."
    ii. Author Paul Zahl says grace is love that seeks you out when you have nothing to give in return.

SURRENDER

In the movie *Shawshank Redemption*, the character Andy Dufresne is wrongfully convicted of murder but over time plots his escape. He forms a close relationship with inmate Red Redding, the only guilty man in the prison. They have the following exchange.

ANDY
Whatever mistakes I made I paid for them and then some. That hotel, that boat, I don't think that's too much to ask.

RED
I don't think you got to be doing this to yourself, Andy. It's just shitty pipe dreams. I mean, Mexico is way the hell down there, and you're in here, and that's the way it is.

ANDY
Yeah. Right. That's the way it is. It's down there and I'm in here. I guess it comes down to a simple choice really. Get

busy living or get busy dying. I guess it comes down to a simple choice really…"[334]

I had just cut a very frustrating day in the recording studio short and was just about to sit down on the couch for a snack when my wife (at the time) walked in the house with a manila envelope in hand and her father behind her. It was a shock as she was supposed to be at work and her dad lived two states away, but I immediately knew what it meant. I had no clue our problems were that serious five minutes before but when I saw that entrance, I knew what was in that envelope. She was divorcing me.

She asked me in the bedroom and told me that she wasn't happy and had not been in a long time. She asserted that I was not happy either. She was right on both accounts. I protested that I knew we were in a slump, but I thought we would pull through it. She told me she did not want to pull through it, but she knew I would want to see the kids so thought it best we work through this amicably. I told her I did not understand. What happened that was so bad that we could not get through it? She said she didn't want to talk about it now. I asked her to write it down, all of it, in a letter so I would know. I asked her to do this and to give me a chance. She agreed to the letter but not the chance.

She stayed at a hotel that night with her dad. She picked up the kids from a non-disclosed location so that we could tell them the next day that we were splitting up. To this day that is the hardest thing I have ever had to do. One of my sons Zion chased me to my car begging me not to leave. All I could say is that I must. I received the letter about a week later, all 16 pages of it. It outlined every wrong I had committed over the past 14 years. Some of them were quite petty, like forgetting my wallet on our first date when I was 17. But most of the wrongs were real, heavy and lay at my doorstep firmly. It smacked me like a ton of bricks. Although I was a Christian (and a for real one) I had been a selfish, self-absorbed, neglectful, temperamental, and often borderline emotionally abusive husband. I had not put her needs above my own. I had not treated her the way Christ treats his church. My ex asserts the entire marriage failing was my fault. I don't agree that I am the only one who ever did wrong in the marriage, on that account we disagree but we do agree on the reason for the marriage failing is mine. I am the reason the marriage failed. I am not the only one who did wrong, but I am the reason it failed.

I was so concerned with making my way in the world and my career that I neglected the relationship all together. Now the reason I wanted to make a name for myself was so that she could be proud of me and proud to be with me, but I forgot to be the kind of man she would want to be proud of along the way. It was my fault, and I could not fix it.

Over the next year I read every book I could on marriage and becoming the kind of man she could love. I came off the road, quit my band, gave up my record deal, and began to work in the corporate world. I went to divorce care; I went to counseling. I was accountable to other men. I stopped being so hard on my oldest boys. I stopped trying to make them the athletes my dad wanted me to be in order to earn his love through them, even though he passed away six months before. I began to strip away the pride I had carried along with me as a crutch for so many years. I tried to give her the space she needed and to serve her where she needed without stepping down as a father. I became a man who was crushed but crushed in all the right ways.

This situation was self-inflicted. I was the villain, and I could not fix it. I have been Andy, innocent and in a prison, so to speak and I have been Red, guilty and deserving of prison. In the failing of my first marriage, I was Red. Whether you are Andy or Red in any given situation you only have one choice. Get busy living or get busy dying. I chose life. Ultimately my attempts to save my first marriage failed. They failed even though I did not fail that last year. I really had become the man she could be proud of, but I became him far too late. It was not too late to be the father my kids needed and that became my focus. The hurt and pain my kids and I were in was real and deep. I stopped asking God to take that pain away. My free will had dug the ditch I now lay in. I just asked God to get us through it and redeem the situation. Simone Weil once said, "We must not wish for the disappearance of our troubles but for the grace to transform them." I knew at a certain point that reconciliation was beyond my ability to bring about but there was always hope for redemption. Redemption could only be achieved by digging through with surgical precision all the faults and failings that had led me to this place. In his book *The Discourse on Imagined Occasions*, Soren Kierkegaard says, "the purest heart is precisely the one most willing to comprehend his own guilt most deeply."[335]

Even though this situation was self-inflicted, and I deserved all the vitriol anyone who knew us could throw at me, that is not what I received. I received grace and care from many Christians during this time. Some lent me money, some let me stay with them for months, others would call to check on me, take me out to lunch, pray with me, cry with me. God's hand spoke to me through people while my family was being wrecked by divorce. Unlike the situation earlier were God loved me through authors, in the breaking apart of my family God loved me through the people around me. It was the most difficult time I have ever had in my life, but it had moments of profound sweetness as well.

The divorce went through. I found out given enough time one person cannot stop another form legally divorcing them. I was laid bare. I had previously thought I had so much to offer God. I had my intellect, my talent, my work ethic to offer God that could really help God further his kingdom. I had a great family that had beat the odds of being married so young. I had three great kids that were high achievers, and we were really going to give God the help he needed. Then it all came crashing down. Like I said in Part 3 of the book in a six-month period I lost my career, my dad and my marriage. I was crushed, I was wounded,

I was humiliated and humbled and I was finally lost enough to be led. Brennan Manning says, "[Jesus] is the savior who saves us from ourselves."[336] I was finally ready to be used by God because I was ready to be saved from myself. I was done with my plans, my agenda, and my preoccupations. It wasn't until I became utterly done with myself. It was not until I realized how eternally useless my intellect or talent is without God that I was ready to be used by him. I learned in this time what Brennan Manning articulates in his book *Abba's Child*, "In love's service, only wounded soldiers can serve."[337]

I moved into an apartment, and I started very clumsily trying to rebuild a life. There were starts and stops and sins, two steps forward and one back but I was on my way. God was changing me, even if it didn't seem that way sometimes to onlookers. My kids were still hurting and in counseling. They had to switch schools for a year on top of everything else. My life became work, kids, and not much else.

About a year and half later unexpectedly I met my now wife. As my son Zeke says "she stepped into a dumpster fire, and I will never know why." My wife was not scared off by the fact that I had been divorced, or that I had kids or a past. She saw the man I could be and did not focus on the man I was. I did not think I would ever find someone else given the vast amounts of failure on my ledger, but she was unfazed by it. If there is a villain in my stories it is always me but if there is a hero (other than Jesus) in my story, it is Summer. Jesus saved our family through her. She was the stabilizing force we needed. Within a year of dating, we were married with the kids blessing. In fact, before we got engaged Summer went to my twins who were 14 at the time and told them that we were planning on getting married but that she was going to have me write a letter to my ex (which I did) asking her to give the family another shot at reconciliation. If my ex (their mom) decided to give our marriage another shot right up until the day Summer and I got married, Summer told the twins that she would step out of the situation in order for God to do a reconciliatory work. However, after Summer and I said our vows, she told them that as a family we had a new covenant and Summer would not back out. The reality is that my ex had zero interest in putting our family back together, but the willingness of Summer to bow out like that went a long way with the twins.

Just a few months after we were married, I was back in music and working on a doctorate with Summers full support and approval. We have been married 12 years, she has a great relationship with our older three kids, and we have an eight-year-old ourselves. God truly gave me what Isaiah 61:3 talks about, beauty for ashes. My life burned to the ground and there was nothing I could do about it. All I could do was put one foot in front of the other and walk. Building myself back as a man surrendered to what ever God wanted. Void of my musical dreams, void of my expectations of my kids, void of what and how I thought life should be. It was during this crushing that I surrendered not for salvation (that was already done) but surrender of agenda, surrender of expectations and aspirations. It is during this time the verse Isaiah 6:8 became a prayer, "Here I am, Lord, send me." I just wanted my life to be an example of what a consistent surrendered life looked like. I wanted my life to be a liturgy.

I learned by coming to the end of myself that God not only loves me, but likes me, when I get out of his way to do so. Brennan Manning recounts this story in his book *Abba's Child*, of a man and his 80-year-old who took a walk along a lake to watch the sunrise. After a long silence the man's elderly uncle began happily skipping down the road.

Nephew: "Uncle Seamus, you really look happy.
Uncle Seamus: "I am."
Nephew: "Want to tell me why?"
Uncle Seamus: "Yes, you see, me Abba is very fond of me."[338]

I learned that by giving up on myself, by giving it all to him that my Abba didn't just love me, but he was very fond of me.

Liturgy

CH.
Let my Life Be, be a Liturgy
For all the world to, all the world to see
All the grace that, the Lord has given me
Let my life be, be a liturgy

V.1
While I was a long way off
You were looking for me
I was swimming in that trough
You were running full speed
Singing my son once was lost
But now he's here with me
now I have a brand-new song to sing

V.2
To my fellow man (amen)
My heart is open to you (amen)
If you need a hand (amen)
Call on me cause I've got two (hallelujah)
You will the taste tears (amen)
Why don't you drink the wine (amen)
Immanuel came near (amen)
So let me glorify (hallelujah)[339]

CONCLUSION

Often our intellectual doubts and deconstructions are birthed from painful personal experience. Likewise, our faith and reconstructions are birthed from positive personal experiences. As we live and gain more and more understanding of our experiences, our perception can change. We can even come to see the redemptive nature of our most painful experiences even if we never fully understand why we had to go through them. It is Kierkegaard that is credited with saying in his journal,

> "It is really true what philosophy tells us, that life must be understood backwards. But with this, one forgets the second proposition, that it must be lived forwards. A proposition which, the more it is subjected to careful thought, the more it ends up concluding precisely that life at any given moment cannot really ever be fully understood; exactly because there is no single moment where time stops completely in order for me to take position [to do this]: going backwards."[340]

The redemptive transformation of all of our experiences is the core message of Christianity. BrennanManning says, "Christianity is not simply a message but an experience of faith that becomes a message."[341] C.S. Lewis supports this assertion when he says in *The Great Divorce*, "Heaven, once attained, will work backwards and turn even agony into glory."[342] In my experience most of the time when I grow in faith it is on the backside of a period of doubt. When I have perceived a mountain elation in God's presence it is almost always after a time of pain and disappointment. All humans will have doubts about their belief system and worldview. All humans live putting their faith in their belief system and worldview. I have deconstructed and reconstructed many of my beliefs. I doubt easy and believe hard. I don't have any delusions that I am done with doubt. I fully expect that I will deconstruct several of my beliefs and have to reconstruct them again (and no pastor Joe I am not sleeping with anyone, other than my wife as often as she lets me). I love this quote from the late singer-songwriter Rich Mullins from a talk he gave in 1997 at Carpenter's Way Church,

"Used to be I'd only get born again about every year—once a year. That was when I was going to camp … those of you that are young enough to go to camp and re-dedicate your life every year, you keep doing it, 'cause about the time you get to college you're gonna learn that you have to re-dedicate your life about every six months. And then you'll graduate from college, and it will become a quarterly thing. By the time you're in your 40s and 50s you'll do it four times a day."

I fully expect I'll doubt again, and you should to. It is okay, doubt is an integral part of faith. It is certainty that is faith's enemy. I think it is important that we put the critical eye on what is causing our doubts as much as the doubting of beliefs we once held firm. I have found that if I give my faith a fair shake it can stand up against and hold its own with any counter view. I have read Hawking and Dawkins, Marx and Nietzsche, Ehrman and Dennet, Harris and Hitchens, Foucault and Derrida, and while I find them to be brilliant people over all; I find the works of Plantinga and Lewis, Aquinas and Augustine, Copan and Adams, Craig and Merleau-Ponty, Kierkegaard and Leibniz, Weil and Manning, Peter and Paul to be much more compelling. If given equal weight and equal criticism I have always been able to reconstruct my faith with more intellectual and experiential integrity than I have in leaving it. My beliefs have changed in some ways for sure but the overarching core themes have remained orthodox to Christianity and I am beginning to doubt that will ever change. If I had to sum up in one sentence where I find myself today it would be found in the Bible John 6:66–69, "From this time many of his disciples turned back and no longer followed him. 'You do not want to leave too, do you?' Jesus asked the Twelve. Simon Peter answered him, 'Lord, to whom shall we go? You have the words of eternal life. We have come to believe and to know that you are the Holy One of God."

Distant Shore

Intro
When I was wash up on that distant shore
I'll trade my rags for some brand new clothes
I know from the belly of my mother he changed my name
I won't end up in no shallow grave
When I wash up on that distant shore

V.1
When I wash up on that distant shore
The waves won't crash against my soul no more
When I find myself out of time and space
The angels may not know my face
For all the marks and scars, all the pain on my calloused heart

Ch.
But the Lord will say this one's mine
And I'm gonna be free from the chains that held my broken life

V.2
When I shed this skin and poverty
Won't be held ransom by what is sold as free
Won't be picking cotton in no rich man's field
Breaking my back or beggin' for my next meal
Grace will break my chains and I'll celebrate freedoms name

Ch.
And I'll strip away what's held me down
And I'll break away free trade my pain for a crown[343]

319

Discussion Questions

1. Why is personal experience so often overlooked?

2. Postmodernists reduce the world only to personal experience. While personal experience and perception cannot be ignored why should it not be the only thing that counts?

3. In the face of doubt how do you take Rilke's advice and love the questions themselves? How is this an important part of faith?

4. How can experience lead us beyond ourselves?

5. Have you ever had a time where a group of Christians failed you through no fault of your own? What impact did that have on you at the time? Has there been reconciliation since?

6. Have you had an author or certain book that has impacted you as profoundly as the author describes with the work of Brennan Manning? If so which author or book and what made it so deeply impactful?

7. In situations where you have been excommunicated for no fault of your own, is bitterness still a choice?

8. The author says, "There is power in the words I am sorry if you aren't too bitter to let them sink in." Do you agree or disagree? If you agree why is there power in the words, I am sorry?

9. The author had a painful experience with a church, Phillip Yancey in *What's So Amazing About Grace?* states on page 16," I rejected the church for a time because I found so little grace there. I returned because I found grace no where else." How does this speak to the authors story? How does it speak to yours?

10. "Breakdowns and Breakthroughs" is a retelling of the prodigal son story (taken from chapter four the book *What's So Amazing About Grace?*), at the end of this same chapter Yancey talks about a Pastor friend who was dealing with a prodigal daughter. He was waiting up for her going through

all the feelings of indignation and rage that a parent would feel about a teenage daughter in full blown rebellion. Yancey says the Pastor said this on page 56, "And yet I must tell you, when my daughter came home that night, or rather the next morning, I wanted nothing in the world so much as to take her in my arms, to love her, to tell her I wanted the best for her. I was a helpless, lovesick father." Have you ever thought of God as a lovesick father? Would this change your doubt any if you could see God as a lovesick father?

11. In the song there is the line "Freedom's dreams are just a lie," have you ever chased after something you thought would bring freedom only to find out it was a lie? How did you come to that realization?

12. Could you make the sacrifice Peter Parker did to save his loved ones? What are the similarities between Peter's sacrifice and the sacrifice Jesus made? What are the differences?

13. How did you personally perceive the authors testimony? Do parts of the authors journey resonate with parts of yours? How do you or can you relate?

14. The author speaks of an encounter with the supernatural. How do you perceive this information? How does it align with your personal experience?

15. Have you experienced abandonment from a loved one like the author did, how has this shaped your ability to have faith in God?

16. The author talks about coming to faith in Jesus, have you ever had a time in your life where you have dedicated your life to religious faith? What was that like for you? Did it have a lasting impact on you?

17. What is the purpose of a testimony? Relate the lyrics of "Beacon for the Fleet" to the purpose of a testimony.

18. The author makes a comparison of the love the Little Prince has for his rose and Jesus love for his people. In what ways are they similar and in what ways are they different?

19. In the *Shawshank Redemption* excerpt Andy asserts there is a free will agency in how we handle our circumstances even when we can't change them. What do you think Andy means by get busy living or get busy dying?

20. How did the author get busy living when his life had falling apart?

21. The author told three stories of personal experience in this part of the book. In two of the three the author is at fault. In the third story the author is not at fault. Does fault matter when juxtaposed to Andy's (from *Shawshank Redemption*) assertion of having a choice in how we live?"

22. The author repeatedly calls himself the villain in his story, what is the message the author is trying to convey in doing this? Do you agree?

23. How does the Soren Kierkegaard quote "the purest heart is precisely the one most willing to comprehend his own guilt most deeply" speak to the authors assertion that he is the villain?

24. How do you take the Manning quote, "In love's service only wounded soldiers can serve"? How would you relate this back to the soul-making theodicy of Part 3 of the book?

25. What is a liturgy and how can your life be a liturgy?

26. In the introduction of the book and here at the end the author quotes John 6:66–69, do you perceive the quote any differently here at the end of the book than you did at the beginning?

BIBLIOGRAPHY

Freeman, Fr. Stephen. "Sin Is Not a Legal Problem - Athanasius and the Atonement." Glory to God for All Things, July 12, 2016. https://blogs.ancientfaith.com/glory2godforallthings/2016/07/12/sin-not-legal-problem-athanasius-atonement/.

Kierkegaard, Søren, and Niels Jørgen Cappelørn. *Kierkegaard's Journals and Notebooks*. Princeton, NJ: Princeton University Press, 2015.

Kierkegaard, Søren, Edna H. Hong, and Howard V. Hong. *The Essential Kierkegaard*. Princeton, NJ: Princeton University Press, 2000.

Kierkegaard, Søren, Howard V. Hong, and Edna H. Hong. *Three Discourses on Imagined Occasions*. Princeton, NJ: Princeton University Press, 2009.

Lewis, C. S. *The Great Divorce*. London, UK: Collins, 2012.

Manning, Brennan, John Blase, and Jonathan Foreman. *ABBA's Child: The Cry of the Heart for Intimate Belonging*. Colorado Springs, CO: NavPress, 2015.

Manning, Brennan. *The Furious Longing of God*. Colorado Springs, CO: David C. Cook, 2009.

Manning, Brennan. *The Ragamuffin Gospel*. CO Springs, Co: Multnomah Books, 2015.

Rilke, Rainer Moira, and Norton M D Herter. *Letters to a Young Poet*. New York, NY: W.W. Norton & Company, 1934.

SAINT-EXUPERY, ANTOINE DE. *Little Prince: And Letter to a Hostage*. S.l.: PENGUIN BOOKS, 2021.

The Shawshank Redemption. Film. United States: Columbia, 1994.

Simpson, Ben. "The Ragamuffin Legacy." RELEVANT, June 7, 2017. https://relevantmagazine.com/faith/ragamuffin-legacy/.

Simpson, Ben. "The Ragamuffin Legacy." RELEVANT, June 7, 2017. https://relevantmagazine.com/faith/ragamuffin-legacy/.

Spider-Man: No Way Home. Film. United States: Sony Pictures Releasing, 2021.

Yancey, Philip. *What's so Amazing about Grace?* Grand Rapids, MI: Zondervan, 2011.

ENDNOTES

322. Rainer Moira Rilke and Norton M D Herter, *Letters to a Young Poet* (New York, NY: W.W. Norton & Company, 1934).

323. Søren Kierkegaard, Edna H. Hong, and Howard V. Hong, *The Essential Kierkegaard* (Princeton, NJ: Princeton University Press, 2000).

324. Ben Simpson, "The Ragamuffin Legacy," RELEVANT, June 7, 2017, https://relevantmagazine.com/faith/ragamuffin-legacy/.

325. Brennan Manning, *The Ragamuffin Gospel* (CO Springs, Co: Multnomah Books, 2015), 16.

326. Philip Yancey, *What's so Amazing about Grace?* (Grand Rapids, MI: Zondervan, 2011).

327. Written by Jason Lee McKinney (Zekers and ZiZi Music (BMI).

328. *Spider-Man: No Way Home* (Sony Pictures Releasing, 2021).

329. Brennan Manning, *The Furious Longing of God* (Colorado Springs, CO: David C. Cook, 2009).

330. Fr. Stephen Freeman, "Sin Is Not a Legal Problem - Athanasius and the Atonement," Glory to God for All Things, July 12, 2016, https://blogs.ancientfaith.com/glory2godforallthings/2016/07/12/sin-not-legal-problem-athanasius-atonement/.

331. Written by Jason Lee McKinney and Alan Moore (Zekers and ZiZi Music (BMI); Alan D Moore music (BMI)

332. Antoine De Saint-Exupery, *Little Prince: And Letter to a Hostage* (S.l.: Penguin Books, 2021).

333. Written by Jason Lee McKinney (Zekers and ZiZi Music (BMI).

334. *The Shawshank Redemption* (Columbia, 1994).

335. Søren Kierkegaard, Howard V. Hong, and Edna H. Hong, *Three Discourses on Imagined Occasions* (Princeton, NJ: Princeton University Press, 2009).

336. Brennan Manning, John Blase, and Jonathan Foreman, *ABBA's Child: The Cry of the Heart for Intimate Belonging* (Colorado Springs, CO: NavPress, 2015), 42.

337. Brennan Manning, John Blase, and Jonathan Foreman, *ABBA's Child: The Cry of the Heart for Intimate Belonging* (Colorado Springs, CO: NavPress, 2015), 25.

338. Brennan Manning, John Blase, and Jonathan Foreman, *ABBA's Child: The Cry of the Heart for Intimate Belonging* (Colorado Springs, CO: NavPress, 2015), 64.

339. Written by Jason Lee McKinney (Zekers and ZiZi Music (BMI).

340. Søren Kierkegaard and Niels Jørgen Cappelørn, *Kierkegaard's Journals and Notebooks* (Princeton, NJ: Princeton University Press, 2015).

341. Brennan Manning, John Blase, and Jonathan Foreman, *ABBA's Child: The Cry of the Heart for Intimate Belonging* (Colorado Springs, CO: NavPress, 2015), 106.

342. C. S. Lewis, *The Great Divorce* (London, UK: Collins, 2012), 67.

343. Written by Jason Lee McKinney (Zekers and ZiZi Music (BMI). Scott Faircloff, Scotfair Music (ASCAP).

Special Thanks

I want to thank the Uncreated Creator and Maker of All That Is for never leaving nor forsaking me, no matter how much I doubt, question, or complain. I want to thank my wife Summer for her patience, faithful love, and unending support. I want to thank my kids (Zeke, Zion, Zakyra, and Zekaiah) for showing me what it really means to love someone with an ache and sacrificial posture I could have only imagined before them. I want to thank my mom for loving me and giving me a far better childhood than what she had. Finally, I want to thank the faculty (especially Dr. Christopher Ben Simpson and Dr. Richard Knopp) at Lincoln Christian University for walking me through formally and academically the big questions I had only experienced deconstructing and reconstructing as a doubting disciple on my own.

About the Author

Dr. Jason Lee McKinney is a professor, internationally touring singer, multiple award-winning songwriter and recording artist, and lay philosopher. Dr. McKinney holds a BA in Management, an MBA, an MA in Philosophy and Apologetics, and an Ed.D in Leadership and Professional Practice. Dr. McKinney resides in Nashville with his wife Summer (a therapist and author) and eight-year old son Kai (a drum phenom). The McKinneys also have two grown sons—Zeke (a recording artist for Tooth & Nail records) and Zion (a worship leader at LifePoint church), one grown daughter, Zakyra (who is studying to be a theater teacher) and one daughter-in-law, Juliana (a middle school choir director and wife to Zion).

also available from

WordCrafts Press

Aerobics for the Mind
Michael Potts, PhD

What's the Big Idea?
Robert G. Lee

Elders at the Gate
Ray Blunt

I AM
Summer McKinney

www.wordcrafts.net